# COUNTERTERRORISM

A Reference Handbook

Other Titles in ABC-CLIO's

**CONTEMPORARY WORLD ISSUES**
Series

*Chemical and Biological Warfare*, Al Mauroni
*Consumer Culture*, Douglas J. Goodman and Mirelle Cohen
*Courts and Trials*, Christopher E. Smith
*Dating and Sexuality in America*, Jeffrey Scott Turner
*Drug Use*, Richard Isralowitz
*Environmental Activism*, Jacqueline Vaughn Switzer
*Forest Conservation Policy*, V. Alaric Sample and Anthony S. Cheng
*Gay and Lesbian Issues*, Chuck Stewart
*Nuclear Weapons and Nonproliferation*, Sarah J. Diehl and James
    Clay Moltz
*Media and American Courts*, S. L. Alexander
*Media and Politics in America*, Guido H. Stempel III
*Racial and Ethnic Diversity in America*, Adalberto Aguirre Jr.
*Racial Justice in America*, David B. Mustard
*Reproductive Issues in America*, Janna C. Merrick and Robert H.
    Blank
*U.S. Immigration*, Michael C. LeMay
*Work and Family in America*, Leslie F. Stebbins
*Women in Prison*, Cyndi Banks

Books in the Contemporary World Issues series address vital issues in today's society such as genetic engineering, pollution, and biodiversity. Written by professional writers, scholars, and nonacademic experts, these books are authoritative, clearly written, up-to-date, and objective. They provide a good starting point for research by high school and college students, scholars, and general readers as well as by legislators, businesspeople, activists, and others.

Each book, carefully organized and easy to use, contains an overview of the subject, a detailed chronology, biographical sketches, facts and data and/or documents and other primary-source material, a directory of organizations and agencies, annotated lists of print and nonprint resources, and an index.

Readers of books in the Contemporary World Issues series will find the information they need in order to have a better understanding of the social, political, environmental, and economic issues facing the world today.

# COUNTERTERRORISM

## A Reference Handbook

Graeme C. S. Steven and Rohan Gunaratna

**CONTEMPORARY
WORLD ISSUES**

A B C 🟤 C L I O

Santa Barbara, California • Denver, Colorado • Oxford, England

Library of Congress Cataloging-in-Publication Data

Steven, Graeme C.S.
  Counterterrorism : a reference handbook / Graeme C. S. Steven and
Rohan Gunaratna.
    p. cm. — (Contemporary world issue)
  Includes bibliographical references and index.
  ISBN 1-85109-666-3 (hardcover : alk. paper)
  ISBN 1-85109-671-X (e-Book)

  1. Terrorism — Prevention. 2. Terrorism — Prevention — Government
policy. I Gunaratna, Rohan, 1961– II. Title. III. Series.

HV6-31.S744 2004
363.32—dc22

                                                              2004009632

08  07  06  05  04  10  9  8  7  6  5  4  3  2  1

This book is also available on the World Wide Web as an eBook. Visit abc-
clio.com for details.

ABC-CLIO, Inc.
130 Cremona Drive, P.O. Box 1911
Santa Barbara, California 93116-1911

This book is printed on acid-free paper ∞.
Manufactured in the United States of America

*To those faceless men and women*
*fighting terrorist groups*

# COUNTERTERRORISM

A Reference Handbook

# Contents

# Preface

After Al Qaeda attacked America's most iconic landmarks on 9/11, a state of perpetual conflict between the Islamists and the West has arisen, where Al Qaeda and its associates periodically strike targets of the United States, its allies, and its friends. Although the pre-9/11 Al Qaeda *group* conducted an average of one attack every two years, the post-9/11 Al Qaeda *movement*—Al Qaeda and its associated groups—mount an average of one attack every three months.

To compensate for the loss of its state-of-the-art training and operational infrastructure in Afghanistan, Al Qaeda is seeking to establish new bases in Yemen, Mindanao in the Philippines, Kashmir, the Pankishi Valley in Georgia, Chechnya, and Iraq. Like bees that disperse when its hive is attacked, Al Qaeda organizers, operatives, financiers, and other experts have dispersed from Afghanistan and Pakistan to lawless zones of Asia, the Horn of Africa (the easternmost projection of Africa, including Somalia), the Middle East, and the Caucusus, increasing the threshold of worldwide terrorism. Dependent on the ability of the United States to manage the deteriorating situation in Iraq and the willingness of Muslim governments to cooperate with the West, the dispersed threat could either escalate or de-escalate.

The security environment became more complicated with the unilateral U.S. intervention in Iraq, a watershed event that has not in any way reduced the threat of terrorism. In contrast to the highly successful U.S.-led global coalition response that gravely weakened Al Qaeda after 9/11, U.S. intervention in Iraq has facilitated the growth of existing and emergence of new Islamist political parties and terrorist groups in the Muslim world. The resurgence of the Taliban, Hezb-e-Islami, and Al Qaeda in

Afghanistan and the post-invasion alliance between secular Saddam loyalist Tawhid Wal Jihad and Al Ansar Al Islami, an Al Qaeda associate group in Iraq, spells continued violence in 2004. The momentum of attacks in Iraq has created an operational tempo for terrorist activities worldwide.

With the steadfast growth of Muslim public anger and rage against the United States, its allies, and friends, Islamist groups in Iraq and beyond are now able to exercise greater influence among the Muslim communities. An American Muslim remarked: "Bin Laden brought down two towers, but George Bush destroyed two countries." Like sharks in search of new opportunities, Al Qaeda and its associate groups are aggressively harnessing the resentment among the Muslims living in the West and in their home countries.

As the memory of 9/11 recedes, the West is likely to witness another mass casualty attack on Western soil. Such targets are numerous, and hence all of them cannot be protected and so will remain the most vulnerable to attack. The November 2003 double suicide attacks in Turkey, the bridge from the Middle East to Europe, is a grim reminder that terrorists can strike amidst security measures. Especially after Turkey, Al Qaeda's hallmark of targeting picture-postcard or emblematic targets in the West is becoming more likely. As terrorists determined to survive and succeed adapt to the post-9/11 security environment, they are likely to identify the loopholes and gaps in Western security architecture and breach its security and countermeasures. The frequency of attacks in the Middle East, Asia, Horn of Africa, and the Caucusus will continue, but for greater impact they are likely to kill, maim, and injure more people. For effect, the terrorists will continue to attack economic, religious, and population targets using the tactic of coordinated simultaneous suicide operations. The sustained global action against Al Qaeda will further force the mother group to the background, thereby empowering its associates to the fore and making it more difficult for intelligence and enforcement agencies to monitor and respond to a numerically larger number of Islamist groups.

U.S. intervention in Iraq has increased the threshold of terrorism worldwide and weakened the resolve of Muslim leaders, their governments, and publics to fight terrorism. Despite the pledges, the failure of the international community to provide more grants and aid to Afghanistan and Pakistan ensures the support for extremist ideologies and the survival of Al Qaeda leadership. Furthermore, Iran is likely to develop into a safe zone for Al Qaeda unless the West strengthens the hand of the moderates over the hardliners in Tehran.

Following are some likely future developments:

- Unprecedented security, intelligence, and law enforcement cooperation; heightened public vigilance; and aggressive hunting of Al Qaeda and associated cells has made it difficult for terrorists to mount another 9/11 scale attack on U.S. soil. Although terrorist capabilities to attack North America, Western Europe, and Australasia have suffered, the terrorist intention to mount an attack on Western soil has not diminished. The attack in Madrid on March 11, 2004, demonstrated that Al Qaeda and its associated cells are likely to continue mass casuality attacks on Western soil in the coming years.
- The bulk of the terrorist attacks will be conducted by Islamist terrorist groups from Asia, the Middle East, the Horn of Africa, and the Caucusus. Most of the attacks will be conducted in Muslim countries but against high-profile, symbolic, and strategic targets of the United States, its allies, and its friends. Furthermore, due to the hardening of American targets (similar to Israeli targets after Munich 1972), the threat shifted to allies and friends of the United States. Germans and French were the targets in Tunisia, Westerners—especially Australians—in Bali, eleven French naval technicians in Karachi, the Italians in Iraq, and the British in Turkey.
- The threat has shifted to "soft" targets—unprotected or poorly defended targets. Due to government hardening of military and diplomatic targets, the terrorist attacks will shift to economic (tourism, hotels, banks) and religious (Christian, Jewish, Hindu) targets and population centers. Almost all the attacks will be suicide vehicle bombings, an Al Qaeda hallmark. The vast majority of the attacks will result in mass casualties, including deaths of Muslims. Nonetheless, the Islamist groups will find sufficient support to continue the fight against the United States, its allies, and its friends.

- Al Qaeda has been gravely weakened. The vast number of attacks will be conducted not by Al Qaeda but by associated Islamist groups. As demonstrated in Turkey, Morocco, Chechnya, Pakistan, Tunisia, Algeria, the Philippines, Jordan, Iraq, and Indonesia, groups trained, armed, financed, and ideologized by Al Qaeda are able to mount attacks as lethal as Al Qaeda. Six groups—Al Ansar Al Islami in Iraq, Salafi Group for Call and Combat in Algeria, Tawhid Wal Jihad, Hezb-e-Islami, Islamic Movement of the Taliban, and Jemmah Islamiyah in Southeast Asia—will likely conduct Al Qaeda–style attacks. Due to the sustained U.S.-led coalition action against Al Qaeda, the group will be able to conduct fewer attacks but will remain in the background inspiring, instigating, and coordinating attacks by its associated groups.

In addition to these significant functional and regional terrorist trends and patterns, terrorist groups are increasingly expressing an interest to acquire, use, and develop dual technologies. In the hands of a terrorist, certain civilian technologies with military applications can enhance terrorist performance. Just as 9/11 suicide hijackers adapted commercial infrastructure as missiles, Al Qaeda members are sighting agricultural farms in search of fertilizer to develop bombs, pharmacies and chemist stores to acquire material to build bombs in garages and kitchens, and hospital and industrial complexes to smuggle out radiological devices.

The recovery of the manufacturing apparatus with ricin traces but not the ricin itself in the United Kingdom in 2003 suggests that Al Qaeda and its associated groups have begun to move down the road of chemical, biological, and radiological (CBR) weapons. In 2002, an Al Qaeda Tunisian member attacked a Jewish synagogue in Djerba, the oldest in North Africa, using a liquid petroleum gas (LPG) vehicle. He killed fourteen Germans, three Frenchman, and five Tunisians. The recovery of three dozen terrorist manuals from Afghanistan and other theaters with formulae to manufacture chemical and biological agents and radiological dispersal devices is indicative of several hundred members with such specialist capabilities. As the Al Qaeda movement continues to recruit from a cross-section of society (rich, poor, educated, and less educated), it will gain access to specialist technologies. Although conventional terrorist attacks (using guns and bombs) will remain the most common, the likelihood of terrorists using dual technologies, particularly CBR agents, is increasing.

The threat of hijacking of aviation and maritime transportation to strike human and infrastructure remains significant. As a proven technique, Al Qaeda and its associated groups have tested and attempted several times—even after 9/11—to hijack aircraft with the intention of attacking ground and maritime targets. A weakness in the transportation chain in a target or a neighboring country is likely to pave the way for success. Despite terrorist failures to destroy commercial airliners in Iraq in 2003 and Kenya in 2002 and a U.S. fighter plane in Saudi Arabia in 2001, the threat continues. With the failure of operational agencies to disrupt the Al Qaeda–linked fleet of merchant ships, where lethal cargo can be transported relatively easily, the future threat posed by surface-to-air missiles (SAMs) remains significant. With the difficulty of hijacking aviation, even a nonsuicide conventional hijacking, terrorists are likely to invest in attacking aviation targets when airborne or while grounded with other stand-off weapons—rocket-propelled grenade launchers (RPGs) and light anti-tank weapons (LAWs). As aerial and ground targets harden, the vulnerability of the maritime domain to infiltration and strike has increased. A vessel could be used not only to transport lethal cargo but also as a bomb to attack a port city. Investing in vigilant vessel profiling is the key to identifying and searching high-risk ships before they reach a port.

# Regions of Concern

With sustained U.S.-led coalition action in Afghanistan since October 2001, the threat posed by Al Qaeda has globalized. Al Qaeda organizers of attacks, financiers, operatives, and other experts now operate with associated groups from lawless as well as hospitable zones in the Middle East, Asia, and the Horn of Africa. Even so, Al Qaeda and its associated members are concentrated in four regions of the world: Iraq and its border regions, Yemen and the Horn of Africa, the Pakistan-Afghanistan border, and the Indonesian and Philippine archipelagos.

- The Islamist ideologues have declared Iraq as a new land of jihad (holy war). In time the scale and intensity

of the fighting in Iraq will increase due to the
unimpeded flow of mujahedin (Islamic guerrilla
fighters) through Iran, Syria, and Saudi Arabia;
collaboration between foreign mujahedin and Saddam
loyalists; increased support from angry Muslims
worldwide; and tacit and active sanctuary and covert
support from Iraq's neighbors to the Iraqi fighters.
Unless Western and Muslim governments invest more
resources and men, the situation in Iraq will deteriorate
even further. Like Afghanistan during the Soviet
occupation, Iraq is emerging as the new land of jihad
for the politicized and radicalized Muslims worldwide.
Although the bulk of the foreign mujahedin at present
are from the Levant (including Syria), with time,
Muslim youth from North Africa, the Horn of Africa,
the Persian Gulf, and the Caucusus, cradle and convert
European Muslims, and Asian Muslims are likely to
enter Iraq. As much as Afghanistan produced the
current generation of mujahedin, the next generation of
mujahedin is likely to be produced in Iraq.

- Al Qaeda has developed significant infrastructure in
the Horn of Africa, including Somalia, and is using that
region as a base to launch operations both in the
Persian Gulf and in Africa. Several hundred Al Qaeda
members in Yemen (only 35 percent of the country is
under government control) are moving back and forth
to East Africa to develop the horn as a theater for
sanctuary. In the coming years, East African Islamist
groups influenced by Al Qaeda will increasingly
participate in international terrorism. Subsaharan
Africa, with incompetent and corrupt governments,
remains the Achilles heel of the Western security and
intelligence agencies.

- Afghanistan was a terrorist Disneyland after Soviet
withdrawal from February 1989 until U.S. intervention
in October 2001. As a result of international neglect, Al
Qaeda, Taliban, and other Islamist groups trained
several tens of thousands of mujahedin in Afghanistan.
Although nearly six hundred Al Qaeda members who
fled Afghanistan and its associate members in Pakistan
have been arrested, the reservoir of trained mujahedin
is huge and is largely located along the Afghanistan-

Pakistan border. As President Musharraf of Pakistan continues to target Al Qaeda and Taliban members, Pakistani support for Islamism and opposition to Musharraf are growing. To prevent a future Islamic government coming to power, sustained western assistance to Musharraf, improved Pakistan-Afghanistan relations, and an international resolution of the Indo-Pakistan dispute over Kashmir are essential at this stage. As Al Hezb-e-Islami, the Taliban, and Al Qaeda seek to develop Pakistan's northwest frontier province as a staging pad to conduct operations into Afghanistan (a repetition of the anti-Soviet Afghan mujahedin model), Pakistan remains the most pivotal state in the fight against terrorism.

- With the United States becoming Iran's immediate neighbor overnight, the hardliners in Tehran advocate support for anti-U.S. insurgency in Iraq. Due to sustained U.S.-led coalition action in Afghanistan, the bulk of the Al Qaeda leaders and members moved to two countries—Iran and Pakistan—in late 2001 and early 2002. An estimated five hundred Al Qaeda members, led by Saif Al Adil and Saad bin Laden, are located in Iran. Although the Iranian moderates call for tougher action against Al Qaeda, the hardliners with previous training ties to Al Qaeda wish to repeat the success of the Lebanese Hezbollah's coordinated suicide attack of October 1983, which killed 241 American and 58 French soldiers and forced the Multi-National Force (MNF) to withdraw from the Middle East. As the West has failed to engage Iran, the duality of Iran's response to Al Qaeda is likely to continue. The United States identifying Iran as "evil" will help neither the West nor the Muslim moderates in Iran.

# Al Qaeda: From a Group to a Movement

To survive and to be relevant, Al Qaeda has transformed through three phases, and it is still changing.

After the Soviets decided to withdraw from Afghanistan, Al Qaeda Al Sulbah (The Solid Base) began as a group to support local jihad movements fighting for suppressed and oppressed Muslims. By providing finance, weapons, and trainers, the group played or attempted to play critical roles in the lands of jihad—Algeria, Tajikistan, Bosnia, Chechnya, Mindanao, Kashmir, and Egypt, among others. In the first phase, they assisted associated groups or directly targeted opposing governments mostly in Muslim countries.

In the second phase, largely due to the close cooperation with the Egyptian groups—the Egyptian Islamic Jihad and the Islamic Group of Egypt—Al Qaeda developed its own capability to mount operations—against U.S. troops in Yemen in December 1992 and Somalia in 1993, at the World Trade Center in New York in February 1993, on eleven U.S. airliners over the Pacific, on U.S. President Bill Clinton and other Oplan Bojinka targets in 1994–1995, on Western targets in Saudi Arabia beginning in the mid-1990s, at U.S. embassies in East Africa in August 1998, on the USS *Cole* in October 2000, and most infamously, through the attacks of September 11, 2001.

Due to post-9/11 security measures in Western countries, Al Qaeda and its associated groups have not been able to strike again on Western soil; in response they have targeted Western (including Israeli and Jewish) sites and people in Muslim countries or Muslim regions. This third phase has borne witness to attacks—mostly car bombings—in a Balinese tourist area and at the Jakarta Marriot in Indonesia, of an Israeli hotel and aircraft in Mombasa in Kenya, of the oldest Jewish synagogue in Djerba in Tunisia, at Jewish and other targets in Casablanca in Morocco, and at a variety of Western targets in Saudi Arabia, Turkey, Pakistan, Chechnya, and Iraq.

In the third phase, the bulk of the post-9/11 attacks were not staged by Al Qaeda but by its associated groups. As they lacked the expertise of Al Qaeda, the bulk of their attacks produced more Muslim casualties than non-Muslims. As a result of the loss of training and rehearsing bases in Afghanistan and the intense networking with its associate groups, Al Qaeda has morphed from a group into a movement. Having successfully performed its vanguard operational role by attacking America's icons, a hunted Al Qaeda is investing in an ideological role, mostly through the Internet. Although the Western governments are largely investing their resources to fight Al Qaeda, the center of gravity has shifted beyond Al Qaeda into its associated groups, posing varying scales of threat in different regions.

# Conclusion

The fight against Al Qaeda and its associated groups, spearheaded by the United States, has met with partial successes and failures. Although declaring war on Iraq was an errant overreaction to 9/11, to withdraw now would be fatal. Indeed, the present deadlines for troop withdrawal from Iraq and Afghanistan are unrealistic. Like the Soviets in Afghanistan in a war-fighting role or NATO in Bosnia in a peacekeeping role, the Western powers and their Muslim partners must remain engaged in these two theaters.

The effectiveness of the fight against Al Qaeda and its associated groups is strictly dependent on the long-term cooperation and coordination to share intelligence and conduct operations against terrorist groups and suppress their support bases. To succeed, it is paramount that the United States maintain a robust antiterrorism coalition, particularly the support of the Middle Eastern and Asian Muslim governments. By resolving the Israeli-Palestinian dispute and by investing in public diplomacy (as opposed to government-to-government relations), the United States can seek to change its image from an aggressor to a friend in the Muslim world.

# Acknowledgments

First thanks must go to Mrs. Mim Vasan for her editorial help with the book. Thanks also must go to Tore Bjorgo, Magnus Ranstorp, and Oscar Becerra for their opinions and assistance. I would particularly like to thank Neill Martin, John Allison, Paul Wilkinson, and especially John Horgan for being such inspirations and for all their help and encouragement over the years. Final thanks must go to my family: Maggie, Pam, Bob, Brian, and Callum, without whose support this book would have never been possible.

—*Graeme C. S. Steven*

I wish to thank Barry Desker, Institute of Defence and Strategic Studies, Singapore; Bruce Hoffman of RAND, Washington Office; Scott Campbell, Maritime Intelligence Group, Washington D.C.; Andrew Coburn, RMS, London; Andy Clarke, CBS, London; Boaz Ganor, International Policy Institute for Counter Terrorism Policy, Israel; Russ Howard, Combating Terrorism Centre, West Point; Nikkos Passas, Northeastern University, Boston; Jesse Finklestein, IDDS intern from Watson Institute for International Studies, Brown University; and Ian Rosenberger, IDSS intern from Cornell University, for their steadfast support. I wish to express my appreciation to production editors Gina Zondorak and Laura Stine, acquisitions editor Mim Vasan, and copyeditor Michelle Asakawa. For their steadfast affection, I want to thank my wife Anne, our sons Kevin and Ryan, my parents, my brother Keith, my sister Malkanthi, and her husband Shanthikumar.

Arabinda Acharya, International Centre for Political Violence and Terrorism Studies, Institute of Defence and Strategic Studies, Singapore, worked as my principal research assistant.

—*Rohan Gunaratna*

Both authors wish to thank the many people who cannot be named for security reasons for their cooperation and assistance.

# 1

# Terrorism and Counterterrorism in the Global Context

"We owe it to all those whose bravery protects us
to enjoy the freedom they secure for us."
*Sir John Stevens, head of the London
Metropolitan Police Force, U.K.*

In order to "counter" something, one must first understand the nature, essence, and dynamics of what it is that is trying to be countered. Therefore, before discussing or examining counterterrorism, one must first be familiar with the phenomenon of terrorism. Furthermore, before defining what terrorism *is* and examining it more closely, it is useful to note what it is *not*, and to dispel some common myths or misconceptions about terrorism, as noted by Stohl (Kegley 2003):

- Political terrorism is exclusively a nongovernmental activity
- All terrorists are insane, psychopaths, or suffering from mental illness
- All terrorists are criminals
- One man's terrorist is another man's freedom fighter
- All insurgent violence is political terrorism
- A terrorist's purpose is to cause chaos

- Governments always oppose nongovernmental terrorism
- Political terrorism is exclusively a problem relating to internal conditions
- Contemporary terrorism is caused by the evil actions of one or two major actors
- Terrorism is a futile strategy

# The Terrorist Threat Today

The face of terrorism is changing rapidly. It has emerged as the single biggest security threat to both governments and societies today. Governments should be using every tool of statecraft—intelligence, law enforcement, military, political, diplomatic, economic, and financial means—to combat and reduce the threat of terrorism. Terrorism has replaced the threat of nuclear confrontation, the predominant threat during the Cold War.

Al Qaeda's coordinated multiple suicide airborne attacks aimed at destroying three outstanding U.S. landmark targets—the World Trade Center in New York City, the Pentagon, and Congress—on September 11, 2001, demonstrated the escalating terrorist threat posed to civilian and military infrastructure. Conducted by nineteen suicide hijackers, the attacks killed about 3,100 citizens from seventy-eight countries. According to Bruce Hoffman of RAND, only fourteen terrorist attacks killed more than one hundred people in the twentieth century; until 9/11, the terrorist attack that killed the largest number of civilians was in Abadan, Iran, when 440 people were killed in 1978; total U.S. fatalities during three decades of international and domestic terrorism were under three thousand. With 9/11, the worst terrorist attack ever, the threshold for terrorism worldwide increased. Terrorism has moved from a tactical to a strategic threat, prompting governments to invest unprecedented resources both in preempting terrorist attacks and in managing mass casualty attacks.

Since the Cold War, most major terrorist groups have developed a presence outside their immediate theaters of conflict, often cooperating and coordinating their actions. With the exchange of ideas, technologies, and personnel, the terrorist intentions, capability, and opportunities for attack have increased dramatically. Moreover, conflict conditions create the milieu for the spawning and growth of terrorist groups. Now two-thirds of the countries of the world are affected by political violence. As of 2002, there were twenty-three high-intensity conflicts (where more than one thousand people die per conflict per year), seventy-nine low-intensity conflicts (where between one hundred and one thousand people die per conflict per year), and thirty-eight violent political conflicts (where fewer than one hundred people die per conflict per year). At the turn of the millenium, according to Dr. Albert J. Jongman of the Interdisciplinary Research Programme on Causes of Human Rights Violations in the Netherlands, there were 612 politically motivated groups, mostly with guerrilla and terrorist capabilities, active in 140 conflicts. Nonetheless, only about forty organizations have developed an external reach and pose a threat to international security.

The geographic region most affected by terrorist violence is the Asia-Pacific region. In scale of violence, South Asia is followed by Southeast Asia, Oceania, and Northeast Asia. Within this region, Afghanistan, Pakistan, India, Sri Lanka, Indonesia, and the Philippines are experiencing high-intensity conflicts; Myanmar, Bangladesh, and Nepal are witnessing low-intensity conflicts. The Asia-Pacific region is closely followed by sub-Saharan Africa, with the Horn of Africa and Southern Africa following Central Africa. In particular, Angola, Burundi, Chad, Congo, Guinea, Nigeria, Rwanda, Sierra Leone, and Sudan are experiencing high-intensity conflicts. Cameroon, Central African Republic, Brazzaville Congo, DR Congo, Ethiopia, the Ivory Coast, Kenya, Liberia, Nigeria, Senegal, Somalia, South Africa, Tanzania, and Uganda are experiencing low-intensity conflicts. In Latin America, Colombia has been witnessing the most violent conflict, with Peru, Mexico, and Guatemala witnessing low-intensity conflicts. In the Middle East, Algeria and the Israeli-Palestinian conflicts produce the highest fatalities and casualties. Iraq, Iran, and Lebanon are witnessing low-intensity conflicts. In the former Soviet Union, the Caucasus is home to high-intensity conflict, notably the conflict in Chechnya; this is followed by low-intensity conflicts in Central Asia. Until 9/11, North America and Europe had the lowest fatalities and casualties.

# Definition of Terrorism

Terrorism is a unique form of political violence, a political campaign backed by threats and acts of violence. It must be systematic and deliberate; it seeks to influence a wide audience by generating fear. Primarily it targets civilians to gain political control of the public. Other forms of political violence include attacks against infrastructure (sabotage), against political leaders (assassination), against military (guerrilla warfare), and genocide (ethnic cleansing). Although attacks against civilians (so-called soft targets) are the most common in the initial wave of terrorist operations, subsequently terrorist groups develop the capability to attack security forces (hard targets). Today, about 45 percent of all attacks staged by terrorist groups are against security forces personnel. The tactical repertoire of contemporary terrorist groups includes forms of political violence other than terrorism. For instance, the National Liberation Army (ELN) sabotaged gas and oil pipelines in Colombia; Basque Fatherland and Liberty (ETA) assassinated moderate politicians in Spain; the Free Aceh Movement (GAM) conducts guerrilla warfare against Indonesian security forces; and the Liberation Tigers of Tamil Tigers (LTTE) have ethnically cleansed Sri Lanka's northern province of Muslims.

Terrorism differs from common crime. Terrorism is driven predominantly by a political motive (ideological, ethnic, religious); crime is predominantly driven by an economic motive. With the decline of state sponsorship, terrorist groups resort to crime to build their capacities and capabilities; but the line blurs between terrorism and organized crime as groups learn increasingly from each other and adopt each other's tactics. The Revolutionary Armed Forces of Colombia (FARC) extorts money from foreign companies in Colombia; the Abu Sayyaf Group (ASG) kidnaps foreigners in the Philippines; the Islamic Movement of Uzbekistan traffics narcotics; the Revolutionary United Force of Sierra Leone (RUF) smuggles diamonds; the Armed Islamic Group of Algeria (GIA) steals cars; and Al Qaeda engages in credit card fraud. Contemporary terrorist groups traverse along the political violence-criminality nexus. In summary, terrorist groups are armed political parties. Strategically, their goal is always political; operationally, they build support and infrastructure; tactically, they build military power, accumulate economic wealth, and gain political strength. Terrorist groups have also learned the benefits of spreading their support, training, procurement, and financing operations internationally so as to make it difficult, if not impossible, for their governments to disrupt them.

There are two forms of terrorism: *Domestic terrorism*—also called national terrorism—refers to acts of terrorism committed within the territorial borders of a country and involving citizens and interests only of that country. *International terrorism* refers to acts of terrorism involving citizens or the territory of more than one country.

Almost all major terrorist groups have developed an external presence during the post–Cold War period. By building robust external support networks, even domestic terrorist groups have developed an international dimension. Therefore, the distinction made during the Cold War between domestic and international terrorism is of lesser relevance today, especially toward understanding and responding to the threat of terrorism.

Four databases collect information worldwide about domestic and international terrorist incidents: RAND, the International Centre for Political Violence and Terrorism Research at the Institute of Defence and Strategic Studies in Singapore, the UN Terrorism Prevention Branch, and the Centre for the Study of Terrorism and Political Violence (CSTPV) at the University of St. Andrews in Scotland. The vast majority of terrorist incidents are domestic, but they are largely unreported in the international press, especially if they occur in the Southern Hemisphere. Incidents of international terrorism constitute about 8–12 percent of all incidents of terrorism. Most government agencies and private research institutions collect data about only a few domestic or regional terrorist campaigns. Traditionally, RAND, the U.S. State Department, and a few other government agencies collected data on international terrorism. The overall terrorist threat is skewed because most analysts map terrorist trends and patterns by examining only incidents of international terrorism. The decade preceding 9/11 witnessed a steady decline in the incidents of international terrorism, largely due to international cooperation. However, the overall incidents of terrorism increased due to an increase in domestic terrorism. The overall increase in terrorist incidents is attributed to the numerical increase and the intensity of intrastate conflicts.

The U.S. State Department defines terrorism as "premeditated, politically motivated violence perpetrated against noncombatant targets by subnational groups or clandestine agents, usually intended to influence an audience." Here, "noncombatant" includes, in addition to civilians, military personnel who at the time of the incident are unarmed or not on duty.

The U.S. State Department also considers acts of terrorism to be "attacks on military installations or on armed military personnel when a state of military hostilities does not exist at the site, such as bombings against U.S. military bases both at home and overseas."

The U.S. Justice Department defines terrorism as "the unlawful use of force and violence against persons or property to intimidate or coerce a government, the civilian population, or any segment thereof, in furtherance of political or social objectives."

The Federal Bureau of Investigation (FBI), an agency of the Justice Department, describes terrorism either as domestic or international, depending on the origin, base, and the objectives of the terrorists: *Domestic terrorism* is the unlawful use, or threatened use, of force or violence by a group or individual based and operating entirely within the United States or its territories, without foreign direction, committed against persons or property to intimidate or coerce a government, the civilian population, or any segment thereof, in furtherance of political or social objectives. *International terrorism* involves violent acts or acts dangerous to human life that are a violation of the criminal laws of the United States or any state, or that would be a criminal violation if committed with the jurisdiction of the United States or any state. These acts appear to be intended to intimidate or coerce a civilian population, influence the policy of a government by intimidation or coercion, or affect the conduct of a government by assassination or kidnapping. International terrorist acts occur outside the United States or transcend national boundaries in terms of the means by which they are accomplished, the persons they appear intended to coerce or intimidate, or the locale in which the perpetrators operate or seek asylum.

The U.S. Defense Department defines terrorism as the unlawful use of—or threatened use of—force or violence against individuals or property to coerce or intimidate governments or societies. It is often used to achieve political, religious, or ideological objectives.

In the U.K. Terrorism Act 2000, *terrorism* means the use or threat of action that is designed to influence the government or to intimidate the public or a section of the public within or outside of the United Kingdom. Terrorism is also the use or threat of action for the purpose of advancing a political, religious, or ideological cause. Terrorism involves serious violence against a person or serious damage to property; endangers a person's life, other than that of the person committing the action; creates a serious risk to the health or safety of the public or a section of the public; or is designed seriously to interfere with or seriously to disrupt an electronic system.

Instead of defining terrorism, twelve UN conventions criminalize a set of specific threats and actions as terrorist. They are in the areas of internationally protected persons, safety of aviation, safety of maritime navigation, safety of fixed platforms at sea, hostage-taking, protection of nuclear material, manufacturing explosives, bombings, and financing. The post-9/11 policy-working group on terrorism delineated the broad characteristics of the phenomenon of terrorism as an act meant to inflict dramatic and deadly injury on civilians and to create an atmosphere of fear, generally for a political or ideological (secular or religious) purpose. The world body is under significant pressure to adopt a universal definition of terrorism.

There are over one hundred definitions of terrorism. As no one definition has gained universal acceptance, we propose a working definition of terrorism: *Terrorism is the threat or the act of politically motivated violence directed primarily against civilians.*

Some supporters of the Palestinian, Kashmiri, and Kurdish struggles have argued that they are legitimate campaigns and that Palestinian, Kashmiri, and Kurdish actions against civilians are not terrorist. They have also argued that when a campaign is legitimate, the fighters are "freedom fighters," not terrorists. In our view, whether a campaign is legitimate or not, deliberate attacks against civilians to achieve a political goal are terrorist. Killing unarmed combatants, including women and children, is not an act worthy of a freedom fighter. Irrespective of legitimacy, perpetrator, location, and time of the attack, terrorism is a method.

What has hampered international counterterrorism efforts for so long is that both agencies and countries have defined terrorism to suit their budgets or interests. A basic starting point for world leaders should be a working definition based on the unacceptability of directly or indirectly targeting or affecting civilians in order to further one's aims or cause. This should be the starting point, as it is hard to imagine heads of state who would publicly advocate such targeting of civilians.

# The Types and Causes of Terrorism

Terrorist groups develop ideologies or belief systems to advance their aims and objectives. Secular and religious ideologies are designed to politicize, radicalize, and mobilize the actual and potential followers of terrorist groups. Terrorist groups seek to advance their objectives by conducting a terrorist campaign within an ideological framework. Although aims differ according to the ideological orientations of each group, their objectives are to gain recognition at local, national, and international levels; intimidate and coerce both the target population and the government; and provoke the government to overreact so as to generate greater public support. Three principal strands have generated the ideological fuel required to spawn and sustain terrorist campaigns around the world.

## Ideological Terrorism

Marxism, Leninism, and Maoism provide the ideological fuel for left-wing terrorist groups to advance their aims and objectives. They seek to overthrow existing regimes and establish communist and socialist states. Most of the groups driven by left-wing ideologies—the Communist Combatant Cells (CCC) of Belgium, the Red Army Faction (RAF) of Germany, the Red Brigades (RB) of Italy, Action Direct (AD) of France—disintegrated at the end of the Cold War and ended with the death of the Soviet empire. A few left-wing groups survived in the poorer regions of the world. They include FARC in Colombia, the Tupac Amaru Revolutionary Movement (MRTA) in Latin America, the Sendero Luminoso (Shining Path) in Latin America, the New Peoples Army (NPA) in the Philippines, and the Peoples War Group (PWG) in Andhara Pradesh, India. Of these groups, FARC, the Nepal Maoists, and the NPA pose a severe national security threat to Colombia, Nepal, and the Philippines. The left-wing groups still active in Europe are the Revolutionary Organization 17 November and Revolutionary Nuclei, both of Greece, and the Revolutionary People's Liberation Party (DHKP-C) in Turkey.

Groups driven by right-wing ideologies include the Ku Klux Klan, Aryan Nations (Church of Christian Aryan Nations, Church of Jesus Christ Christian), the Aryan Liberation Front, the Aryan Brotherhood, the Arizona Patriots, the American Nazi Party (National Socialist Party, United Racist Front), and the United Self-

Defense Forces of Colombia (AUC). A right-wing group bombed the Alfred P. Murray Federal Building in Oklahoma City on April 19, 1995. Overall, groups driven by right-wing ideologies pose a low threat compared to other categories of terrorism. In contrast to the left-wing groups, the bulk of the right-wing groups are located in North America and in Western Europe. Most right-wing groups are neo-Nazi, neofascist, anti-Semitic, and racist groups dominated by skinheads, attacking immigrants and refugees, mostly of Asian and Middle Eastern origin.

## Ethnonationalist Terrorism

The first wave of ethnonationalist campaigns was by national liberation movements directed against colonial rulers. They included the Irgun and Lehi opposing the British rule in Palestine in the 1940s and French rule in Algeria in the 1950s. Contemporary groups driven by ethnonationalism can be divided into three subcategories—groups fighting for autonomy, for unification, or for reunification (irredentism). The Al Aqsa Martyrs Brigade, the Jammu and Kashmiri Liberation Front (JKLF), and the Liberation Tigers of Tamil Eelam are fighting for independence from Israel, India, and Sri Lanka, respectively, and are motivated by Palestinian, Kashmiri, and Tamil nationalism. Two other groups, Continuity and the Real IRA, are fighting for unification or reunification with the Republic of Ireland. The PKK is fighting for linguistic and cultural autonomy for the Kurds in southeastern Turkey. In comparison to other categories, ethnonationalist conflicts produce the largest number of fatalities and casualties, internally displaced persons and refugee flows, and the biggest human rights violations. Groups that have adopted virulent ethnonationalist ideologies pose a significant threat to their opposing ethnic communities and governments.

## Politico-Religious Terrorism

Groups driven by religiosity include those from the Christian, Jewish, Sikh, Hindu, Buddhist, and Islamic faiths. They include the Army of God in the United States; Kach and Kahne Chai of Israel; Babbar Khalsa International of Punjab, India; Aum Shinrikyo (recently renamed Aleph) of Japan; the Islamic Resistance Movement (Hamas); the Palestinian Islamic Jihad (PIJ); and the Armed Islamic Group of Algeria. Aum, an apocalyptic group, aimed to take over Japan and then the world until its leader Soko Asahara was arrested after a deadly sarin attack in the Tokyo subway in 1995. In contrast to other Islamist groups campaigning within their territories, Al Qaeda and Lebanese Hezbollah (to a lesser extent) have a global or a universalistic Islamic agenda. To justify violence, politically motivated religious leaders propagate corrupt versions of religious texts, often misinterpreting and misrepresenting the great religions.

Of the religious category of groups, *Islamists,* or groups motivated by radical Islamic ideology, are predominantly the most violent. This is mainly because most religious terrorists often believe they are supported by God, or they draw support from religion. Groups often use religious clerics to interpret religion to the aims of the group, justifying the leadership and causing anyone who questions the leadership or group to appear as "apostates" or "unbelievers," those who would question God and not carry out his bidding. Two pivotal events in 1979—the Islamic Revolution in Iran and the Soviet intervention in Afghanistan—led to the increase in the number of groups driven by Islamism. By holding on to U.S. hostages for 444 days, the Islamic Republic of Iran in 1979 defied the United States. The anti-Soviet multinational Afghan mujahedin defeated the Soviet Army in 1979, after which the Islamists turned their energies toward building a capability to defeat the remaining superpower—the United States—along with its allies and its friends in the Muslim world. With martyrdom becoming widespread and popular among Islamist groups throughout the 1980s and 1990s, the scale of violence unleashed by Islamist groups has surpassed that of secular ethnonationalist and left-wing and right-wing groups. For instance, the Palestinian Liberation Organization (PLO), Popular Front for the Liberation of Palestine, and Abu Nidal Organization killed far fewer people than their Islamist counterparts—Hamas and PIJ.

## Other Categories

Terrorist campaigns are also driven by ideologies that lack mass appeal and therefore are not very common. These can include state-sponsored, anarchist, and single-issue terrorism. Because terrorism is a "low cost–high impact" form of violence, states wishing to advance their foreign policy goals have supported terrorist groups to attack their inimical states. Due to sanctions imposed by the international community against states that sponsor terrorist groups, this clandestine surrogate form of warfare has declined throughout the 1990s and into the twenty-first century. Although the U.S. government has accused a range of countries of supporting terrorism, there is no evidence that North Korea, Iraq, Sudan, Libya, or Cuba sponsor terrorism today, though in the 1990s, Sudan and Libya were active sponsors of terrorism. Iran, Syria, and Lebanon continue to support terrorism, albeit in reduced scale. The U.S. list of countries can be seen as "politically colored," as it does not include a dozen other countries that clandestinely support foreign terrorist groups.

Single-issue terrorist groups include violent animal rights and anti-abortion groups that seek to change a specific policy or practice rather than the political system. Anarchist terrorists seek to overthrow established governments by a wave of bombings and assassinations. State response to anti-globalization movements will determine whether we are likely to witness the emergence of terrorist groups espousing the cause of anti-globalization, although there are already fears in intelligence communities that anti-globalization groups have been networking with terrorist groups with similar beliefs.

Some of the groups have overlapping ideologies. The ethnonationalist PKK has a strong Marxist-Leninist orientation; the original ideological disposition of the LTTE was Marxist-Leninist; Hamas and PIJ are religious but have a strong nationalist dimension; and Al Aqsa Martyrs Brigade is ethnonationalist but has a strong religious dimension. In order to survive, the ideologies of groups tend to shift with the changes in the political environment. Groups driven by left-wing ideologies operating in North America and in Western Europe declined in strength and size at the end of the Cold War. The post–Cold War period witnessed a resurgence of ethnicity and religiosity. As a result, groups driven by ethnicity and religion now account for about 70–80 percent of all terrorist groups. Furthermore, the ethnonationalist and religious groups have the greatest staying power. Unlike left-wing or right-wing conflicts, ethnonationalist and religious conflicts are protracted.

Although the different *types* of terrorism allude, to some degree, to the motivation or causes of such activities, one must be careful not to solely consider the ideological factors driving the group. A group might be primarily motivated by religious reasons, but that is not to say that it is not affected by external factors or that its members did not join for other reasons, as we shall see in the section on why people join and support terrorist groups. Although the FARC in Colombia is ostensibly an ideological group, it has realized the wealth and improved standard of living that can be accrued from illegal activities such as drug trafficking. Thus, if one tried to counter such a group solely on the basis of its ideological issues, then one would be highly unlikely to resolve the situation. One must also take into account external factors that may affect the drive to undertake in such violent activities. It is also important to treat each case individually. These points become particularly important in a counterterrorism context and are apparent when one realizes, for example, that measures used to counter or resolve one *type* of terrorism in one country would not necessarily work on the same *type* of terrorism in another country. Thus, for instance, you would not expect to respond to ideological violence in Italy in the same way as ideological violence in Africa, because not only would the ideologies probably differ, but the context would be different. Certain factors that contribute to the drive to undertake or partake in such action would be present in one example but not in the other. To further illustrate this one might consider that in developing world countries, environmental factors such as the availability of food, water, and resources may affect the motivation of certain groups, and that membership in a group might mean that through pillaging, members can acquire such resources that they would not be able to obtain as individuals.

The causes of political violence and terrorism should not be viewed in isolation but in relation to five major sectors: military security, political security, economic security, societal security, and environmental security.

> Generally speaking, *military security* concerns the two-level interplay of the armed offensive and defensive capabilities of states, and states' perceptions of each other's intentions. *Political security* concerns the organizational stability of states, systems of government and the ideologies that give them legitimacy. *Economic security* concerns access to the resources, finance and markets necessary to sustain acceptable levels of welfare and state power. *Societal security* concerns the sustainability, within acceptable conditions for evolution, of traditional patterns of language, culture and religious and national identity and custom. *Environmental security* concerns the maintenance of the local and the

planetary biosphere as the essential support system on which all other human enterprises depend. These five sectors do not operate in isolation from each other. Each defines a focal point within the security problematic, and a way of ordering priorities, but all are woven together in a strong web of linkages. (Buzan 1991, 19–20)

It is important to respond to the problem of terrorism based on the type of terrorism, to recognize external factors, and to treat each case individually rather than to use broad generalizations. One must realize that many groups use ideology as a front, or façade, in attempts to either cover or legitimize their activities to their supporters. Thus because a group is a certain type of group (e.g., ideological), it does not mean to say that the group is *actually* driven by that ideology, or that it was ideology alone that caused all of its members to join. If we understand more about the causal factors that drive the group to act—and about the individuals who join the group that undertakes such actions, as well as the environment/context in which they operate—we can better understand how to respond, resolve, and counter such terrorism.

# Motivations for Joining or Supporting a Terrorist Group

Since 9/11, much speculation has taken place over the role of religion in terrorism. This is another example of focusing on the *type* of group, and not taking into account any other factors. Religion can and often does play a significant part, but it is imperative to recognize the roles and degrees of influence of other factors involved and not focus solely on one aspect, such as religion, to the exclusion of the others, as doing so will ultimately lead to misunderstanding. When looking at factors that motivate entry, and that encourage or deter exit, one must remember that just because a group or individual is religious, for example, it does not mean that other factors cannot cause members to join or leave. For instance, there were rumors of a case a few years ago of one of the regional chiefs of Al Qaeda who left the group citing economic factors, as he found out that his opposite number in another region was getting paid more than he was! Also, when looking at suicide missions and "martyrdom," there is the example of the LTTE, which effects suicide missions based not on religion and the belief of automatic access to heaven, but on indoctrination. Members are indoctrinated with the belief of becoming a martyr/legend/hero, doing something to be remembered by, and making others proud. Promises of their family being paid and supported (so they won't need to worry about food, money, etc.) if the individual undertakes the suicide mission further increases the motivation to do so.

Although the factors that affect the aspects involved with entry to and exit from terrorist groups can vary depending on region, culture, and type of group (whether ethnic, ideological, religious/cult), the following brief and general summary of the most common themes provides a basic working knowledge of the factors involved.

# Theories of Psychology

## Are Terrorists Mad or Irrational?

Let's look briefly at what psychologists suggest: psychopathology theory claims the notion that terrorists are mad or psychopaths (suffering from a psychopathological disorder), and thus are *irrational* actors. Proponents of this line of thought do not take issue with the suggestion that terrorists reason logically. However, they argue that political terrorists are driven to commit acts of violence as a consequence of psychological forces. Jerrold Post (*Origins of Terrorism*, 1996) suggests that they have a special psycho-logic that is constructed to rationalize acts they are psychologically compelled to commit, and that "individuals are drawn to the path of terrorism in order to commit acts of violence, and their special psycho-logic, which is grounded in their psychology and reflected in their rhetoric, becomes the justification for their violent acts."

The question is whether this theory can be applied to *all* terrorists. This theory is possibly more relevant when looking at low-level thugs, such as some of the paramilitaries, who have perhaps been bullied and have insecurities that might drive them to get involved in such activities. There are interesting parallels with studies conducted by the FBI's behavioral science unit (Douglas et. al 1997) in Quantico on serious criminals such as rapists and in other studies of people who become involved in paramilitary activities, serious crime (rape, murder, etc.), and the more "thuggish" elements of organized crime, in their motivations and backgrounds. Many, bullied while young, developed "them and us" syndromes, feeling that the world is against them; they felt insecure and so developed macho or "bad" reputations in order to ward off potential aggressors. Such sentiments often motivate such people to train obsessively, sometimes take steroids, turn into bullies, and feel secure in a group with a "dangerous" reputation. Although this theory may help explain some of the thuggish elements in an organization, it cannot be applied to the whole organization. One must bear in mind the sophistication of many terrorist groups. Many such groups have research and development wings, for example. The LTTE actually developed stealth boats and was in the process of building mini-submarines for its maritime division, the Sea Tigers. Many groups also have legal wings investigating international and domestic legal loopholes, as well as operating very astute political fronts. Therefore, if all terrorists were mad or suffered from psychopathological disorders, such organizations would not be so successful at evading capture, continuing to operate, or achieving some of their aims. Although there may be elements of these factors or symptoms involved in the motivation to become a terrorist, they often vary in their extent. For these reasons it is often better to take a "case-by-case" approach rather than generalize.

## Are Terrorists Rational?

The basis of Rational Choice Theory is the notion that the decision to both become a terrorist and commit terrorist acts is influenced by factors in the environment, and that the actor is a rational one who responds and reacts to these environmental factors. This theory opposes the common misconception that "all terrorists are mad" and looks at external as well as internal factors in trying to understand and explain such behavior. Many psychologists, such as Taylor, Horgan, and Silke, for example, have conducted interviews with terrorists and found them to appear rational and "normal," with no signs or histories of psychopathological disorders.

One must be aware of the dangers of generalizing on such topics. There is no "one size fits all" theory, and the motivating factors can depend on thespecific case study; indeed, the best explanation is often a kind of "pick-n-mix" combination of a number of different factors.

As it would be wrong to fully discount the theory that all terrorists are mad, it would be equally wrong to state that all terrorists are rational; there will always be counterexamples to every example put forward. There will always be some *mad* terrorists, and there will always be some *rational* terrorists; it is not a question of either/or, but a question of discerning where the boundaries lie.

Due to the parallels of terrorism with racist and right-wing youth groups in Europe over *entry* and *exit*, as found by Bjorgo (1997), we shall apply his framework and findings to the case of the terrorist in the following sections.

## Reasons for Joining Terrorist Groups

Many people join terrorist groups in their youth, and indeed it is in the interests of groups to "get them when they're young," as that is when they are most impressionable and most vulnerable to group manipulation and indoctrination. Some are also likely to join in an act of adolescent rebellion, making it easier for the group to take them physically, as opposed to resorting to coercion. In terms of manipulation and indoctrination, an interesting example is that of the Tamil Tigers (LTTE), which as part of its youth recruit training regularly shows *Rambo* videos in between weapons training. Such a technique reinforces the idea of invincibility and machismo by exploiting adolescent feelings. Although most recruits are youths, it would be wrong to say that adults are not recruited. As is true with adolescents, adults often can be manipulated through propaganda and by exploiting any vulnerabilities they may have.

One common factor that motivates people to join or support a group is belief in the cause of the group—sympathy with the aims, ideology, religion, or politics of the group. Factors that can affect the degree of members' "sympathy" with the cause can be formed by the whole socialization process—their upbringing, education, friends, family, community, what they see on TV, and so on. The belief that the political process has failed and that the only way to achieve the end goal is to support or use terrorism, and the belief that by employing terrorism (as opposed to democratic means) it is feasible to achieve the end goal, can also drive someone to support or join terrorist groups.

Terrorist propaganda often purports that the community has been wronged or deprived and that community members are the victims of unprovoked and unjustified attacks or efforts from an oppressive "bullying" opponent. Provocation and anger can motivate people to support or join terrorist groups. A feeling of hopelessness (and the sense that terrorist groups are "bullied underdogs" of "David and Goliath" proportions) can drive people to join. Revenge is another powerful motivation; it is often triggered when security forces or another group harms individuals, their loved ones, or property. Often the most committed members of terrorist groups are those who have been directly affected by political violence, often by a state or a state-sponsored group. Those who have suffered the loss of family members and friends, their schools or their homes, become the most committed because they have direct and tangible personal justifications as opposed to an ideological cause. They are likely to have a personal vendetta or battle with what they perceive as "the enemy." Joining or supporting a terrorist group is often perceived as the only avenue for extracting revenge.

Although *conscription* is not widespread (and is often highlighted and exaggerated by governments for propaganda purposes), terrorist groups also coerce some recruits to join or support them. In Colombia and some African countries there are accounts of terrorist and paramilitary groups raiding villages and kidnapping children, recruiting them, and inducing terror to ensure villager support. In an atmosphere of fear and uncertainty, a potential recruit can be threatened by a terrorist group to join or support a group, and indeed have no real choice. Such recruits harbor the belief that joining or supporting a terrorist group would facilitate protection of his or her family from the terrorist threat. Likewise, if a family member has been taken away to join the group, the group will often blackmail the remaining family, threatening to kill the taken family member if demands are not met. In places such as Northern Ireland many individuals join terrorist or paramilitary groups for protection from opposing groups. If individuals have been bullied or feel threatened by gangs or criminals, even though there may not be any real threat, they may also be driven to join groups for protection.

Terrorist groups often use propaganda to legitimize their cause, and to display their members as freedom fighters and charismatic folk heroes standing up for what they believe, undeterred by the vast odds against them, and taking on the full might of the "enemy" with no regard for their personal safety. This propaganda is also designed to attract potential recruits who might have a boring or mundane life with no sense of purpose, those who feel like a "nobody." Such people often perceive the opportunity of joining such a group as an opportunity for becoming a mythical hero, martyr, or living legend, with a life of excitement and action. A common theme among adolescents is that they often strive to be taken seriously as adults. Groups such as the FARC exploit this by approaching such youths and treating them seriously—showing them respect that perhaps others do not. FARC recruiters will befriend the youth and then get him/her to go with them, ostensibly to see if they would like to join the group, although few, if any, get the choice of not joining. They are then taken into the jungle and continually moved around so that it is physically impossible for them to return home. Once these new members have acquired the necessary jungle survival and navigational skills that would aid them in returning home, other techniques are employed to ensure they do not leave the group (threats to families, involvement in killings, guilt, criminal implications).

Some individuals join or support a terrorist group for social recognition or social acceptance. Clark (*Terrorism*, 1983) found when investigating ETA that in the Basque region of Spain, mixed-parentage children (those not "pure Basque") are reviled, and that only 8 percent are of mixed Basque-Spanish origin. When Clark investigated the background membership of ETA he found that over 40 percent of the terrorist group were from such mixed-parentage families, thus suggesting that they were trying to show that they were so Basque that they would go to the extremes of fighting for Basque independence; in other words, they were attempting to "out-Basque the Basques" (Reich 1996, 29). Many members of terrorist groups join because they are attracted by romantic fantasies of a secretive "James Bond" lifestyle or are excited by prospects of receiving illegal weapons training; others are attracted by the tribalism of being part of a group with its own distinctive uniforms, fear-inducing symbols, and so on. Psychologists (e.g., Douglas and Olshaker 1997) have documented numerous terrorist group members who were drawn to positions of authority, dominance, and control.

Some individuals join terrorist groups for economic reasons, much as one might choose a career due to its perceived benefits. Because contemporary terrorist groups engage in organized crime—from trading in diamonds to trafficking in narcotics to human smuggling and credit-card fraud—to fund their existence and operations, joining a terrorist group can be lucrative. In conflict zones, areas affected by drought, and areas with little or no prospects for its residents, the opportunities for livelihood are often limited, and there may be no alternatives or better prospects than to join and stick with a terrorist group. The phenomenon of "war economies," where groups receive more money than they ever would if there were no war, compound this problem, for if a "war economy" exists, not only are people more likely to join, but they are equally unlikely to leave. For example, groups such as the Tamil Tigers or FARC may be receiving so much funding that if their political demands (e.g., of independence) were achieved there may be no jobs or income to revert to; thus it is a more prosperous and stable option to continue the war economy.

Some scholars believe that people join terrorist groups because they have failed to achieve their political goal by political means; that in their minds the use of violence is justified because there is no other path available. This is simply not true. By turning straight to terrorism, it can be argued, one saves a lot of time and effort because it is easier to present a cause by terrorist, rather than democratic, means; to organize and achieve a political party and aim, one needs significant resources (finances, personnel, etc.) as well as sophisticated organizational skills to run the party and mobilize public support through various events, and delicate handling and courting of the media.

Unlike most democratic political parties that tolerate dissent, many terrorist groups are totalitarian movements led by dictators. The internal and external political environments of members are often controlled with no or limited access to the outside world. Events are interpreted through the group's viewpoint until its members share certain values and beliefs. Singularly and collectively, members believe that they can accomplish the aims, objectives, and goals of the terrorist group. We now turn our attention to understanding what happens when a person joins a terrorist group.

## Recruitment Techniques

Theorists have long argued that poverty, lack of education, and unemployment produce terrorist recruits and supporters. However, Osama bin Laden comes from the richest nonroyal Saudi family, and his principal strategist, Dr. Ayman Al Zawahiri, is from one of the most educated families in Egypt. Although those who live in poverty, are unemployed, or underemployed are most vulnerable to ideological indoctrination, it also generates recruits and supporters for terrorism in developed countries, as well as among wealthy and educated classes. However, because the socioeconomic and political conditions in Asia, Africa, the Middle East, Latin America, and the former USSR are conducive to the inculcation of terrorist ideologies, the bulk of the terrorist groups are located in the poorer regions of the world. Both territorial and migrant communities harboring actual and perceived grievances and aspirations provide significant political, economic, and military support for terrorist groups. However, causal factors of terrorism can be very diverse, as they often depend on various, sometimes interrelated, factors—individual circumstances, external environments, psychology, upbringing, and so on. It is necessary to consider how groups recruit members and the often very sophisticated manipulative process that groups utilize.

In a situation where unemployment was over 50 percent, medical supplies and food staples were scarce, and much of the population had no education, the Armed Islamic Group of Algeria (GIA) operated through mosques by giving food, medical handouts, and offering accommodations. This gave the GIA a very credible humanitarian dimension to attract potential recruits and *legitimize* its cause. Keeping in mind that both the Sharia and Qur'an prescribe the notion of Muslim brotherhood—that it is wrong not to equally share resources among Muslims—and that there was, or at least was perceived to be, in Algeria a corrupt government seen by the populace as benefiting from the oil industry while the the greater population suffered (it has been estimated that the entire wealth of Algeria's 28 million residents is in the hands of only about 5,000 people), one begins to understand how religion was manipulated to play an important part in driving people to join terrorist groups as well as justifying their actions.

Protracted socioeconomic and political conflicts create the conditions for the spawning and sustenance of virulent ideologies. Through propaganda (word of mouth, sermons and lectures, leaflets and booklets, print media, radio, TV, and the Internet), terrorist ideologues indoctrinate members, supporters, sympathizers, and potential recruits. Those indoctrinated join, collaborate, support, or sympathize with terrorist goals, aims, and objectives. Sustained terrorist indoctrination can construct new grievances (insecurity) or exacerbate existing grievances (education, employment opportunities, cultural rights, land settlement and colonization, regional autonomy). Similarly, through heightened propaganda, the aspirations of an affected community can be elevated.

Indoctrination is particularly important in long-term operations, suicide operations, or where a terrorist becomes a "sleeper agent"—residing in the target country for a number of years, living a normal life, and waiting to be activated as and when the group wishes. This is particularly relevant in the case of 9/11, when many observers wondered how the terrorists could sustain their beliefs for so long in the target country. The answer is clearly this: If a terrorist from an impoverished background comes to, for example, the United States as a sleeper agent and sees the luxury Americans live in compared to his or her family and friends at home, his or her commitment to the cause and suicide mission will often be reinforced. Prior long-term indoctrination in terrorist training camps also keeps these types of agents focused on their missions. An interesting parallel is the Cold War, whereby the Soviet intelligence agencies let only their most committed ideological spies and agents come to the West for long-term assignments to ensure they wouldn't be swayed by life in the target country. The same principle exists with terrorist groups, whereby only the most committed (and indoctrinated) are allowed to undertake such assignments.

The processes and uses of indoctrination not only help explain motivations to join but also explain the transition to extremism or suicide bombing—where extreme indoctrination, propaganda, and interpretation of external events through the group viewpoint occurs, often because the individuals are removed from reality. Instead of the idea that it is a *madman* or *fanatic* who gets recruited and then executes a suicide mission, we now see that the more likely scenario is that of a rational person who goes through the recruitment process (including manipulation and indoctrination) of the group and ends up with a mindset that allows him (or her) to conduct such acts. A famous example is that of Zacarias Moussaoui, who was recruited by Al Qaeda at a time when he was very vulnerable: living in a foreign country, with nowhere to stay, no job, no friends, and little money. The extent of indoctrination was such that he later wasn't recognized by his brother, who remembered him as a "kind, caring, moderate person," not someone with extreme religious beliefs who had the urge to "fight for and with his Muslim brothers."

Moussaoui is now in U.S. federal custody pending trial on allegations that he was to have been the twentieth active Al Qaeda terrorist in the 9/11 attacks.

A particular danger for youths in the early recruitment stages is that they may focus so much on becoming a part of the group that they miss what it is they are actually getting into, what life will be like, what the consequences may be. The escalation of violence is often gradual; it takes time before members reach the extremes of murder. Some may exit because they have realized that things have "gone too far," but more junior members may not do so because they are gradually sucked in. The real danger, though, is that by this stage it is perhaps too late, and there are no credible exit opportunities available as they may already be stigmatized or involved in crime. It is this notion of "no return" that is so important:

> Becoming socialised into a new community, with a world-view and value system completely at odds with mainstream society, and building bonds of loyalty to the new "family," represents one fundamental process individuals go through when they join such a group, and occurs in tandem with the severing of ties to normal society, and often, society, family, [and] friends burn the bridges behind them. (Jamieson 1989)

Research shows that once inside a group, many find they are not instantly accepted into the "secret circle,"[1] core, or clandestine activities, and are involved in overt activities to weed out those who are committed from those who are not (Bjorgo 1997). Although many get bored and leave, others who are curious about the inner circles, crave acceptance, or desire to prove themselves push for this inner circle. This is the beginning of a process designed to invoke absolute loyalty and "burn all other bridges"—when regular or full-time members openly mistrust irregular or part-time members. Because part-timers have already risked social isolation, this treatment by group members often makes them want to prove themselves and pushes them further into the group. Many go through processes of inclusion and socialization into a new reclusive and stigmatized community, having ties severed to the normal community outside (Bjorgo 1997). As the dual processes of inclusion and socialization occur, it becomes harder to leave the group the further and longer they continue. Usually it takes time—and a long and gradual process of "bridge-burning"—for recruits to become full members, or "regulars." Terrorist groups use different methods. Based in northern Ireland, the Provisional Irish Republican Army (PIRA) does not pay members unless they have been chosen to become full-time. The small allowance that is sometimes given to other members is so little that many are forced to divide their time between PIRA activities and earning more money to live, leaving little spare time for external relations that might conflict with the group's interest. "Full-time" members may be expected to regularly move around the country to various "posts," thus minimizing the development of external social relations.

To summarize, when one becomes a member of a terrorist group, one experiences a new identity, isolation, stigmatization, criminality, and a sense of purpose. The process and shared experiences of the group can build up a collective psychology—a passive or indirect form of indoctrination or brainwashing. One PIRA member noted: "We confirmed each other's opinions all the time as we lived in our own closed world, marginalized and isolated from others" (Jamieson 1989).

If there is no community of supporters or the group has to recruit externally, usually the group will first pick out vulnerable targets (youths or those who are "down on their luck" or depressed), as they are vulnerable to approaches and thus easy to manipulate. In the case of religious groups, people who are more ideologically committed are also targets, as they are easy to manipulate through clerics interpreting religion to the aims of the group. The techniques used to manipulate can include blackmail, propaganda, promises of both tangible rewards for self and/or family (cash, food, medicine), and intangible rewards (becoming a martyr and going to heaven).

Once the targets have been approached, their commitment is tested. The techniques employed are that of *intensive* testing through a rigorous selection process (requiring that they show up for 5 A.M. prayers, or complete a training camp, etc.). Another technique used is, for want of a better term, a *boring* process (such as handing out flyers for hours) to test a recruit's commitment. There is no immediate weapons training or access to secrets because the recruitment process is designed to weed out undesirables—fantasists or "loose cannons" who are easier for the authorities to notice/catch, as well as those who are unpredictable and undisciplined.

Those who complete each stage of the recruitment process and remain are socialized into a new community in an isolated and often stigmatized group that binds them together. Throughout the process, individuals are indoctrinated and adopt the group's values, perspective, views, style, and behavior. They also adopt the group's enemies (opposing/rival groups or state security forces). A further test of commitment is participation in illegal activities or in violent confrontations wherein recruits become criminals; the group's knowledge of this is a threat against individuals if they decide to leave or betray the group (Bjorgo 1997).

Bjorgo noticed these processes and identified the important aspect he described as "bridge burning"—cutting ties to "normal" society. He noted that the process of burning bridges is often inherent in the recruitment process: recruits are expected to go where they are told, when they are told, and are instructed that their ultimate loyalty must be to the group and to the cause. As this occurs, they become dependent on the group (they have no other friends outside, and thus no conflicting loyalties).

It is not only the "cause" or religion that is solely important. One must take into account environmental, as well as social and psychological, factors, along with the methods that groups use to attract and recruit potential members. It is often pointless trying to explain the mindset of terrorists without knowing about their backgrounds, previous situations, and how the group recruits or operates.

Often, the reality of life as a terrorist is very different from the image or motivating factor that caused the individual to join in the first place. The factors that drive individuals to join a group can also become the factors that make them want to leave, if membership of the group ceases to satisfy or fulfill that need that caused them to join in the first place.

# Common Motives for Wanting to Leave a Terrorist Group

Bjorgo (1997) suggests that factors encouraging exit can be divided into *push* factors (internal factors that drive the individual to want to leave) and *pull* factors (external factors that drive the individual to leave).

## Push Factors

*Negative reactions from social surroundings:* Suspected as terrorists, individuals are often avoided, even by sympathizers, due to the danger and hassle. Some may find that instead of becoming a folk hero they have become even more isolated. This may cause some individuals to wish to leave if their motivations to join were to win friends and gain status.

*Losing faith in the group's ideology and politics:* If individuals joined for ideological reasons, they may become disillusioned on realizing that they are not engaged in a political war but are killing innocent civilians rather than strictly military or opposition targets. Or they may realize that they cannot achieve their initial aims or that their initial aims and beliefs were wrong.

*The feeling that "things are going too far":* If innocent people are getting killed, or there are too many casualties, the perceived risks and "cons" may outweigh the "pros," causing the individual to realize that "this wasn't what I joined for."

*Disillusionment* about group and comradeship can cause individuals to want to leave, especially if they joined for social reasons. Although there is often a close camaraderie in the group due to massive external pressures acting as a cohesive, there is also a great deal of paranoia and "backstabbing" due to the constant fear of being infiltrated. Such fear, paranoia, backstabbing, and accusations are magnified in a small close-knit group and thus felt more strongly and personally because there is no other social support network. Thus, social factors can also affect the operational or "professional" aspects of the terrorist group. Furthermore, a loss of status, confidence/trust, and position in the group can cause people to want to leave if they are sidelined or excluded.

*Exhaustion* from the constant pressure of threat of injury, imprisonment, or death can also cause some individuals to want to leave the group. As members of the Red Brigades stated, "When you join, your whole life changes; you are a political terrorist '24: 7' with no respite, no fun, no babies, no cinema, and so you begin to miss your previous conventional life" (Jamieson 1989). If you are always looking over your shoulder—even to go round the corner for a paper—you often increasingly want a break or a normal life. These pressures cause many to "burn out" and some to commit suicide, as they see no alternative.

## Pull Factors

External factors that cause members to leave include the longing for the freedoms of a normal life. Often as members grow older they find they don't have the same need for excitement anymore, or they may get the feeling that they are "too old for this." Other pull factors can include the fear of (further) jeopardizing personal future and career, finding a girlfriend or boyfriend outside the group, acquiring new responsibilities for a spouse and children, and any other conflicting loyalties (although in many cases this is not often the case, as the organization is extremely strict and disciplined). Pull factors become increasingly attractive because a terrorist lifestyle is a full-time one with little or no respite. A key point is that even if members want to leave, it is seldom possible for them to do so.

# Factors Inhibiting or Deterring Disengagement

Again, Bjorgo's studies on youth and extremist gangs are relevant, as they have parallels with the factors involved in terrorist groups, and so his framework and findings have been applied to the phenomena of terrorism.

One factor deterring exit is that there is nothing to substitute for the *positive characteristics* of the group—comradeship, loyalty, understanding, and excitement. This sentiment is reflected in many ex-terrorist accounts. According to his well-publicized quote, Sean O'Callaghan, the former head of the IRA southern command, for example, stated, "In essence, the reason why so few republicans quit is that they cannot imagine that there is life, fun, decency, and honour outside the ghetto or group." Although one might question the notion of terrorists referring to or being affected by decency and honor, one must not discount the fact that it is a sentiment that they *feel;* thus it cannot be ignored when dealing with terrorists.

This problem is compounded by *time;* the longer a member remains, the more the group becomes his or her social universe—providing community, a substitute "family," identity, a sense of purpose, security and protection against external threats and enemies, and excitement and adventure. Leaving the group thus means forfeiting these things. A shared collective experience results in an intimate understanding and bonding and becomes part of the character of the individual. The importance of having someone you can talk to, who is either going through the same thing or can relate to it, should never be underestimated. This parallels documented experiences of former and serving Special Forces soldiers, where the pressures of not being able to tell anyone (even your spouse) about your job and life cause a great rift in other social situations, and can lead to not being able to form proper relationships with others; this reaffirms the value of group membership and understanding. This problem is amplified when the individual knows he cannot reenter the terrorist group and can act as an effective deterrent against those considering leaving the group.

The fear of *negative sanctions* from the group or the community, if the community supports the terrorist group, also acts as a deterrent to leaving. It is usually in the group's interest to kill individuals who want to leave the group to deter others from defecting and to safeguard any secrets individuals may have. Individuals may be open to blackmail at a later date, or run the risk of people in their "new life" finding out about their past activities and crimes. Even if individuals manage to evade the group, their families may not.

Fearing the *loss of protection* from former enemies can also deter people from leaving the group. As members they may only worry about the group's enemies; even then they have or may feel that the group affords them some degree of protection. If they leave the group, they have no protection, and depending on how they leave, they may also need to worry about reprisals from their former group.

An additional consideration is that of the belief that they are doing something honorable or fighting a noble cause and the *sense of importance or purpose* that this gives while they are members of a group. This is an especially significant factor in the case of when the individual wants to leave, as this sentiment is first *felt* and then *taken away*. How does one make the transition from feeling that he or she is a "freedom fighter," as they often see themselves, to a supermarket shelf stacker, or office worker, for example? This is a question that needs to be addressed by those involved in witness protection or relocation programs.

Another factor deterring exit is the fear that one's future and career are already ruined. Terrorists often have no personal bank accounts, social security number, national insurance number, and so on, as these are all means by which they can be traced—once an individual is made a full-time member of a terrorist group, his or her identity often disappears for operational requirements. Employability is thus diminished, as there are no employer's references. In addition, passports and other documents required to travel and settle abroad are unavailable. Many members of terrorist groups feel that their future prospects are so limited by their membership that they might as well stay in the group.

And as mentioned earlier, in developing or undeveloped countries where there is a "war economy," not being a member of the group might mean not having food, water, money, or other life essentials.

# Applying These Findings to Counterterrorism

In order to motivate people to disengage from terrorist groups, one has to reinforce the "push factors," which make continued belonging to the group less attractive; reinforce the "pull factors," which make belonging to "normal" society more attractive; and reduce the factors that inhibit potential defectors to disengage from the group. When continued adherence to the group seems unattractive, and when life outside the group seems attractive, the probability for disengagement increases (Bjorgo 1997).

From examination of the aforementioned factors that motivate entry, as well as those encouraging and deterring exit, one can formulate a checklist of prerequisites to be met to ensure an effective exit by an individual from a terrorist group. By using such a checklist, one can evaluate different exit strategies and formulate better ones (such as more effective witness protection or relocation schemes). Following is a list of criteria based on Bjorgo's (1997) research on when and how terrorists exit their group:

1. Positive characteristics of the group need to be substituted (alternative social support structure)
2. Fear of negative sanctions from the group are removed/nullified
3. Loss of protection from former enemies is substituted

4. Problems of social isolation and nowhere to go need to be resolved
5. A sustainable career, income, and future need to be developed
6. Negative reactions from society need to be dealt with/social reintegration
7. Lost faith in the group's ideology and politics, the feeling that things went too far in the group, and disillusionment regarding the group and comradeship often need to be replaced with the feeling of a sense of purpose and a cause to fight for
8. Lost status, confidence, and position in the group may require the encouragement of a new feeling of confidence, status, and position in another group
9. Exhaustion from the stress of life in a terrorist group needs to be countered by rest and recovery of confidence from assured protection
10. Physical separation from the group, often being moved to another area

The above criteria can differ depending on the individual, region, culture, and economy. However, these are general guidelines that can be referred to when examining specific cases.

There are likewise requirements for terrorists to reassure the public about their exit from the terrorist group and reintegration into society. They must:

1. Renounce violence and the use of terror, and perhaps ideology (publicly) to ensure they can't go back to the group (otherwise there might be public outcry and suspicion that the individual has not really left the group)
2. Cooperate with authorities against the terrorist group (to prove further that they have left and renounced terror, as well as earning any state help in terms of relocation and protection)
3. Serve a (minimum) sentence or punishment for their crimes (otherwise there would be public outcry)—this time can be used to train them for another career, arrange new identities, and give them the isolation from the group to change their views independently

As noted earlier in this chapter, some recruits are driven by altruistic reasons whereas others have a genuine desire (perhaps for revenge or from promises of financial rewards for themselves and their families) to sacrifice their life for the people, the land, or for any other ideal that could drive a recruit or a serving member to commit an act of terrorism. Terrorist propaganda that inculcates the belief that sacrificing one's life will create a better future for the community or religion attracts fresh recruits and increases the commitment of existing recruits. Inculcating the belief that death is inevitable and that government troops would harm a potential recruit because of differences in ethnicity, religion, or ideology can drive a recruit to join a terrorist group and contribute to the cause before dying. This highlights the importance of having an effective counterpropaganda capability.

Research suggests that a terrorist group by its own action alone cannot be successful. Often, government overreaction or underreaction generates overwhelming support and recruits for terrorism. Internment without trial, curfews, mass arrests by the security forces—including arrests on mistaken identity or on false information provided by a personal enemy—can humiliate and turn a non–terrorist sympathizer into a terrorist sympathizer. Furthermore, terrorist propaganda claims of the state being a bully and unjustified become more credible. Many groups when organizing demonstrations and riots, for example, encourage members and supporters to engage security forces with only sticks and stones so that when the security forces respond it instantly looks (to the media and onlookers) like the security forces are overreacting by using force when the "rioters" are only using stones. It is thus important for security forces to have media liaisons and to use water cannons instead of live ammunition in such circumstances.

Similarly, collateral damage by security forces (e.g., the death of one's mother, father, brother, or sister) motivates people to join terrorist groups. Intelligence (along with cultural and linguistic understanding) is paramount in order to accurately identify and pinpoint the terrorist and the terrorist infrastructure. When a terrorist is captured, it is important to release information of what they were involved in (bombings that killed children, recruiting children to kill targets, etc.) so that the public can see what the group is really like; this has the effect of reducing potential and actual support, deterring potential recruits, and possibly "turning" current members. However, there is the risk that too much sharing of this information with the public could damage the individual's odds at a fair trial, with the possible result of a court case being thrown out.

If the terrorist group can recruit five new members for every terrorist killed or captured, the battle against the terrorist organization is lost. Often when a colleague is killed, security forces will enforce collective punishment. As shown in the policy of collective punishment meted out in Israel, this has proved to be counterproductive. To prevent such counterproductive actions, especially overreactions, there should be accountability and oversight at all levels in the counterterrorist organization. Targeting the terrorist rank and file with counterpropaganda and offering irresistible incentives for desertions and *surrendees* can weaken a group from within. Nonmilitary methods are equally or more important than military methods because political and economic measures are enduring and can have a lasting impact on a terrorist group and its support base.

It is hard for a terrorist group to grow in strength and size. It needs an effective propaganda capability as well as a strong support base. Terrorist groups often provoke security forces to overreact to generate sympathy and support. A restrained law enforcement response is therefore critical to prevent terrorist groups from expanding its support bases, essential for both recruitment and sustenance.

Another factor to consider when looking at how and why people join terrorist groups, and how to counter or prevent more from joining, is the actual physical opportunity to do so. Many groups openly recruit, and if one lives in a community supportive of the group that provides many recruits then it may be seen as natural for people from that community to "join the cause and fight for their community." The availability and ease of access to the group must therefore be reduced, if not removed entirely. Furthermore, the state must reduce any positive aspects of group membership while increasing the negative aspects, thus deterring possible recruits from joining and encouraging potential "leavers" to leave.

Religion plays an apparent role in motivating individuals to join terrorist groups. The ostensible line is that people volunteer for suicide attacks, that everyone inside the organization has freedom of choice, and that sheer conviction of both religious belief and the organization's "cause" are the sole factors in motivating an individual to act. The reality is that a calculated and intelligent use of different strategies attracts and manipulates individuals into joining and acting for a group's ends under the banner of religious belief.

When discussing counterterrorism, one must first understand what motivates those whom the counterterrorist is trying to defeat; in this way we can treat the causal factors as opposed to the symptoms. It is thus important to adopt a holistic approach and take into account the environmental factors surrounding the individual prior to membership in the group as well as currently, as well as the behavior or psychology of the individual or group.

Currently the area of exit and disengagement programs is a weak one in counterterrorism terms, as many of our democratic legal and penal systems remain extremely ill-suited to the specialized tasks of encouraging and effecting disengagement from terrorist groups. It is an area of very high potential return, given the intelligence that can be gathered and the overall weakening of the group as a result; thus it should be paid more attention and resources.

## Trends and Evolution of Terrorism

Since 9/11 many consider terrorism a *new* phenomenon or threat. Although one can argue that the scale of 9/11 was unprecedented, the concept, risk, and threat of such an attack was not new. Years ago Ramzi Yousef, for example, had planned to plant bombs (and detonate them during flight) on board eleven U.S. airliners over the Pacific. The Lockerbie, Scotland, disaster of 1988 is another example of a large-scale aviation terrorist incident. Although analysts have talked of a *new* terrorism that began in the 1990s, the idea, along with information on how to conduct such incidents, has been around for some time. This is the case not only for aviation terrorism but also for nuclear-biological-chemical (NBC) weapons and other forms of attacks. Although the *level of risk* may be new, the *forms* themselves are not; thus, one should not hysterically panic at the existence of a perceived *new* threat. It is helpful to realize that the capability and idea to undertake such actions as an NBC attack, for example, have been around for decades, and that terrorists have taken advantage of them only a few times. Furthermore, mass panic is only likely to increase the attractiveness of such an attack due to the publicity any group doing so would attract.

Terrorism is not new. As early as A.D. 66–70, Jewish zealous sects engaged in terrorist acts, as did the "Assassins" at the end of the eleventh century. The modern concept of international terrorism can be traced back to the hijacking of the El Al plane by PFLP members on July 22, 1968 (Hoffman 1999). This spawned the *internationalization of terrorism*—the process of previously isolated groups developing an international status, developing contacts with each other, and helping each other in terms of procurement, training, and so on. This phenomenon began to grow toward the end of the Cold War; it included the development of more sophisticated overseas support structures, diversification in fundraising and procurement, and the ensuing blurring between terrorist and organized crime activity. Thus some analysts talk of a "New Terrorism" emerging in the 1990s. Was this *new* or not? Let us first look at how and why these and other trends occurred and at the impact of changes in the world system.

Although ethnic tensions were restrained during the Cold War, one could not say that they did not exist; likewise there still existed state-sponsored terror, state terror, and LICs (low-intensity conflicts). The risk of nuclear Armageddon during the Cold War kept many ethnic or self-determination issues mostly under control. But when the world system shifted from a bipolar to a multipolar one, previously contained ethnic issues arose. States that had been satellites of one of the Cold War sides suddenly became independent players in a multipolar world system, able to adopt and pursue their own agendas. The same occurred at a sub-state level, with many groups better able to pursue dreams of independence. Decolonization exacerbated these problems, causing many countries such as India, Congo, Pakistan, and Sri Lanka to suffer from the consequences of ethnic and religious conflict. The new political environment freed up previously contained ethnic tensions and led to new political, geographic, economic, and environmental debates.

Features of the post–Cold War world included economic globalization, moves toward global free trade, international mobility of capital, and an easier cross-border movement of people. The latter resulted in a side effect of mass migration and ensuing cultural clashes. The proliferation of technology that also occurred at this time increased the ease and lethality of international terrorist activities and procurement; as a result there was a greater potential for more individuals to be involved with or to benefit from terrorism. The creation and increased accessibility/

availability of the Internet and global communications increased the audience worldwide and, simultaneously, the potential for more people to be involved or to benefit from terrorism.

Fundamentalism can also be attributed to the rise in economic globalization. Sheehan (1996) notes that economic globalization has produced rapid social change and social dislocation. Although overall standards of living have risen in many areas, he notes that growing economic inequality and injustice have exacerbated social instability and provided a seedbed for armed conflict.

Many of the moves toward economic globalization and free trade were designed to make it easier for individual and corporate investors to move assets, whether money or production facilities, across international borders. The implications of this resulted in the phenomenon of "capital flight" due to global capital mobility under a global system of free trade. The possibility of capital flight means that countries are forced to compete with each other, to attract and keep capital investors in order to avoid investors "uprooting" their investments and reestablishing elsewhere. The main problem with capital flight for "developing" countries is that they must compete against each other, usually by lowering environmental, social, and labor standards. Further worries on this theme emerged when it was realized that one move toward free trade (Multilateral Agreement on Investment [MAI]) meant that corporations would be able to challenge local laws before an international tribunal, but governments or their citizens will have no corresponding right to take action against offending corporations. They will have no right to conserve their environment or protect people against the harmful effects of foreign investment (Pilger 1998).

The effects of globalization undermine local industries as governments would have had no powers to protect them from external competition. Such a system of "free trade" did not seem to imply "symmetric" or "even" development, as called for in the 1974 UNESCO conference, but "asymmetric" or "uneven" development.[2] It is for these reasons that economic globalization seemed undesirable for undeveloped, and certain developing, countries. It seemed that it would not result in "fairer distribution" of wealth, as globalization means integration and the dropping of barriers, and thus more likely that the strongest or the biggest companies would dominate.

The moves made by the "global establishment" toward global free trade seem to fit the picture portrayed by "dependency" theorists and subscribers to the "core-periphery" model of neocolonialism or neoimperialism. It is the reaction and effects of the "devaluing of social rights and conditions" in developing and/or undeveloped countries, as a result of the globalization of free trade, that should be paid more attention to, namely, the effects on society. This is significant when the result can be nationalism and even terrorism, as many terrorist groups in such countries seem to adopt this view.

Although most of the world's former colonial states are formally independent, their economic, social, cultural, and even political relations are dominated by the former colonial power(s) (Viotti and Kauppi 1993).

This "imperialism without colonies" was characterized by Ghanaian president Kwame Nkrumah in his book *Neo-Colonialism: The Last Stage of Capitalism* (1965) when he wrote that neocolonialism involves a state theoretically independent and sovereign, but whose economic system and political policy are in reality controlled by an outside power.

An interesting example of this neocolonialism is that of Algeria in the 1990s, where the French term *desclassement* has been used to describe the social, political, and economic factors involved in the "fueling" of militant Islam. As they lose out to the business classes, the working and middle classes are disaffected. Unemployment was also a major contributing factor in the rise of terrorism in Algeria. Although there was obviously money in the country, due to its oil reserves and the Western presence extracting it, few in the middle classes could find jobs, even if they had graduated from university. The wealth from the oil industry was blatantly unevenly distributed, and those in the street "are convinced that much of the country's oil wealth is spirited off to private Swiss bank accounts" (*Economist* 1999, 53). Furthermore, the injection of "petro-dollars" meant that Algeria's government was not accountable to the people. The government relied on foreign oil companies, French financing, and the army, rather than votes or taxes, to keep it in power. Some Algerian Islamists have campaigned against oil companies, demanding control of the nation's resources and self-determination.

Over the last 100 years Islam was used to express protest leading to resistance. According to Gellner (1985) this has certainly been connected with a position of powerlessness—political, economic, technological, but also social and cultural vis-à-vis the dominating West. Many people in Algeria and other countries saw multinational corporations as agents of the West enforcing neocolonialism and draining the resources from a country where the public would not benefit. If one looks through the rhetoric of terrorist groups in developing and undeveloped countries, particularly those involved in the oil industry, one sees that this is a common theme that terrorist groups state as being a motivating factor. The FARC in Colombia and factions of the GIA in Algeria are some of many such examples.

If Western presence is seen as neocolonial—as it may be in the West's vested interests to remain in the region, supporting the oppressive regimes in order to protect and ensure the availability of affordable energy—then one can see how terrorist groups may be motivated to target the West. This also helps explain the significance of the targeting of the Twin Towers and the hub of the U.S. economy on 9/11.

The end of the Cold War and the rise of economic and technological globalization have led to an apparent increase in ethnic, religious, and cult groups—which see violence as an end in itself and are less likely to be constrained morally from more lethal attacks (Hoffman 1999). In the 1970s all active international terrorist groups had secular goals and beliefs, with the majority having a Marxist variant. A major trend of the 1980s and 1990s, however, was an increase in the number and severity of ethnic and religious conflicts. In the 1990s, one-third of all active international terrorist groups were religious, and the majority were Islamist; a high percentage of the remaining international terrorist groups was motivated by ethnicity. Features include using mass terror against a designated enemy either to rid the enemy from "their" country or as an end in itself on the principle that "one less unbeliever" is good. The religious fanatics or those waging a holy war are unlikely to be inhibited by the prospect of causing large-scale carnage (Wilkinson 2001). In summary,

> [T]he escalation of ethnic conflicts into savage warfare involving extensive use of the weapon of mass terror is the more striking feature of the patterns of terror worldwide in the late 1990s. Moreover, owing to the intractability of such conflicts and the international community's repeated failures to find effective ways to prevent or resolve them, this form of warfare and its concomitant mass violations of human rights are likely to spawn major eruptions of terrorist violence well

into the next century....The close examination of trends in terrorism worldwide does not lead one to conclude that we now confront an entire new phenomenon of postmodern terrorist regimes and movements of the 1970s and 1980s. The regimes using terror against their own populations have been doing so for decades. State-sponsored terrorism has been apparent for over three decades. The majority of the secular international terrorist movements active in the later 1990s were established in the 1970s and most of those motivated by religion emerged in the 1980s. It is significant that only 10 of the 41 active major terrorist groups listed in the U.S. State Department's patterns of global terrorism 1998 were founded in the 1990s: most of these groups have known aims, organisational structures and leading activists, and various links with like-minded organisations and/or states.

Since many of these ideological groups have been more domestically focused, they have not received the same international attention.

The main continuing trends that have been identified and confirmed by analysts and statistics are as follows:

- International terrorist activities are increasing in lethality
- International terrorist acts are decreasing in number
- Domestic terrorist acts are increasing in number and lethality

Although this book focuses on international terrorism, globalization and the end of the Cold War may also help explain why there has been a rise in domestic terrorist acts. As to why international terrorist acts are declining in number, there is perhaps too much speculation, and thus no solid explanation can be given. Perhaps counterterrorism efforts have paid off, and it is thus harder for such acts to be planned and executed. What we shall focus on in this book is perhaps the most worrying: the trend of increasing lethality.

In recent years there has been a dramatic fall of recorded international terrorist attacks, yet a dramatic rise in fatalities. In aviation terrorism, for example, there has been a shift from hijacking to sabotage bombing of jumbo jets, as well as growing evidence of attempts to acquire—and some success in acquiring—surface-to-air missiles. In vehicle bombs there has been an escalation from small car bombs to huge truck bombs. In the United States there have been attempts to bring down whole buildings for maximum death, such as Oklahoma City in 1995, and the attacks of 9/11.

Why is there increasing lethality? Terrorism has become an easier tactic due to improvements in technology—it is now easier to access information, make contacts, and acquire equipment, weapons, and training; it also is easier to access terrorist groups through their Web sites. More groups also seem to see violence as an end in itself rather than as a means to an end. Cult or religious fanatics or those waging a holy war are unlikely to be inhibited by the prospect of causing large-scale carnage. Governments and private-sector targets learn from the past and harden their security, so terrorists look for easier targets, such as civilians, again to maximize publicity through atrocity. As the public becomes desensitized through repeated media viewings of the more spectacular disasters and atrocities, terrorists use even more dramatic and spectacular methods and attacks to maintain media attention. Other groups recognize that they must play "one-upmanship" in order to attract publicity for their cause. Likewise they may realize that if there is a significant amount of fear regarding a certain tactic, they are guaranteed publicity if they employ it. As Bowyer Bell (1998, 20) noted, "Often it is our reactions to terrorism which may constitute the primary danger, not terrorism itself." The current "super-terrorism" scare over the use of NBC weapons is an excellent example of this (Sprinzak 1998).

There is a popular rumor that after President Clinton read *The Cobra Event*, a fictional account of an attack on the United States using NBC weapons, he ordered preparedness exercises and contingency planning for the major cities in the United States. The irony is that in trying to find whether a city can cope, and in trying to make all the preparations for such an event, these actions tend to heighten the fear factor, thus increasing the reaction to and thus likelihood of a terrorist attack of this nature. Any small group wanting easy publicity or large group wanting maximum damage and a propaganda victory would thus only need to launch even a small attack using these methods to be assured instant notoriety. To see the disruption and fear such attacks cause, one need only look at the example of the post-9/11 anthrax letters, or the Aum Shinrikyo 1995 subway attack in Tokyo using the nerve agent sarin.

Such fears have caused many to ask whether we will see more use of NBC weapons in terrorist attacks in the future, especially as it may be easier to get chemical/biological weapons (CBWs) than to acquire guns or explosives. It is of obvious concern to many that states believed to sponsor terrorism have CBW programs. There are nuclear materials in Israel, India, Pakistan, China, Britain, France, North Korea, Russia (and former Soviet states), Libya, Iran, Iraq, Ukraine, the United States, and South Africa; and there is always the risk of proliferation of technology into unauthorized hands. Recent media reports attest to evidence that groups such as Al Qaeda have attempted to smuggle uranium and plutonium and to acquire and develop such NBC technology and materials, and that there are plans to use substances like sarin in the London underground.

Groups such as the LTTE have used chlorine on military bases in Sri Lanka, U.S. extreme right groups have been caught with anthrax and ricin, and Aum Shinrikyo used sarin. However, one must bear in mind that there are problems in employing such methods as well as reasons why many groups have not used them (Claridge 2000). First, a great deal of sophistication is needed to develop and *weaponize* such materials (usually requiring someone with university-level training to deal with such material and resources such as laboratories and specialized equipment). Deploying such materials also carries great risks (methods are often unpredictable and can be affected by wind, weather, etc.), posing a risk to those disseminating the substances, a risk of the direction of the substance, if airborne, being altered and perhaps affecting nontargets. Targets for optimum use, therefore, are likely to be contained areas with little ventilation and little influence from factors such as weather (the likely targets for CBW attacks are areas such as underground tube/subway networks). Nuclear or dirty bombs, however, can be used anywhere, and likely targets are largely populated urban areas for maximum damage and disruption, as the affected area cannot be used due to long-term irradiation. Another factor affecting the use of such methods is negative publicity. If a group were to use NBC weapons, it would likely alienate itself and damage its credibility, support, and funding. However, it is debatable whether Al Qaeda would be as affected by such considerations.

In terms of the *internationalization of terrorism*, it is useful to note that the concept of transnational terrorism is also not *new*.

The notion of a Muslim brotherhood and the idea of traveling to other countries to fight with and support other Muslim brothers can be traced back to Egyptian Islamists in the early 1900s. As mentioned earlier, examples of networking, alliances, and international training camps after events such as the PFLP hijacking (1968) and the Munich Olympics (1972) are evident from the 1970s onward. What was different from the 1990s onward, however, was the *scale* of internationalization, through new technology and globalization. In terms of technology (apart from new developments in arms), one of the main factors has been the development and accessibility of the Internet. The Internet is used to disseminate propaganda; to procure funds; for information/cyber warfare and sabotage; for swapping and acquisition of knowledge of tactics, techniques, and bomb making; for dissemination of orders to terrorist cells and for meeting other like-minded terrorists; and for setting up strategic alliances and recruitment. The process of globalization and the development of global communications ensures easier publicity. Likewise, free trade made it easier to move funds, equipment, and people. Groups thus took advantage and began setting up and sustaining overseas structures for financing, procurement, rest and recuperation, propaganda, training, forging documents, and so on.

Although there are some effective multilateral measures that states can use, international terrorist organizations and networks are so diverse and widespread that they can be likened to a balloon—if counterterrorist efforts squeeze the balloon in one part, the balloon will reduce in the area under pressure and expand in other areas. Furthermore, the problems of multilateral intelligence sharing and compromise of sources, as well as the reluctance for multilateral intelligence sharing, make terrorism extremely difficult to counter. Chapter 2 examines some difficulties in countering international terrorism.

A key trend that has not yet been mentioned is the reciprocal nature or relationship between the terrorist and the counterterrorist. Terrorism and counterterrorism are evolutionary processes. Once one side gets used to certain tactics and developed countermeasures, the other side has to innovate and develop new ones, and so it goes. For example, the 2001 hijacking of planes caused a "hardening of security," which caused the terrorists to instead start planting bombs, in response to which the authorities hardened security again, which resulted in terrorist attempts to acquire SAMs. Another example is in Northern Ireland, where security forces developed jamming measures to prevent terrorist bombs from being detonated, after which the terrorists responded by developing counterjamming measures; the security forces then developed counter-counterjamming measures. This theme is evident throughout the history of terrorism and is evident in the conventions and political moves following such actions, as can be seen in the chronology in Chapter 3. Thus the relationship between terrorist and counterterrorist seems a cyclical one whereby one continues to learn from the other. What becomes important, then, is to reduce terrorists' capacity to learn, research, develop, procure, and finance themselves by making it as hard as possible for them to operate. Their support structures, both domestic and international, have to also be reduced if not destroyed. It is important that people realize that an effective counterterrorism capability does not only mean having elite military forces but also the capability to take on terrorists at every level of operation: military, political, economic, social, and legal. The counterterrorist must not only learn from the terrorist but also look to other countries and how they have responded to counterterrorism to identify what works and what does not. The experience of countries such as the United Kingdom, Italy, and Israel, for example, can prove extremely useful in these respects.

## Terrorist Organization and Infrastructure

A terrorist organization consists of the terrorist group and its support base. This group includes the leadership, middle-level cadres, and the recruits who are constantly trained and retrained and assigned political and military activities. The lifeblood of a terrorist group is dependent on the support it generates from its like-minded ethnic or religious brethren. A terrorist support base can consist of collaborators, supporters, and sympathizers who provide political, financial, and military support. Not all support is voluntary. Coercion, intimidation, robbery, and organized crime are the usual methods for generating finances. The strength and the size of the group depend on the support base. The ability of the group to sustain its operations depends on the capacity of the support base to replenish the group's human losses and material wastage.

Terrorist groups have two operational wings—an overt or semicovert political wing, and a clandestine military wing. The political wing engages mostly in support functions; the military wing engages in operational functions. The political wing operates through front, cover, and sympathetic organizations that appear as commercial, socioeconomic, educational, cultural, religious, welfare, humanitarian, and human rights organizations. These terrorist-affiliated infrastructures, some of which are legally registered as charities and nonprofit organizations both within and outside the conflict zone, build political and financial support for the military wing. Terrorist groups will use these affiliated infrastructures to disseminate propaganda; generate recruits, supporters, and sympathizers; raise and launder funds; secure forged, adapted, and genuine idendities; hire, rent, or buy safe houses and vehicles; gather intelligence; procure weapons, dual technologies, and other supplies; and transport supplies to the theater of conflict.

The terrorist operational network in the military wing is responsible for mounting final reconnaissance or surveillance of the intended target and executing the operation. To ensure operational security, terrorists assigned to conduct intelligence and military operations are organized into compartmentalized cells. Although most active terrorist groups are from the Southern Hemisphere, they have established significant support networks in North America, Europe, and Australasia. Liberal democracies are open to terrorist groups to establish state-of-the-art propaganda, fund-raising, procurement, and shipping infrastructures. Some of the support networks mutate into operational networks that conduct assassinations, bombings, ambushes, and direct attacks. It is important to recognize, however, that any democratic "weaknesses" are also their strength and that counterpropaganda can and should be used. Furthermore, draconian measures will benefit terrorist propaganda and often push the public to favor the terrorist.

## Terrorist Training and Weaponry

Terrorist groups pose a significant threat to domestic, regional, and international security because they provide professional training and weaponry. The quality of training and weaponry available to terrorist groups has changed dramatically over the years. During the Cold War, the USSR and its satellite states, as well as the United States and its allies, provided training to a number of terrorist and guerrilla groups. The superpowers controlled the level of training, weapons, and targeting to ensure that the conflicts did not escalate from a Cold War to a "Hot War."

In the past three decades, terrorist training infrastructure has moved generally from the Middle East to Asia. In the 1970s and 1980s, the Syrian-controlled Bekka Valley in Lebanon was the main center for training for over forty foreign terrorist groups. Due to the Oslo Accords, the center of gravity in international terrorism shifted from the Middle East to Asia in the 1990s, at which point Afghanistan became the major center for training for at least two dozen groups until the U.S. intervention in October 2001.

## Training

Today, many terrorist groups have access to similar levels of training available to security forces personnel. Five main factors have facilitated terrorist access to professional training. First, U.S. and allied sponsorship of anti-Soviet mujahedin groups throughout the 1980s included provision of field manuals (FM series) reserved for the U.S. military, including the U.S. Special Forces. For instance, in the New Jersey home of Sayeed Nosair, the FBI recovered secret U.S. military manuals originating from the J. F. Kennedy Center for Special Warfare in Fort Bragg, North Carolina.

Second, several former security forces personnel from Egypt, Algeria, and the United States participated in the anti-Soviet and the global jihad campaigns that followed. For instance, an Egyptian captain named Ali Mohommad (who later joined the U.S. Special Forces as a sergeant) was Al Qaeda's principal military instructor in Afghanistan, Sudan, Somalia, and Bosnia and also trained Osama bin Laden's bodyguard contingent.

Third, the privatization of security and proliferation of security companies and former security forces personnel willing to serve as both trainers and mercenaries increased at the end of the Cold War. For instance, when the Sri Lankan government purchased landing craft mediums (LCMs), the LTTE clandestinely hired experts from Swan Hunter, the manufacturers of LCMs, to understand their vulnerabilities and limitations.

Fourth, certain government intelligence agencies continue to provide training to foreign terrorist groups to advance their foreign policy against inimical states. For instance, the Revolutionary

Guards of Iran continues to train Hezbollah. Thus do well-connected or well-endowed terrorist groups gain access to high-quality training hitherto reserved for professional militaries.

Fifth, due to the end of the Cold War the development of globalization, with its attendant freedom of movement of trade, capital, and information; the lowering of trade barriers and borders through agreements such as NAFTA and the Schengen Agreement; and the invention of the Internet increased the reach of the terrorists.

Terrorist groups provide both ideological and physical training to their recruits. Although governments tend to focus on disrupting terrorist access to physical training, countering ideological indoctrination is paramount.

## Ideological Training

Ideological training is continuous during membership in the group. Often both the motivation and endurance of terrorists, especially to survive in a hostile zone, depend more on their commitment to ideology than on physical training. For instance, most of the 9/11 suicide hijackers lived in the United States for over a year without changing their minds about their mission; this was undoubtedly due to the high-level indoctrination they had received for years. Even after Zacarias Moussaoui was captured, three weeks before 9/11, his belief in Al Qaeda's objectives kept him from divulging the organization's elaborate plans and preparations, as well as the identities and location of Al Qaeda members and leaders in the United States.

Ideological training differs from organization to organization. If the group is driven by ethnonationalist ideology, its members will be indoctrinated about the suffering of their ethnic brethren and the need to sacrifice their lives so that future generations will be able to live in safety. The opposing ethnic community will be portrayed as subhuman, evil, and destructive. Members will be indoctrinated to the point that they will believe that only by waging a sustained terrorist campaign will they be able to recover their homeland. Members of an Islamist group will be made to believe that it is a Muslim duty to wage jihad. Almost all the Islamist terrorist groups waging jihad in Palestine, Algeria, Kashmir, Bosnia, Chechnya, Afghanistan, Eritrea, Somalia, and the Philippines are driven by the Salafi school, whose members are indoctrinated to worship and love Allah above all else. They do not follow the teachings of the imams and the sheikhs; instead they pledge their allegiance only to Allah and his messenger. Contemporary ideologues draw from the writings of Sayed Abdul A'la Maududi, the founder of the Pakistani political party Jamat-I-Islami, and Sayed Qutb, the ideologue of the Egyptian Muslim Brotherhood who sanctioned the use of violence for the establishment of Islam. They appeal for the return of the Koran and Sunnah, with the principles of Islam applied to modern society through the use of rational judgment in religious matters. Maududi and Qutb reaffirmed the function of Islam in politics and civilized societies under the control of secularism and the Western development paradigm of democracy. Aligned against Western political thought, especially the concept of sovereignty, both called for the establishment of a "revolutionary vanguard of true believers" to organize Islamic states. Citing the successes of the Iranian revolution of 1979 and the anti-Soviet Afghan jihad (1979–1989), they urge taking on their enemies—Muslim regimes friendly to the West and the West itself.

### Physical Training

Physical training of terrorists takes three forms: basic, advanced, and model. *Basic training* (or recruit training) involves physical and weapons training. The training course lasts from one week to four months, depending on the opportunities available for training and the sophistication of the terrorist group. A Hamas or a Palestinian Islamic Jihad member living in the occupied territories may train for a few days before embarking on a suicide mission. As the execution phase of a suicide attack against an Israeli target is short, the Palestinian suicide terrorist does not need extensive physical training. A member of Al Ansar Mujahedin in Chechnya who is assigned to infiltrate Moscow and conduct a spate of bombings will receive extended training so that he will be psychologically and physically prepared to meet the numerous challenges likely to face him in his long-range deep-penetration mission.

The type of training, recruitment, and time involved in terms of access to weapons training depends also on the location. In a conflict zone the process and techniques used are likely to differ from those used in a developed country. Members usually must prove themselves before they are allowed to advance to the next level of training and operations.

Although the training to be a guerrilla can differ from that of a terrorist, the terrorist curriculum is very similar. This is because most terrorist recruits trained to attack civilians must learn how to engage security forces when confronted by them. For instance, a terrorist tasked to plant a bomb in Srinagar, infiltrating across the line of control in Kashmir, must learn how to move at night and engage Indian border guards if or when confronted. Terrorist training for rural and urban environments is very similar. Most terrorists learn on the job—they survive and progress not according to plan but opportunity. Nonetheless, the sophisticated terrorist groups train their members about how to fight in built-up areas. The training to be a terrorist can be shorter than the training to be a guerrilla, but many terrorists receive both terrorist and guerrilla training. Terrorists primarily attack soft targets; guerrillas primarily attack hard targets. Terrorist training and guerrilla training both aim to build confidence in their recruits.

The curriculum and duration of recruit training depends on their environment and role. If the terrorist has to survive a longer period in the battlefield in a guerrilla role, training is for a longer period in order to prevent demoralization, desertion, injury, or death. A poorly trained terrorist in a guerrilla role is likely to suffer injury and die, demoralizing other members, facilitating desertion, and restraining recruitment. Training and retraining are the keys to success for a terrorist group, whether operating in a terrorist or a guerrilla context. Therefore, most sophisticated groups emphasize continuous training to ensure that their members are mentally and physically prepared for battle at all times. Thus the disruption of training facilities and expertise is paramount in countering terrorism.

The *advanced training* by a terrorist group is sometimes akin to government special forces or commando training. It is like an advanced infantry-training course where terrorists receive harder training to increase their confidence and endurance. Usually, the best members are given the limited opportunities available for advanced training. Many who receive advanced training end up as group or subgroup leaders or as trainers. Specialized training ranges from communication know-how to intelligence gathering or to the use of specialized weapons or weapons systems (sniper and heavy-caliber weapons). Terrorists are cost-conscious; they handpick certain members in relation to their special qualities, orientation, and aptitude for special missions.

Sophisticated terrorist groups also offer a third category of training for specific missions, called *model training*. The terrorists assigned for 9/11 were trained to fly commercial aircraft; terrorists assigned to bomb the U.S. diplomatic targets in East Africa in August 1998 were trained to drive vehicles; terrorists assigned to ram an explosives-laden boat in to the USS *The Sullivans* in January and USS *Cole* in October 2000 were trained to pilot boats. Model training also helps terrorists to gain stealth, speed, and surprise. The numbers who train in the higher training categories—advanced and model training—are kept small to reduce the risk that a trainee will be captured and to protect the secrecy of the operation. Many terrorist groups often have separate wings and separate camps for each type of training. For example, the LTTE has a maritime wing (the Sea Tigers) that trains separately from the land forces; it also has the secretive Black Tigers, who conduct suicide operations.

Some recruits have served in the military and the police and thus have had professional training. For instance, Ahmad Jabril, the leader of the Popular Front for the Liberation of Palestine–General Command (PFLP-GC), is a former captain in the Syrian army; Namangani, the founder and leader of the Islamic Movement of Uzbekistan, was a former Soviet paratrooper; and Said Bahaji, an Al Qaeda member of the German cell, was a former soldier in the Bundeswehr. The two Al Qaeda military commanders, Muhammed Atef and Abu Ubadiah al-Banshiri, had served in the Egyptian police and the army. Both the Algerian and Chechen terrorist groups had several former military officers occupying important positions in their ranks. Some terrorist groups ask supporters and sympathizers, including those living in Western Europe, to join security forces in order to obtain police and military training—how to mount surveillance or reconnaissance, manufacture explosives and explosive devices, and use firearms. Terrorist groups that relied heavily on the training infrastructure in Afghanistan are likely now to join security forces for professional training.

The seven-thousand-page, multivolume *Encyclopaedia of the Afghan Jihad* outlines the cumulative body of knowledge in the possession of contemporary terrorist groups. The first ten volumes are on tactics, security and intelligence, handguns, first aid, explosives, grenades and mines, tanks, manufacturing (improvisation of arms and explosives), topography and land surveys, and weapons. The cover of each volume shows a belt-fed machine gun on a window ledge next to a copy of the Koran. The treatment of each subject is extensive and detailed. The encyclopedia covers operations in rural, urban, mountain, and jungle terrains. It is simply written, authored by veterans of the Afghan war; it has trained a new generation of post-Soviet mujahedin to fight in regional conflicts such as Kashmir, Mindanao, Chechnya, and Algeria as well as in terrorist campaigns. Every theater has its own manual.

Al Qaeda uses a manual of the Islamic Group of Egypt for its terrorist training. A copy recovered in Manchester, United Kingdom, has the title *Declaration of Jihad Against the Country's Tyrants (Military Series)*, superimposed on a drawing of the globe with a sword piercing the continent of Africa and a section of the Middle East. The manual is dedicated to the "young Moslem men who are pure, believing and fighting for the cause of Allah. It is [the authors'] contribution toward paving the road that leads to majestic Allah and establishes a caliphate according to the prophecy." The eighteen lessons include "Necessary Qualifications and Characteristics for the Organization's Members," "Counterfeit Currency and Forged Documents," "Means of Communication and Transportation," "Information-Gathering Using Covert Methods," "Assassinations Using Poisons and Cold Steel," and "Torture Methods." The manual draws heavily from United States, British, and other field manuals—especially those used by elite forces—as well as the widely distributed *The Terrorist Handbook*, produced in the West. Al Qaeda follows the principles of "need-to-know" and "operational security" meticulously when disseminating such information, showing why security forces have found such difficulty finding these manuals.

The training of Ahmed Saeed Omar Sheikh, the terrorist accused of kidnapping and murdering the American journalist Daniel Pearl, provides insight into terrorist training. Omar Sheikh went with twenty other recruits to a training camp in Afghanistan staffed by both Harakat-ul-Mujahedin and visiting Al Qaeda instructors. The Khalid bin Waleed camp—previously known as Salman Farsi camp—offered a forty-day "Istakbalia" course. After morning *namaz* (prayers) in the mosque, Omar Sheikh engaged in physical exercise until 8 A.M. After breakfast, he received instruction in the use of small and medium firearms until lunch. After resting for two hours and namaz in the mosque, religious education and physical training followed. For firing practice each recruit including Omar Sheikh was provided six rounds daily.

Recruits were also given night security duties. Of the eight instructors, Omar Sheikh mostly stayed with Ayubi, alias Abu Anjwari, from Karachi, an educated *muhajir* (migrant).

After completing basic recruit training Omar Sheikh was selected for specialized training from September to December 1993. According to claims made by Omar Sheikh to his Indian interrogators, he received training from serving members of the Special Services Group of Pakistan (SSG). (It is likely that he received training from former members and not serving members of the SSG.) His specialized terrorist training course matches the standard course tailor-made for the mujahedin provided by former members of SSG. Omar Sheikh told his interrogators that he received training in surveillance and countersurveillance, the art of disguising, interrogation, cell structure, secret meetings, secret writings, cryptology and codes, free wrestling, and moving (e.g., how to enter a room by kicking the door open, falling on the floor and shooting if somebody suspicious is in the room). He was trained in reconnaissance, checking of equipment, selection of persons for an operation, assignment of tasks, approaching the target, method of attack, use of signals for withdrawing, systems of communication, and first aid. He also received training for urban warfare, use of assault rifles, light machine guns, rocket launchers, night movement, and raids and ambushes.

There is a generation of terrorists with knowledge comparable to that of regular soldiers in government service. Well-funded groups have hired some of the best available special force trainers in the world. To fight terrorism today, it is essential that troops assigned for counterterrorism work receive highly specialized counterterrorism training. Because most terrorists are better trained, better armed, and better motivated, regular troops and police are likely to be unsuccessful without specialized training. The response of the German police to the massacre of Israeli athletes in the Olympic village in Munich in 1972 provides an insight into the difficulty of fighting terrorism without creating elite forces. Training and equipping highly specialized counterterrorist forces remains at the heart of sound planning and preparation to fight contemporary terrorism. This also reinforces the value and need for disrupting and denying terrorists access to training as well as information and expertise, as well as the importance of intelligence.

## Terrorist Weapons

Terrorist weapons include factory-manufactured and improvised explosives, small arms, and light weapons as well as dual technologies. A few terrorist groups seek to develop, acquire, and use chemical, biological, radiological, and nuclear weapons. Nonetheless, the bulk of the weapon types used by terrorists consists of conventional weapons, especially firearms and improvised explosive devices.

### Explosive devices

Terrorist groups obtain factory-manufactured explosives through theft or from a terrorist state sponsor. In addition, they sometimes manufacture their own explosives. Sophisticated terrorist groups purchase both military and commercial explosives using forged and adapted end-user certificates. Under the cover of transporting general cargo, terrorist groups transport the explosives by land, sea, and air. Terrorist groups have gained access to both fragmentation and incendiary types of explosives. The availability of explosives, associated technologies, and expertise enables terrorist groups to build improvised explosive devices (IEDs) to attack land, sea, and aerial targets.

Terrorist recruits can master bomb-manufacturing skills in a short period of time, and knowledge of how to handle and manufacture explosives and explosive devices is widely available on the Internet and in *The Terrorist Handbook*. The threshold for terrorism has been raised dramatically through the popularization of terrorist devices on the Internet. Security and intelligence agencies have monitored e-mail communications between terrorist groups, such as Hezbollah providing Hamas and Palestinian Islamic Jihad with information on how to manufacture explosives and make improvised explosive devices. Because IEDs can be designed and built for use in various situations, they are the favored weapon of many terrorists. Molotov cocktails and pipe bombs are the oldest form, and often most frequently used by terrorists worldwide, because the fuel for Molotov cocktails and the gunpowder for pipe bombs are easily obtainable and inexpensive, and the device is easily manufactured. Letter and parcel bombs are the most common examples going back to the end of the nineteenth century. The threat of letter and parcel bombs is very real because only a fraction of the millions of letters and packages passing through post offices and courier companies annually can be scanned.

Terrorists usually prefer high-velocity explosives, which are more destructive, more stable, and can be molded to any shape and size. The scale of destruction to humans and infrastructure depends on the quality of the explosive, the way it is packed, and the nature of the target. Almost all the explosives demonstrate fragmentation, blast pressure, and incendiary effects. The shrapnel—glass, nails, spikes, ball bearings, barbed wire, and other pieces of metal—in the device makes it more lethal. Furthermore, if placed in a metal container, the fragmentation is even greater. If the target is an enclosed structure of concrete with windows, the fragmentation will include shattered pieces of concrete and flying glass. Sometimes Hamas, PIJ, and Al Aqsa Martyrs Brigade have added rat poison, an anticoagulant, to the bomb device to ensure that the injured bleed to death. Blast pressure can be positive—the outward wave of air—and negative—the vacuum created that sucks air into the point of explosion. With the explosion, building walls and complete floors collapse, and objects and people are flung at great speed. On occasion those exposed to a blast appear unaffected but in reality suffer major to minor internal injuries, with hemorrhaging that takes time to take effect. Often their lungs are ripped apart, their liver and other internal organs are damaged, and their eardrums and eyes are injured. Lasting a fraction of a second, the incendiary effects ignite skin, hair, and other inflammatory material. Some devices are specially designed to start a fire. The victims suffer from physical and psychological consequences: shock—pale face, abundant sweating, and slowed pulse; loss of consciousness—concussion, meningeal hemorrhages, and encephalic lesions; and panic attacks—trembling and amnesia.

Terrorists continue to develop new technologies and tactics to improve the efficiency and efficacy of their explosive devices, just as counterterrorists work tirelessly to offset them. The *Afghan Jihad Encyclopedia* provides a plethora of information, including how to booby-trap everyday items. The mujahedin consider explosives the "safest weapon" because it enables them to get away from the area and avoid arrest.

Guerrillas or terrorist groups engaged in guerrilla warfare also often employ mines. Although some groups have acquired mines by theft or by raiding military facilities, most groups operating in rural and jungle terrains manufacture them. Terrorists manufacture land mines to target vehicles, enemy soldiers, and civilians. The psychological impact of an antipersonnel mine attack that leads to injury can demoralize a target. Attempts by the International Committee of the Red Cross (ICRC) and nongovernmental organizations such as International Alert in London to influence or seek an agreement with terrorist groups to totally abandon the use of mines have met with partial success. Security forces must disrupt and destroy the access to, expertise in, and resources relating to mines, terrorist manufacture, and training.

Terrorist groups, especially those operating in rural areas, use land mines (mostly antipersonnel mines) against counterterrorists, especially against search-and-destroy teams. After exploding a primary device, some terrorist groups place a secondary device aimed at targeting reinforcing troops. In most countries, the technology to detect land mines is primitive, and though it has improved recently, the use of mine-detection equipment slows down military operations. Thus most counterterrorist forces do not use mine detection equipment. In contrast, mine detection equipment is widely used by serving or retired explosives ordinance disposal personnel in mine-clearing operations mounted by governments and by humanitarian organizations in post-conflict situations or during periods of cease-fire.

Terrorist groups use both hand-thrown and rocket-propelled grenades frequently. Some terrorist groups even manufacture their own grenades. Terrorists lob grenades into vehicles, schools, homes, offices, and public meetings. Usually the impact of a grenade is multiplied if it explodes inside a vehicle or a building rather than in an open space—so when traveling in conflict zones, it is wise to shutter vehicles fully and to protect the windows of premises with a wire mesh.

As noted earlier, information on how to manufacture explosives or an explosive device is widely available in the public domain. However, manufacturing and transporting explosives and explosive devices require specialized training and extraordinary skill so that the bomb maker or the bomber doesn't die or suffer injury during the manufacturing or the transportation phases. Even experts such as Ramzi Ahmed Yousef, the February 1993 World Trade Center bomber in New York, suffered injuries. Although most terrorist recruits are taught the theory of explosives, only a handful are selected to become explosives experts. Before the training begins, almost all training manuals emphasize the need to identify a correct type of person to undergo the highly specialized explosives course: someone calm, quiet, and intelligent, not a hothead who might kill himself/herself or others.

To overcome enhanced security measures at airports and seaports aimed at preventing the transportation of explosives to the target location, contemporary terrorist groups are training their recruits to build bombs by using material commercially available in the vicinity of the target. After training terrorists in manufacturing bombs using commercially available material, they are dispatched to target zones without any bomb-making material. The terrorists, who have memorized the bomb-making instructions and formulae, rent apartments and use their rooms, garages, and kitchens to produce the explosives and the explosive devices. The bombs Al Qaeda planned to build to destroy the U.S. Embassy and the American Cultural Center in Paris soon after 9/11 used commercially available chemicals.

With higher detonation rates, military explosives have a greater shattering effect than do homemade ones. They are also stable and insensitive to heat, shock, impact, and friction. Nonetheless, a homemade explosive device can be as devastating as a military explosive device, as shown by the explosives type found in the shoes worn by Richard Reid, who planned to bomb Flight AA63 from Paris to Miami on December 22, 2001. The explosive TATP is manufactured in terrorist bomb factories in the Israeli-occupied areas of Palestine. It is also the favored explosive of the Palestinian terrorist groups—Hamas, PIJ, and Al Aqsa Martyrs Brigade—including that of its suicide bombers. Al Qaeda trained its explosives experts to manufacture TATP, but it requires expert handling.

Every bomb has the signature of a terrorist school, if not a terrorist group, due to a number of factors (the way it is constructed, the components used, etc). Every explosive device provides an understanding of the technical competence of the terrorist group. The type of explosive and the method of its manufacture can help to identify the group responsible and, sometimes, the bomb maker. The study of the technical capability of a terrorist group can provide clues about where terrorists obtain their supplies and about the identity of their trainers. Furthermore, it helps to trace the origin and to predict the terrorist group's technological trajectory.

Contemporary terrorist groups obtain explosives from security forces, state sponsors, and manufacturers via deceptive measures. The Kosovo Liberation Army obtained 80 percent of its firearms, including its explosives, from corrupt officers of the Serbian military. PIRA (the Provisional Irish Republican Army) obtained Semtex from Libya from a 1,000-ton consignment Tripoli received from Czechoslovakia. The LTTE received fifty tons of TNT and ten tons of RDX from Ukraine's Rubezone chemical plant by presenting a forged end-user certificate signed by the secretary of defense of Bangladesh. Although the French intelligence service and navy interdicted only one PIRA consignment, the LTTE consignment reached Sri Lankan shores. Access to explosives enabled terrorist groups to step up their terrorist campaigns. Even if stringent measures are introduced, there are already several tens of thousands of tons of explosives in the hands of terrorist groups, criminal groups, and militaries. The key to reducing the threat of terrorism should be a multia- gency task: denying terrorist groups access to funds, punishing corrupt military officers, instilling sanctions against state spon- sors, requiring state verification of all transactions, limiting ter- rorist access to precursor chemicals, and, most important, im- proving international security, intelligence, law enforcement, and judicial cooperation.

### Manufactured and Improvised Firearms
With the end of the Cold War, the international arms market be- came saturated. Although there are grave legal and operational limitations that constrain governments from combating interna- tional arms procurement and shipping, there is no centralized controlling body that regulates transactions to counter illicit arms procurement and shipping. The widespread availability of firearms, notably small arms and light weapons, has increased the threshold for terrorist attacks. In a July 1999 study, the Inter- national Committee of the Red Cross estimated that over 50 per- cent of the casualties of armed conflicts were civilians. Next to ex- plosives, this category of weapons—including the AK-47, Type 56, M-16, general purpose machine gun (GPMG), light machine gun (LMG), submachine gun (SMG), pistols, revolvers, and rocket-propelled grenade launcher (RPG)—remains the most widely used by terrorist groups. There are nearly fifty million copies and variations of the A. Kalashnikov rifle (AK/AKM), the most used weapon in the world.

Weapons such as the Russian PP-90 submachine gun are perfect for terrorists. Easy to procure, conceal, transport, and use, small arms and light weapons will remain the weapons of choice of terrorists in the foreseeable future. Therefore, limiting their availability by denying easy access to conventional weapons is likely to reduce the threat, as well as incidents, of terrorism.

The widespread availability of weapons has provided terrorist groups access to weapons of all sizes: small, medium, and heavy infantry. Small arms include rifles, pistols, revolvers, submachine guns, and light machine guns. Medium-size infantry weapons are mostly belt-fed machine guns, smaller sized mortars, RPGs, light antitank weapons (LAWs), and small-caliber wire-guided missiles. Heavy infantry weapons includes heavy-caliber machine guns, heavy-caliber mortars, large-caliber wire-guided missiles, shoulder-held antitank missile launchers, and some rockets below the category of artillery. The more sophisticated groups have procured and used standoff-weapons—RPGs, LAWs, surface-to-air missiles (SAMs), and small-, medium-, and large-caliber mortars. Only limited training is needed to use most of these weapons. Groups with standoff capabilities attack not only land targets but also sea and aerial ones. They enable terrorists to preserve their strength and conduct mass fatality and casualty attacks both of combatants and civilians. The terrorist propensity to procure and employ standoff-weapons increased during the 1990s.

With easy access to the saturated weapons market, groups have replaced their improvised weapons with commercially manufactured weapons. Improvised or homemade weapons tend to be less reliable than commercially manufactured standard factory-made weapons. In the Northwest Frontier Province in Pakistan, a replica of any small arm and light weapon can be manufactured. Other regions in the world are awash with weapons: there are huge Soviet and Western stockpiles in Afghanistan and Pakistan; and many countries in Southeast Asia, sub-Saharan Africa, and the Balkans (mostly Croatia) are known to sell weapons without proper verification. In these regions terrorist groups have gained access to sophisticated weapons, dual technologies, and professional trainers. Saturated arms markets in Eastern Europe, the southern belt of the former Soviet Union, and in other regions where Cold War conflicts have ended feed the international arms pipelines of several terrorist groups. Although the industrialized world produces the bulk of light weapons today, the emerging trend is for developing countries to invest increasingly in light weapon production. Because developing states have less control over arms production and trade, it is likely that the illicit arms markets will grow exponentially in the future.

Often terrorist groups accomplish large-scale purchase of arms through the connivance and condoning of governments of the manufacturing countries. To counter this proliferation, it is necessary to minimize or supervise the role of unscrupulous private arms dealers. The international community should encourage arms transactions at a government-to-government level. But due to the enormity of the illicit arms trade and the profits that accrue to the manufacturing countries, they may not be acceptable limitations. Alternatively, governments of the manufacturing states should nominate their arms dealers, renewing their licenses to trade annually after reviewing whether their transactions have complied with international and domestic rules and regulations. Yet there is no international tribunal that can try violations of conventions that regulate illicit arms transactions and transportation, and no central data bank that can collect, collate, and disseminate information on illicit transactions.

There is no way to monitor those involved in the illegal arms trade continuously and adequately. Instead, arms dealers are changing their modus operandi and adopting more sophisticated methods and machinery to elude detection. Action to counter illicit arms trade should encompass the trafficking of arms both across national borders and on the high seas. The bulk of terrorist weaponry is transferred by sea, but it is not an offense for a terrorist group to traffic arms in international waters. There is no international maritime police organization like Interpol to monitor and to counter arms shipments activity by identification, interception, and arrest of crew and vessels.

## Dual Technologies

Dual-user technologies, or dual technologies, are civilian equipment that can also be used for military applications. Terrorist groups procure dual technologies mostly from Western Europe, North America, and the Far East. Terrorist groups experiment and adapt modern dual technologies (GPS, mobile phones, and pagers) to improve and enhance their performance or as a "force multiplier." When Osama bin Laden moved from Sudan to

Afghanistan in May 1996, the Al Qaeda cell in the United States purchased a satellite phone for its leader in New York. Al Qaeda also purchased scuba-diving equipment, range finders, night vision goggles, and communication equipment from the United States, United Kingdom, Japan, Kuwait, and Saudi Arabia. Terrorist groups with maritime terrorist and support capabilities (Hezbollah, Al Qaeda, and the LTTE) have purchased speedboats, communication gear, semiclosed-circuit underwater scuba, and antennas from Thailand, Malaysia, Australia, Holland, United Kingdom, France, and Germany.

Most terrorists are adept at improvisation rather than innovation. Terrorists can turn most dual technologies into improvised weapons or into a component of an improvised weapon. The world watched with horror when aircraft were used as guided missiles to attack U.S. civilian targets on 9/11. Likewise terrorists use commercially available technologies such as pretty good privacy (PGP), an encryption program, to communicate messages. PGP cannot be decoded by government security agencies. Perhaps the most dangerous aspect of terrorist use of dual technologies is the use of laboratory equipment intended to produce medicines for curing the ill; instead, the equipment is used to produce biological and chemical agents to kill and injure.

Terrorist procurement of dual technologies is difficult to prevent. By monitoring terrorist support activity and targeting terrorist groups it is possible to deny those groups access to dual technologies. As most governments target the criminal activities of terrorist groups and not terrorist groups per se, many foreign terrorist groups procure dual technologies from countries around the world. Procuring a dual technology even by an acknowledged foreign terrorist group is not a criminal offense in most countries. This shows the importance of human and technical intelligence in countering terrorism.

## CBRN Weapons

Chemical, biological, radiological, and nuclear (CBRN) weapons are not synonymous with mass casualty weapons. Similarly, CBRN attacks are not synonymous with mass casualty attacks. Although CBRNs are classified as weapons of mass destruction (WMD), not all CBRN terrorist attacks have resulted in mass casualties. With the exception of the nerve gas attack by Aum Shinrikyo of Japan that killed twelve people, no other chemical, biological, or radiological attack to date has resulted in significant casualties. Most terrorists have not used CBRN material due to problems of access. However, even terrorist groups with access to chemical, biological, and radiological materials are reluctant to use them as weapons due to problems of delivery, lack of control (its effects on one's own population), fear of overwhelming retaliation, and, in some cases, concerns over loss of public support. The trend is for terrorists to conduct mass casualty attacks using conventional means (hijacked fully fuel-laden passenger aircraft used as guided missiles or coordinated simultaneous bombings of high-rise buildings and population centers). Nonetheless, a handful of terrorist groups such as Aum Shinrikyo and Al Qaeda have shown a sustained long-term interest to acquire, develop, and use CBRN weapons.

Al Qaeda paid $1.5 million to a Sudanese military officer and acquired a uranium canister in 1993. Although Al Qaeda tested the canister, irradiated from outside, with a Geiger counter, the group was duped. Al Qaeda also purchased a T-389, a military aircraft, for $230,000, and bin Laden's personal pilot, Essam Al-Ridi, flew it from Tucson, Arizona, to Khartoum, Sudan. Bin Laden asked the Egyptian-born American pilot to learn crop-dusting techniques with the hidden intention of launching a chemical warfare attack. In addition to employing an Egyptian physicist, Al Qaeda persisted in its attempts to purchase CBRN material through Russian and Ukrainian organized crime groups. At the time that the United States intervened in Afghanistan, Al Qaeda had established links with Pakistani nuclear physicists and established a series of front companies to obtain components to develop a CBRN capability. Furthermore, Al Qaeda had established a special camp next to the Derunta complex for research into high explosives and CBRN weapons; it is likely that the complex was experimenting on the impact of a radiological dispersal device. From Al Qaeda camps and safe houses, U.S. troops, CNN reporters, and other journalists recovered documents on CBRN material. The computer diskettes of Zacarias Moussaoui, the would-be twentieth 9/11 hijacker, contained information about the aerial dispersal of pesticides. On the pretext of launching a crop-spraying company he had inquired about crop-dusting equipment, suggesting that the 9/11 operation could have been wider in scope. It is not possible to prevent a determined group like Al Qaeda from building a CBRN capability. Even after the Al Qaeda training infrastructure in Afghanistan was destroyed, the trajectory of Al Qaeda clearly demonstrates that the group has been considering using unconventional weapons. On February 20, 2002, Italian police arrested an Al Qaeda cell consisting of four Moroccans with nine pounds of cyanide and a map pinpointing the location of water pipes that lead to the U.S. Embassy in Rome. On April 11, 2002, seventeen people, including twelve Germans, were killed when Al Qaeda members detonated a liquid petroleum gas truck next to the oldest Jewish synagogue in Djerba, Tunisia. On May 8, 2002, U.S. authorities arrested Jose Perdilla, alias Abdullah al Muhajir, a Muslim convert and an Al Qaeda–trained former American gang member planning to detonate a radioactive dispersal device in the United States. It is just a question of time until Al Qaeda or another terrorist group will acquire, develop, and use a CBRN weapon. Indeed, a new volume to the *Encyclopaedia of the Afghan Jihad*—a separate CD-Rom reserved for a few handpicked Al Qaeda members—details CBRN weapons, especially chemical and biological warfare. Unless a state sponsor provides a nuclear weapon to a terrorist group, it is highly unlikely that a terrorist group will be able to gain access to a nuclear weapon. However, it *is* likely that a terrorist group will acquire, develop, or use a chemical, biological, or radiological weapon. Because preserving biological agents is difficult, a chemical or radiological weapon is the most likely weapon of the CBRN categories.

**Chemical Weapons.**    Terrorist groups have copied state actors that use chemicals as weapons. In World War I, state actors used choking agents—chlorine and mustard gas—producing nearly 100,000 deaths and 900,000 injuries. In World War II, Nazis used zykon-B gas against Jews, gypsies, and Soviet prisoners. Since the beginning of the contemporary wave of terrorism, two groups have used these weapons effectively. After besieging the Sri Lankan military detachment in Kiran, Eastern Sri Lanka, the LTTE employed chlorine recovered from a nearby paper mill in Valachchinai against the Sri Lankan troops in 1990. There was neither international outrage nor a close study of the chemical terrorism event (because winds shifted and no one was killed) until the Aum Shinrikyo successfully used chemical agents five years later. Aum Shinrikyo used or attempted to use sarin (a nerve gas), VX, mustard gas, and phosgene gas against Japanese civilians. After Aum killed twelve people and injured 5,500 in the Tokyo subway on March 20, 1995, police raided the group's premises and production facility and recovered chemicals sufficient to kill 4.2 million people. Aum scientists also manufactured anthrax (fortunately not weapons-grade) by visiting a sheep farm in Australia and planned to acquire a thermonuclear device from Russia.

**Biological Weapons.** Biological, bacteriological, or germ warfare has the potential to kill more humans than nuclear warfare. Of 395 biological toxins, a threat analysis by David Franz in 1988 revealed that seventeen are *weaponizable*. During World War II, biological warfare killed several hundreds of thousands of persons. Plague (the Black Death), a rodent-to-human transmitted disease that began in India, created the first known epidemic in China, in 1330. A pestilence occurred when Mongol Tatars catapulted plague-infested corpses into the besieged Crimean city of Caffa. When a few survivors escaped by boat to Genoa, the rats from the ship spread the plague, resulting in the death of a quarter of the European population by 1349. Laboratory samples of the plague still exist in government research facilities in the United States and in Russia. In another example, sixteenth-century Europeans reduced Mexico's native population from 30 million to 3 million in just fifty years by unwittingly introducing measles and smallpox. In 1754, the Native American population in the United States was decimated when traders in Pennsylvania gave them blankets exposed to the smallpox (cowpox) virus. Although smallpox, caused by the variola virus, was eradicated worldwide in 1977, it remains a highly contagious disease that kills 20 percent of all people contracting it. Ethnonationalist terrorists have been afraid to use emerging pathogens—microbes to which few individuals have gained resistance—due to the risk of infecting their own population. But with the advances in biotechnology and terrorist access to scientists, terrorist ethnic targeting is a likely future scenario. Since 9/11 Western governments have been manufacturing and stocking the smallpox vaccine because young people have never been vaccinated and because older people lose their immunity after twenty years. A terrorist group could always manufacture these agents under the pretext of manufacturing vaccines. A contemporary use of biological warfare was seen when Oregon's Rajneeshee Sect wanted to sway the outcome of an election in 1984. According to RAND expert John Parachini, the Rajneeshees obtained a strain of salmonella from the American Type Culture Collection in Maryland with the intent of poisoning ten salad bars in areas where they believed the vote would not favor them. Although 751 people fell ill, no one died. As demonstrated in the post-9/11 anthrax attacks, bacteria-induced diseases can vary in rate of infection and lethality. In addition to bacterial agents (anthrax, brucellosis, tularaemia, and plague) and viral agents (Venezuelan equine encephalitis), terrorist groups have expressed an interest in using toxins (ricin and botulism). In the 1980s, both the Bulgarian and South African secret services used biological material, including ricin, to kill domestic political opponents. Al Qaeda's Islamic Group of Egypt training manual, recovered in Manchester, England, lists ricin as one of its toxins. The French police found a canister of botulism in the safe house of the Red Army Faction in 1980. After receiving news that a Japanese tourist had developed hemorrhagic fever upon returning from a game park in Zaire, Aum scientists traveled to Zaire to obtain infected material either from living persons or corpses. At the turn of the millennium, a U.S. member of the Aryan Nations was arrested for obtaining three vials of yersinia pestis bacterium, which causes bubonic plague. In early 2002, the Russian secret service is believed to have used a biological agent in an envelope to kill Ibn-ul-Khattab, the head of Al Ansar mujahedin in Chechnya, who was also the leader of the mujahedin in the Caucuses.

Both chemical and biological agents can be obtained from government laboratories through the terrorist-organized crime nexus. By developing links with rogue scientists, terrorist groups can also produce them in laboratories. As the equipment is dual technology, terrorist groups can also purchase the equipment required to produce these agents in the open market. Although some biological agents are relatively difficult to produce, production is within the reach of contemporary terrorist groups who have access to university-qualified members, collaborators, supporters, and sympathizers. Biological toxins, produced by bacteria, fungi, algae, and other plants and animals, are more lethal than their chemical counterparts. Terrorist groups face a challenge over the dispersal of these agents; they are nonvolatile solids that need to be dispersed by a fine aerosol cloud suspended with droplets containing nerve, blister, blood, and choking agents. *Nerve agents* (fast-acting organophosphate compounds affecting the central nervous system) that are absorbed through skin and the respiratory tract kill immediately (examples are sarin, soman, tabun, and VX). *Blister agents* (affecting eyes and lungs and blistering the skin upon contact) are persistent agents that remain in the target area for a considerable period of time (examples are sulfur mustard, nitrogen mustard, and Lewisite).

*Blood agents* are highly volatile and dissipate rapidly in air when in a gaseous state and affect the normal exchange of oxygen and carbon dioxide, rapidly damaging body tissues (examples are cyanide, cyanogens cyanide, arsine, and hydrogen cyanide). *Choking agents*—a heavy gas delivered at ground level—tend to fill low areas, causing the lungs to fill with fluid and the victim to choke and cause corrosive effects on the respiratory system (examples are chlorine and phosgene). According to a post-9/11 Brookings Institute study titled "Protecting the American Homeland," dispersing smallpox, anthrax, ebola, or another deadly agent in a large city could kill one million people and cause a loss of $750 billion to the economy. The study rates the likelihood of a biological attack as extremely low.

**Nuclear Weapons.** Construction of a nuclear device (as opposed to a "dirty bomb") is not believed to be currently within the reach of a terrorist group. However, the U.S. government has expressed concern over a state sponsor, especially Iraq, providing a nuclear device or radiological material to a terrorist group. Saddam Hussein used nerve gas against Iraqi Kurds and VX against troops in the 1991 Gulf War, and was considered unlikely to hesitate to use CBRN weapons against U.S. troops. Nonetheless, unknown to the international intelligence community, international measures had effectively degraded and destroyed Saddam's CBRN capabilities throughout the 1990s. Although several hundred portable nuclear suitcases and nuclear batteries have disappeared over time and the black nuclear market is active, terrorist groups are more likely to attack a nuclear plant or trigger a radiological dispersal device than detonate a nuclear warhead. Nuclear reactors are hardened targets protected by sixteen feet of concrete, a missile shield, and backup cooling tanks with 600,000 gallons of water. Nonetheless, maps of U.S. nuclear facilities were recovered in Afghanistan, and potassium-iodide pills are being distributed to residents within ten miles of U.S. nuclear plants to try prevent thyroid cancer. U.S. nuclear plants are well protected by containment facilities, but plants in Europe and elsewhere are less well protected, and waste and spent fuel there could be a target. According to statistics released in 2003, the International Atomic Energy Agency estimates that between 1993 and 2003 there have been 175 cases of trafficking sensitive nuclear material. A radiological dispersal device or a dirty bomb could be constructed using nuclear material, such as uranium or plutonium from dismantled warheads or from a nuclear power plant. These devices are unlikely to kill large numbers but would render a large area uninhabitable for considerable time and generate mass panic. According to the Federation of American Scientists, the legacy of radiation lasts for years. Only a few terrorism groups have engaged in radiological warfare in the past. A Chechen terrorist group placed a cesium–137 device in a Moscow park in late 1995, and an unknown person dispersed radioactive uranium–235 in the New York City water supply in 1981. The radiological dispersal events did not produce any fatalities. Compared to deaths resulting from a biological attack (one million), a nuclear explosion is likely to produce low fatalities (100,000), and a radiological explosion is likely to produce the lowest fatalities (10,000). Climatic conditions disperse the fallout in different directions and distances.

More effective measures should be taken to prevent terrorists accessing these materials by more monitoring and security where they are stored, such as in hospitals (which store radioactive materials) and swimming pools (which store chlorine).

# Terrorist Tactics and Targets

*Tactics* are methods employed by terrorist groups to conduct operations. *Targets* are either personnel or infrastructure attacked by terrorist groups. Terrorists select their tactics from a tactical repertoire and their targets from a wide range of opportunities. Ideologies often provide the justification and framework for the selection of certain tactics and targets, but the availability of resources and expertise determines whether a group can engage a certain target. Tactics vary tremendously from high-tech bombings to the simple machete. The repertoire ranges from manufacturing and using IEDs (victim-operated magnetic switches on mines targeting ordnance-disposal personnel) to simple pipe bombs or clubs. Terrorist tactics include bombing, assassination, collective attack, maritime attack, mortar attack, mining attack, and ambush. For a tactic to be effective it need not be high-tech, complex, and expensive. Simple low-tech, low-cost tactics such as arson can be theatrical and effective.

Hijackings, kidnapping, and hostage taking belong to one subcategory of tactics. Because terrorists are copycats, hijackings, hostage taking, and kidnappings become fashionable (if they are effective and hard to counter) during certain periods and are used to gain publicity and income to further a group's aims. Terrorist groups also use threats to advance their aims and objectives. The threat of violent action (bomb, assassination) to cause fear or coerce an action or inaction is also an act of terrorism. Terrorist targets include humans and infrastructures in land, air, and sea. Human targets include political leaders, administrators, military personnel, business leaders, and large populations; infrastructure targets include aviation, maritime, symbolic, and other national critical infrastructure. Favorite terrorist targets are symbolic and invested with the high prestige that will magnify terrorist power and influence.

Terrorist targets include diplomatic (personnel and infrastructure of embassies, high commissions, consulates, and interest sections), foreign or domestic businesses (personnel or infrastructure such as Shell Oil or McDonalds), domestic or foreign military (including UN, NATO, and other peacekeeping missions), transportation assets (buses, trains, train tracks, airplanes, ships, ports), domestic government (personnel and infrastructure such as the police chief or the mayor's office), foreign government (nondiplomatic personnel or infrastructure), foreign (nondiplomatic, tourists, and students and infrastructure), religious (personnel or infrastructure such as mosques, gudwaras, kovils, temples, churches, synagogues), ethnic or racial (by nationality, linguistic group, color, or geographic religion), the general public (random attacks on population centers, such as malls), and humanitarian workers (local and foreign personnel and infrastructure of relief and aid NGOs, including the ICRC). Because it is impossible to protect all likely targets, governments and corporations adopt target-hardening measures (alarms, sensors, close-circuit television [CCTV], special glass, metal detectors, X-ray technology, space or vision barriers, quality training of personnel) that make it costly and difficult for a terrorist group to attack the protected target. However, the key to thwarting a terrorist attack is intelligence, often advanced information of terrorist plans and preparations, developed by infiltrating a terrorist group using human agents.

## Assassination

Assassination is a common tactic when a specific person is targeted for a political purpose, retribution, or retaliation. This is not a random killing, but one focused on an individual for perceived grievances. Executions by self-imposed substate courts, "kangaroo courts," or judges fit into this category. Traditionally, assassination has been used on heads of state to topple the government (e.g., Anwar Al Sadat of Egypt, Aldo Moro of Italy, Indira Gandhi of India, Rajiv Gandhi of India, Yitzhak Rabin of Israel, and Ranasinghe Premadasa of Sri Lanka). By assassinating strong leaders, especially those who fight terrorism steadfastly, terrorists often bring to office weak leaders willing to compromise or follow a course of inaction. Leadership targets are strategic targets aimed at bringing about strategic change. As it has been difficult to target protected persons, terrorists have assassinated important government functionaries, including party leaders, political officials, and diplomats (e.g., Ahmed Shah Masood, Northern Alliance leader of Afghanistan; Ri'fat al-Mahjub, the speaker of the Egyptian Assembly; Shykh Muhammad Husayn al-Dhahabi, former minister of Awqaf in Egypt; Lalith Athulathmudali, Democratic United National Liberation Front leader of Sri Lanka; and Ranjan Wijeratna, minister of state for defense of Sri Lanka). Despite the Convention on the Prevention and Punishment of Crimes Against Internationally Protected Persons, the threat to very important persons (VIPs) has persisted and is likely to grow. Terrorists have also targeted moderates and journalists to eliminate support for a negotiated political settlement against a terrorist group. By selectively assassinating important leaders, terrorists demonstrate society's vulnerability to terrorism. Through assassinations, terrorists seek to break public will. The loss of good leaders who enjoy mass support has led to mass demoralization. The assassination of military commanders demoralizes their troops, especially frontline troops.

Assassination has become a common terrorist tactic. Terrorists also use more specialized weapons to breach VIP security (sniper and high-powered rifles, land-mine attacks, and vehicle bombings). Aware that the assassination of a leader leads to massive retaliation, terrorists often refrain from claiming assassinations. Some groups conduct suicide terrorist assassinations because they do not want the terrorist who perpetrated the assassination to be caught alive. Before launching the assassination operation, many terrorist groups tend to criticize the target of assassination and to portray the target as an unjust person or human rights violator. Often if there is public revulsion at the political murder, the terrorist group refrains from claiming responsibility for it on grounds that the group will suffer loss of public support.

## Armed Assault

The success of an armed assault depends on two factors: (1) initial continuous and final terrorist reconnaissance/surveillance of the intended target, and (2) training, retraining, and model training to gain surprise, speed, and stealth for the strike team. Terrorist planners design a model for the terrorist strike team to ensure that each member is fully prepared. Often operational commanders participate in the final reconnaissance or surveillance of the target before the strike team goes into combat. Planning and preparation are the longest phases in an operation and are key to the mission's success. Examples include Maoists in Nepal attacking police stations in Rolpa, the LTTE attacking civilian settlements in Eastern Sri Lanka, PIRA firing mortars at Heathrow on three occasions over five days, and the Abu Nidal Organization attacking Rome and Vienna airports. A form of armed assault is collective attack. This includes tactical maneuvering on an objective involving coordination and tactics, such as an attack on a strategic settlement or a border outpost. It normally involves attacks against protected civilian settlements or military targets.

Most armed assaults are direct attacks involving the use of bombs, grenades, and guns. Bombs remain the most favored terrorist weapon and account for about 67 percent of all terrorist attacks. Many groups favor the tactic of bombing because the terrorist is far removed from the event and the elements of surprise and shock can be preserved. Bombs differ from mines, rockets, mortars, artillery, or munitions launched from aircraft or ships. Pipe bombs are used also, but not in all theaters of conflict. Vehicle bombs—packaged inside cars, vans, or trucks—can be either random victim weapons or personal attack weapons. With random victim attack bombs, the bomb is detonated with a timer or a remote control device and is likely to kill several hundred persons, depending on the quantity of explosives and attack environment. But if the car bomb is positioned strategically, it could kill more people. The plan of Ramzi Ahmed Yousef, who parked the car in the basement of the World Trade Center in February 1993, was to topple one WTC tower on top of the other and kill 250,000 people. Terrorists can also target and kill individuals by placing a bomb in the car's hood or under the seat or chassis. Some groups use several bombs detonated after each other in places where people are likely to run from the previous bomb to seek shelter, thus maximizing casualties.

In contrast to armed assault, nonarmed assault includes physical attacks upon a person or persons by a person or group. However, this does not belong to the category of tactical operations. Examples are drive-by shootings, "punishment beatings," random shooting of tourists, and beating up citizens attempting to vote.

## Ambush

In terms of volume of attacks, terrorist ambushing follows terrorist bombing. In contrast to armed assault, an ambush is also a coordinated surprise attack, but the attacker lies in wait for the target. If the ambush is well planned, those coming within the kill zone are unlikely to survive. In a guerrilla situation, there may be mines and mortars; a mine attack directs an explosion against on-foot personnel or a vehicle carrying troops or civilians; a mortar attack uses indirect fire against the intended target. An ambush against civilians is categorized as an act of terrorism; an ambush against military personnel is categorized as a guerrilla attack.

## Hostage-Taking

International law defines hostage-taking as the seizing or detaining of a person and threatening to kill, injure, or continue to detain that person in order to compel a third party to do or abstain from doing any act as explicit or implicit condition for the release of the seized or detained person. The December 1979 convention followed the hostage-taking of ninety-six Americans in Iran. The U.S. failure to respond decisively led President Jimmy Carter to lose his presidency and gave rise to the policy of "no negotiations with terrorists."

Terrorists can take hostages either from an aircraft or by barricading a building, for example, to negotiate demands or to gain world attention. After taking hostages, the terrorist group sets forth demands, usually including money and safe passage. International attention enables the terrorists to highlight their cause. In a few cases families, businesses, insurance companies, and even governments yield to hijacker demands, further increasing the threat of terrorism. For instance, the Islamic Movement of Uzbekistan kidnapped American tourists after a Japanese businessman paid to seek the release of Japanese geologists kidnapped in Kyrgyzstan. After Libya paid ransom money for the release of one batch of hostages, the Abu Sayyaf Group kidnapped even more hostages. When India freed Ahmed Saeed Omar Sheikh after Harakat-ul-Mujahedin took passengers in an Indian airline flight hostage, he was involved in the kidnapping and murder of Daniel Pearl, the first U.S. terrorist casualty since 9/11. Appeasement rarely works with a terrorist group.

Some terrorist groups, such as Hezbollah, FARC, ELN, AUC, and Al Ansar mujahedin, are notorious for takings and holdings. Although most hostages are freed eventually, a few groups kill their hostages whether their demands are met or not. Hostage-taking for large cash ransoms is the fastest growing form of terrorist activity in Colombia, Chechnya, Mexico, Yemen, and the Philippines. Even UN peacekeepers, officials, and aid workers have been taken hostage in Bosnia, East Timor, and Sierra Leone. Many of these countries lack either the resources to control the security environment or the elite units to respond to a hostage taking.

Before hostage-takers start to kill their captives, highly trained hostage negotiators and rescue commandos with the skills to help end hostage situations are essential. By investing in training, equipment, and in sharing experiences, nations can lower the threat of hostage-taking worldwide. In hostage situations, governments must work together with the media to forestall coverage of a hostage situation that takes away the element of surprise and prevents a successful storming of an aircraft or an embassy. Most hostages freed by a group or rescued by the authorities must be treated psychologically for shock and trauma. Some hostages rarely overcome their ordeals and eventually commit suicide.

## Hijacking

A hijacking occurs when a vehicle or transportation system is forcibly taken over by a terrorist or a group of terrorists. The vehicle or transportation system can be public or private. In contrast to other tactics, hijackings offer the terrorists mobility, the opportunity to highlight grievances, and unparalleled media attention. The hijacking of aircraft beginning in the late 1960s has been the single biggest threat to public safety in recent years. By the early 1970s, Israelis greatly reduced hijacking threats through sky marshals and a range of other initiatives.

Hijacking is not limited to air or road transport but is also possible with maritime transport. Muhammad Tokcan, a Turkish citizen of Chechen origin, on January 16, 1996, seized a Turkish Black Sea passenger ferry in the Turkish port of Trabzon. When hijacked, the Panama-registered ferry, the *Eurasia*, was about to depart for the Russian port of Sochi. The terrorists took more than two hundred hostages, including ninety-five Russian citizens, and threatened to blow up the ship if Russian forces did not stop their attacks on the Chechens. The hostages were released unharmed after four days. Tokcan was imprisoned after surrendering, but under amnesty he was released by Turkey in 2000.

## Kidnapping

A kidnapping occurs when one or more individuals are abducted by force to be used for ransom or coercion. To increase the ransom payment or coercive power, some terrorist groups refrain from immediate publicity about the abduction. Often the target is a prominent political or military figure, wealthy person, businessman, or opponent. Kidnapping is a lucrative industry in many countries, and terrorist groups may even subcontract kidnappings to other organizations. Al Qaeda and some other groups conduct specialized courses on kidnapping for their members and for members of other groups. Terrorist kidnappings are motivated by publicity, to gain political concessions, to release terrorist detainees and prisoners, and for revenge, retaliation, and funding.

Most sophisticated terrorist groups expend significant resources and time planning kidnapping operations. They monitor the times and routes taken by a potential target. Thus kidnappings can be reduced by countersurveillance and varying the routes and times of journeys. Some terrorist groups infiltrate a target's home or office in preparation for the kidnapping to learn about their target's security measures. Sophisticated terrorists develop contingency plans, check their vehicles or backup vehicles, and study the security of getaway route or routes.

Although governments may prohibit families and businesses from negotiating the release of kidnapped victims by paying ransom, experience shows that this is virtually unenforceable. Permitting families and companies to pay ransom for the release of a family member or employees provides the law enforcement authorities the best possibility of capturing the kidnappers. A highly trained professional police force can monitor the contacts between the captors and the negotiators. The success of U.S. police has led to a remarkably low incidence of U.S. kidnapping.

European elite counterterrorist forces were created as a direct result of the German police's failure to respond to the Black September Organization (BSO) kidnapping members of the Israeli Olympic team from the Olympic Village in Munich on September 5, 1972. Eleven Israelis were killed. In response, West Germany formed GSG9, and other European governments created their own counterterrorist forces. Within two years, MOSSAD, Israel's foreign intelligence service, launched a worldwide manhunt, assassinating all but two of the Munich kidnappers.

The most publicized terrorist kidnapping of an individual was that of Aldo Moro, a former prime minister of Italy, by the Red Brigades on March 16, 1978. His death resulted in a political crisis prompting the Italian government to strengthen the legal framework for fighting terrorism. Four years later, when the Red Brigades kidnapped U.S. general James Dozier, he was summarily released.

## Suicide Terrorism

This is one of the most difficult forms of terrorism to counter. A suicide attack is nearly impossible to thwart once the bomber has been launched because the terrorist is focused on destroying his target and not on protecting himself. But, if intelligence detects an oncoming suicide attack in the planning and preparation stages, it can be disrupted. Suicide terrorism enabled terrorist groups to inflict severe damage to the U.S. Marine barracks in Beirut, Lebanon, U.S. diplomatic targets in East Africa, the USS *Cole,* the World Trade Center, and the Pentagon. Suicide terrorists retain a high potential to destroy asymmetric targets that cannot be attacked successfully by nonsuicide operations. When suicide terrorism is used in the CBRN realm, the potential for destruction will be unprecedented.

About 400 suicide attacks committed by over 30 terrorist groups have taken place since the early 1980s and the beginning of the contemporary wave with Hezbollah in Lebanon. Although the largest number of groups that conduct suicide attacks is Islamist, secular groups, especially ethnonationalist groups, have conducted the largest volume of attacks. Today, fourteen terrorist groups have developed the capability to conduct suicide operations: Al Qaeda, Jayash-e-Muhammad,

Harakat-ul-Mujahedin, Islamic Group of Egypt, Egyptian Islamic Jihad, Al Ansar mujahedin, GIA, Hamas, PIJ, Al Aqsa Martyrs Brigade, BKI, LTTE, PKK, and DHKP-C. The number of terrorist groups developing this capability is growing dramatically because it is cost effective and hard to defeat. In addition to Al Ansar mujahedin of Chechnya, there is unverified information that other Chechen groups, as well as Uigurs separatists, have conducted suicide attacks. In addition to Hezbollah, there are other Lebanese, as well as Syrian, groups that conducted suicide attacks in the 1980s; these groups are not active in a terrorist context at this time. The Revolutionary People's Liberation Party (DHKP-C) in Turkey, a left-wing terrorist group, is the latest group to adopt suicide tactics. A DHKP-C suicide bomber killed himself and a police officer and injured seven others at a regional police headquarters on January 3, 2001. Another suicide bomber detonated himself at a police booth in Istanbul's public square, killing two policemen, injuring an Australian tourist (who succumbed to his injuries), and wounding more than twenty others on September 10, 2001.

A suicide bomber may be launched to reach the target either on foot or in a land, sea, or aerial vehicle. The six types of suicide improvised explosive devices (IEDs) operational at present are: (1) a suicide body suit; (2) a three-wheeler vehicle, car, van, or lorry-borne suicide IED; (3) a motorcycle-borne suicide IED; (4) a naval craft–borne suicide IED; (5) a scuba diver–borne suicide IED; and (6) a micro-light aerial vehicle, glider, mini-helicopter, or passenger aircraft–borne suicide IED. All these categories have been used or tried in South Asia and the Middle East. The first suicide attack in the United States occurred on September 11, 2001. Because the tactic of crash-diving passenger aircraft is cost effective, it is likely to be repeated. Suicide bodysuits have been used mostly by female suicide terrorists, who evade standard security checks by concealing the device in their lower abdomens.

There have been only a handful of terrorist attempts to buy aerial vehicles, train pilots, and conduct airborne attacks because they are costly and difficult. Suicide terrorist attacks with a light aircraft or a passenger aircraft are the most difficult to detect or thwart. Al Qaeda used passenger aircraft to attack ground targets such as the World Trade Center, the Pentagon, and the White House because it would have been more difficult to launch a land attack against such high-profile targets. Terrorist groups continue to develop methods against security forces' countermeasures. (An

Asian terrorist group hired a dog handler to add repellents to explosives to shield the suicide bombers from detection.) In addition to intelligence operations and protective security measures to counter terrorist threats, governments and nongovernmental organizations need to develop nonmilitary operations to reduce the threat of terrorism. Educators, clerics, and other prominent figures need to counter misrepresentations of Islamist ideology and corrupted versions of the Koran. Islamic clerics who are terrorist group leaders intertwine Islam with earthly force and increase the appeal of martyrdom operations. Those spreading terrorist propaganda should be criminalized. Otherwise, suicide terrorism will persist and grow as a phenomenon especially in rich Western countries.

## Aviation Terrorism

The first wave of hijackings began in the early 1960s with Cuban refugees armed with grenades, bombs, and guns and grew steadfastly after 1967. The hijackings that began with one hijacker increased gradually to a group of hijackers, and they developed more know-how about the functioning of the aircraft and crew, concealed their weapons better, and used more sophisticated weaponry. Although the hijackings continued until the end of the Cold War, the antihijack pact of 1973 between the United States and Cuba reduced the threat significantly.

The contemporary wave of terrorism began when three PFLP members armed with pistols and grenades hijacked an Israeli El Al commercial flight en route from Rome to Tel Aviv on July 22, 1968. This was the first flight to be hijacked inbound or outbound to the Middle East. The flight was diverted to Algeria, a country unfriendly to Israel. The PFLP intended neither to kill the ten crew members and thirty-eight passengers nor to destroy the aircraft, but to humiliate Israel; the hijackers injured the copilot but freed the passengers on landing. Through increased security and a policy of retaliation El Al was never again a victim of a successful hijacking. When an El Al flight was taxiing to take off from Athens to Paris on December 26, 1968, two terrorists armed with grenades and machine guns attacked, killing one passenger and injuring another and setting one engine on fire; in response, helicopter-borne Israeli commandos raided the Beirut airport and blew up twelve Lebanese-registered aircraft. Multiple hijackings and mass seizure of hostages took place when PFLP terrorists commandeered four jet airliners in September 1970: one plane was blown up in Egypt after an emergency evacuation; the other three flights were diverted to the Jordanian desert, evacuated, and simultaneously blown up.

Terrorist groups continue to develop new hijacking methods to evade airline security countermeasures. The Black September Organization (responsible for the 1972 Munich massacre) hijacked SABENA airlines Flight 517 from Brussels with the aid of two unsuspecting Palestinian women smuggling firearms and explosives in their cosmetic cases and in special girdles. When the aircraft (a Boeing 707) stopped in Vienna, two BSO male members boarded and took control of the aircraft; the terrorists became bolder as they commandeered the plane to Israel. At the Lodi Airport on May 9, 1972, the hijackers threatened to blow up the plane, demanding the release of more than three hundred imprisoned Arab terrorists; Israeli commandos disguised as mechanics burst into the cabin and opened fire, killing the two male hijackers and capturing the two female hijackers. At Heathrow airport in London, another terrorist, Nizar Hindawi, duped his pregnant Irish girlfriend to take a bomb on board her flight to Israel, but an alert El Al security officer discovered it. Every incident has led to new countermeasures (metal detectors, searching passengers and their baggage before boarding, and sky marshals), and hijackings have declined. The introduction of highly trained, motivated, and tough sky marshals with a mandate to negotiate, capture, or kill hijacker(s) drove fear into many hijackers. But only Israel has at least one sky marshal on each El Al flight; most countries do not post sky marshals on all flights. Measures such as magnetometer archways, x-ray machines, passenger profiling, a bulletproof partition between the cockpit and the cabin, and armored luggage and cargo areas have reduced the threat further. Airlines that do not adhere to strict security guidelines have a higher proportion of hijackings. Under the auspices of the International Civil Aviation Organization (ICAO), a cooperative response against aviation terrorism was developed in Tokyo (1963), The Hague (1970), and Montreal (1971), resulting in a series of UN conventions.

Nonetheless, the threat persists. Because aircraft have a limited supply of fuel and food, the duration of aircraft hijackings is limited. However, national flag carriers in particular remain vulnerable despite a constant upgrading in aviation security. During the past thirty years Middle Eastern and other terrorist groups have used a range of weapons and diverse methods to attack civil aviation (planting IEDs in cargo, carrying firearms on board, firing surface-to-air missiles, and using grenades and knives). A grenade in an airplane is an effective suicidal weapon that causes immediate structural damage and depressurizes the aircraft, usually causing the aircraft to crash. More people have been killed in aircraft IED bombings than in aircraft hijackings and accidents.

Since Babbar Khalsa International (BKI) perpetrated the single worst act of aviation sabotage, on June 23, 1985, the technology to detect explosives has improved markedly. The motivation of that act was to avenge the Indian security force attack on Golden Temple in Amritsar, Punjab, to flush out Punjabi terrorists, and to avenge the massacre of five thousand innocent Sikhs following the assassination of Indian prime minister Indira Gandhi by her Sikh bodyguards. The Air India flight from Montreal to Bombay exploded and fell into the sea about 110 miles east of Cork, Ireland, killing 329 passengers, mostly Canadian citizens of Indian origin. Authorities recovered the bodies of only 132 victims and just 35 percent of the wreckage. Although the BKI poses a lesser threat today, the group continues to operate in the West, drawing support from radicalized members of the Sikh community.

The bombing of the Pan Am flight over Lockerbie, Scotland, a few days before Christmas 1988 demonstrated the role of state sponsors in targeting civil aviation, a threat the Western intelligence community took seriously. In the case of the Lockerbie incident, the bomb—hidden in a cassette player and killing 269 people—was a direct retaliation to the 1986 U.S. bombing of Tripoli, Libya, in which the adopted daughter of Colonel Muammar Gaddafi (also spelled Gadhafi) was killed. The covert operation by the Jamahariya Security Organization (the Libyan intelligence service) prompted the Central Intelligence Agency (CIA) and its British counterpart, the SIS (MI6), allegedly to launch operations to assassinate Gaddafi.

Technologically savvy terrorist groups continue to develop explosives and methods to evade detection. For instance, Ramzi Ahmed Yousef, the February 1993 World Trade Center bomber, developed an explosive device with nitroglycerine that was virtually undetectable at airport controls. The detonator of the bomb, activated by an altitude meter, caused the midair explosion of the bomb. Yousef tested the bomb on a flight bound for Tokyo, Japan, from Cebu in the Philippines on December 11, 1994, with the intention of destroying eleven U.S. airliners over the Pacific Ocean in early 1995. The test explosion, occurring at 30,000 feet above sea level on board a Philippine Airlines Flight 434, killed one passenger, injured ten others, and blew a hole in the fuselage; the plane landed safely in Okinawa. Together with the first Al Qaeda pilot, Abdul Hakim Murad, Yousef planned separate attacks to crash-dive aircraft into the Pentagon and the CIA headquarters in Langley, Virginia. Similarly, the GIA hijackers after hijacking an Air France flight from Algiers with 283 passengers planned to ram it into the Eiffel Tower in Paris on December 26, 1994. In Marseille when the terrorists called for a refueling, the GIGN, the French antiterrorist commandos, stormed the plane, killed all four terrorists, and freed the passengers. The operation injured thirteen passengers, three crew members, and nine commandos.

The continuing threat of airliner bombing and hijacking has prompted governments to enhance x-ray and other advanced explosive and metallic detection systems. Other effective security systems that do not require high-level investment to enhance airport security checks have been adopted by a number of developing countries. Comprehensive positive passenger baggage matching, first done manually and later electronically, has ensured that unauthorized unaccompanied bags are not loaded onto airliners. With the privatization of security, standards of management, training, and morale of airport security have tended to decline. This has resulted in security lapses in Europe, North America, and around the world. Although it has become increasingly difficult for hijackers to smuggle a gun onto airplanes, it has not been difficult to smuggle improvised explosive devices, grenades, knives, and box cutters. Until 9/11, largely due to lax security, the rate of detection of these weapons was low. Considering the detection and confiscation of several hundred sharp instruments at airport controls every day, a repeat of a scaled-down version of 9/11 is not unlikely. If the threat persists, hand searches of all luggage and frisking passengers will become a necessity. The 9/11 tragedy has led to an erosion of the public confidence in the aviation industry, but the enduring need to fly is likely to improve aviation security further. One of the biggest problems is the substantial difference and inconsistency in security levels and measures between international airports. In February 2003, heightened security fears, due to intelligence on impending terrorist attacks connected to expected U.S. and U.K. military operations in Iraq, led to the unprecedented posting of U.K. military at several U.K. airports. Because many countries cannot afford the same levels of security, it is hard to counter aviation terrorism; a Venezuelan who boarded in Colombia managed to get a hand grenade into the United Kingdom despite heightened security.

During the 1990s, terrorists were trained in flying schools in Western Europe and in North America and also in Australia, Pakistan, and Sudan, with authorities turning a blind eye to terrorists and known local supporters learning to fly. A number of terrorist groups, including Al Qaeda, have attempted to infiltrate airports to plant bombs in airline cargo; an Al Qaeda cell from northern Germany penetrated airport security in Amsterdam during the planning stage of 9/11, intending to plant bombs in American passenger planes. There have been terrorist attacks on airline staff; Hesham Mohamed Hadayet, armed with two pistols and one knife, killed two and injured four at the El Al ticket counter in the Los Angeles international airport on July 4, 2002. Although he is unlikely to have had a direct link with Al Qaeda, it appears that he was influenced by Al Qaeda jihad ideology. The shooting prompted authorities to screen all passengers at a remote site before entering the airport, and it is likely that tight security prevented Hadayet from boarding an aircraft with a firearm. Due to increased airport security and the concern for passenger safety of passengers at high altitude, terrorist groups now are likely to invest in missiles to shoot down airplanes. The proliferation of surface-to-air missiles (SAMs) is gradually threatening commercial aviation. Two dozen terrorist groups have gained access to SAMs. Several hundred high-speed military jets and helicopters fell prey to SAMs during and after the anti-Soviet Afghan period. The most popular of the aerial weapons can target only low-flying aircraft or on takeoff or landing.

Although the U.S. Congress in 1985 approved the transfer of SAMs to the Afghan mujahedin and to UNITA in Angola, the CIA expressed reservations and unsuccessfully tried to buy back Stinger missiles that survived the anti-Soviet Afghan campaign (1979–1989). During the same period, many terrorist groups purchased SA-14s, an advanced version of the SA-7. The LTTE office in Paris in 1994 purchased SA-14s from Bulgaria and used them against both military and commercial aircraft in the second half of the 1990s. In December 2001, a Sudanese member of Al Qaeda fired a Stinger missile at a U.S. warplane near the Prince Sultan airbase in Saudi Arabia. By enhancing perimeter security, flying over the missile bubble, and using antimissile flares, military aircraft have minimized the threat, but commercial aircraft remain vulnerable to terrorist attack. With the decline in hijackings due to increased security, the threat of SAMs to the aviation industry is likely to increase.

The single biggest threat to the aviation industry will remain the terrorist use of explosives. As such, both governments and corporations continue to invest significant resources to improve the rate of detection of explosives. Post-9/11 explosive detection equipment and trace explosive detection equipment have a success rate of over 90 percent. In contrast to the explosive detection equipment that tests bulk explosives, the trace explosive detection equipment detects minute amounts of explosives. Trace explosive detection equipment was introduced at airport controls after an Al Qaeda operative named Richard Reid tried to destroy a U.S. airliner in December 2001. This lab-style equipment analyzes passenger items (money, tickets, etc.) to find out whether they have come into contact with explosives. Thus the threat of an attack from the West is likely to recede, though the threat against the West will not. When terrorists cannot target a national carrier from a Western country, they are likely to penetrate security in a developing country and successfully target a carrier providing passage to Western nationals. Although national authorities throughout the international aviation system are enjoined to abide by ICAO security standards, most developing countries lack the resources to implement a well-designed, well-managed, and adequately resourced national aviation security system. An international authority in aviation security, Paul Wilkinson, recently called for a thorough system of international inspection and enforcement of aviation security and safety standards.

## Maritime Terrorism

The maritime security environment was altered significantly even before 9/11, when two Al Qaeda suicide bombers rammed an explosives-laden skiff into the USS *Cole* off the coast of Aden, Yemen, killing seventeen U.S. naval personnel and injuring forty-two others while inflicting extensive damage to the Arleigh-Burke–class destroyer on October 12, 2000. The international alarm and publicity generated by the *Cole* incident triggered two other terrorist groups (one Asian and another Middle Eastern) to mount similar terrorist attacks. Four LTTE suicide stealth boats breached the heavily fortified defenses of the Trincomalee naval port on October 23, 2000. The explosives-laden boats destroyed one fast personnel carrier and damaged a second. A Hamas suicide boat attempting to ram an Israeli naval craft exploded prematurely, with insignificant damage to the naval craft, on November 7, 2000. Three attacks within four weeks demonstrated the copycat effect, a phenomenon not uncommon among modern terrorist groups. The low-cost, high-impact attack prompted several terrorist groups to plan and prepare for targeting objects at sea.

Although a relatively new environment for most terrorist groups, the application of land techniques and tactics at sea is not too difficult. The idea of attacking a U.S. warship was born in May 1998, when the USS *Mount Vernon* visited Aden for three days. When Osama bin Laden was informed of the visit by the leadership of the Islamic Army of Aden Abayan, an associate group of Al Qaeda, he dispatched an operational commander to plan a long-term operation. On January 3, 2000, Al Qaeda's TNT-laden boat was brought from an Al Qaeda safehouse by a trailer and launched into the sea, but due to excess weight, the explosives-laden boat sank within minutes. Deprived of high-grade intelligence on Al Qaeda, the U.S. intelligence community failed to realize that it had been targeted. Within ten months, Al Qaeda mounted a second operation, this time using C-4, a plastic explosive. Like most sophisticated terrorist groups, Al Qaeda too had a steep learning curve whereby it improved its know-how constantly. In keeping with its doctrine of maximizing its successes and minimizing its failures, Al Qaeda dispatched the USS *Cole* masterminds to Kuala Lumpur to plan an attack on another U.S. ship visiting a Malaysian port in 2000.

Since the closure of U.S. bases in the Philippines in the early 1990s, Singapore has become the U.S. military's most important resupply point in Southeast Asia; an average of one hundred Navy vessels stop each year, and several thousand sailors take shore leave. Although the Singaporean Internal Security Department (ISD) has disrupted the Jammah Islamiyyah (JI) organization in Singapore, and Malaysia and the Philippines have followed suit, Indonesia's failure a to disrupt the JI organization and arrest its leadership continues to threaten security in Southeast Asia and Australasia. In addition, Al Qaeda's successful attack on the USS *Cole* and attempted attacks on the USS *The Sullivans* and other U.S. warships off Malaysia, Singapore, and Gibraltar demonstrate the continuing threat posed by this one group. Hezbollah has also mounted surveillance of U.S. warships in Southeast Asia.

Prior to 9/11, the U.S. and the international community had no effective system to monitor the movement of terrorists operating across borders. In preparation for the USS *Cole* bombing, Khalid Almihdhar and Nawaf Alhazmi visited Kuala Lumpur in January 2000 and met with Al Qaeda's Asian leadership, Hambali and Sufaat, planning a similar operation in the Malacca Straits. Despite their visit to Malaysia coming to the attention of the CIA, Almihdhar and Alhazmi entered the United States under their own names and participated in 9/11.

The lessons of 9/11 are being incorporated into the U.S. counterterrorist doctrine but slowly; the U.S. Federal Bureau of Investigation (FBI) is laying the foundation for an international terrorist tracking system. The preparedness of the international community to fight the post–Cold War wave of terrorism has been poor. Post–Cold War terrorists are highly mobile, well educated, and willing to die for their beliefs. In many ways, international and national security, intelligence, and law enforcement agencies only began the framework for fighting the new terrorism after 9/11.

Terrorist know-how and technology for attacking ships have proliferated. A manual about sea mines was recovered in Afghanistan. A 1,086-page Harakat-ul Mujahedin terrorist training manual in Arabic ("Mujahideen ki Lalkaar—War Cry of the Mujahideen") was found near Kabul by Sandeep Unnithan and Mohammad Waqas. Under techniques for disabling ships, the manual reads: "A warship can be immobilised by placing 1.2 kg of plastic explosive on the propeller shaft. A mere 1.3 kg can destroy the engine . . . 4 kg on the base can sink it." Although Afghanistan is landlocked and over three hundred miles from the nearest sea, the Harakat family of terrorist groups operates from Australia to the Balkans and from the United Kingdom to Canada. All the major terrorist groups active today have established external networks; as such they influence the conduct of each other directly and indirectly. Like governments, most contemporary groups learn from one another, either by direct transfer or indirect emulation of technology, techniques, and tactics. The threshold for maritime attacks has escalated with the increased interaction between Caucasian, African, Middle Eastern, and Asian terrorist groups in Afghanistan and elsewhere.

In addition to targeting ships and other objects at sea, a terrorist group can use a ship both to transport supplies and personnel and as a weapon. After 9/11, the International Maritime Organization (IMO) warned that terrorists "could use hijacked oil tankers or liquefied natural gas carriers." The New York port, the third largest port in the United States, is located in the middle of New York City. It is impossible to check each container that arrives there. The carnage from detonating a conventional or a nonconventional device on board a ship inside the harbor is likely to kill and injure a number far exceeding the death toll of 9/11. This illustrates the need for increased, maintained, and universal maritime security.

Despite the looming threat, less than 5 percent of all terrorist groups have developed maritime support and attack capabilities. Yet any determined terrorist group can develop a maritime terrorist capability in a short period of time. Replicating land capabilities in the maritime environment is not difficult, but the maritime infrastructure of terrorist groups is vulnerable to detection. Therefore, only a few terrorist groups with maritime capabilities have attacked commercial and military shipping in a sustained manner. Most terrorist groups have emulated pirates and staged surface attacks both to send a political message and to accumulate general cargo. Aboard fast power boats, terrorists have fired at ships mostly with RPGs, LAWs, and heavy machine guns. The attacks have been infrequent because most commercial and military ships navigate the deep oceans, and because most terrorist groups can operate only within the coastal or territorial waters.

When ships divert from shipping lanes and navigate to ports of call, the marine police, coastguard, or navies of host countries protect them. Therefore, the risk of terrorist attack on commercial and military shipping is low except when they navigate along narrow sea-lanes that are not secured or well policed. Examples include the Islamic group of Egypt that conducted terrorist attacks against cruise liners sailing on the Nile River in the 1990s; POLISARIO, which staged similar attacks off Morocco; and Al Qaeda and its associate groups, which planned to stage suicide attacks and destroy U.S. and British warships in the straits of Malacca in 2000–2001 and off Gibraltar in 2002. Terrorists have also fired at ships from low- and high-trajectory weapons based on land. For instance, the Portuguese terrorist group FP-25 claimed responsibility for an unsuccessful mortar attack on six NATO warships in the port of Lisbon on January 28, 1985. There have been similar attacks off Greece. Therefore, commercial and maritime shipping is vulnerable to terrorist attack by sea (on the surface when moving and underwater when stationary) and by air.

Anchored or berthed ships especially when in port are vulnerable to underwater attack by terrorist groups. Maritime terrorist attacks involving the use of underwater explosives are few but lethal. Only a few groups with access to military explosives, essential to construct an underwater explosive device, can stage an underwater attack. Furthermore, only a handful of groups have members trained as skin or scuba divers (e.g., the "Sea-Tigers" of the LTTE). Al Qaeda manuals recovered in Afghanistan and intelligence of an attack in the making in the United States indicated that the group had access to trained divers willing to die. It is mostly groups with past and present access to state sponsorship that conduct underwater maritime terrorist attacks. They place underwater explosive devices on the hulls of vessels, especially under the engine room. Damage to any part of a ship can be repaired without much difficulty except for the ship's engine. In the past, U.S., Soviet, Middle Eastern, and Indian intelligence agencies, together with their naval counterparts, provided underwater demolition training to a number of terrorist groups. Underwater maritime terrorist attacks inflict significant damage to boats and small ships, but not big ships. This is because terrorist groups have not yet perfected the art of transporting large underwater explosive devices and attaching them to the hulls of large ships. The LTTE has used underwater scooters purchased from Denmark to attack Sri Lankan and foreign ships off northeastern Sri Lanka. As most ships do not have hooks in the hull to attach an explosive device, terrorist divers tie the device to the ship's propeller. To inflict greater damage, suicide divers position the device under the ship's engine and detonate the device. Therefore, using the commonly used underwater explosive device, a terrorist group cannot inflict a mass casualty attack on crew and passengers. In underwater warfare, only terrorist groups with access to military explosives pose a sustained high threat to maritime security. However, a terrorist group can strategically place a sea mine on a shipping lane or ram a boat laden with explosives. Therefore, the threat to commercial and military shipping is high from terrorist mine warfare and maritime surface warfare.

Using front shipping companies and flags of convenience, and by changing their names frequently, terrorists use ships to smuggle members, weapons, and supplies as well as to smuggle humans, narcotics, and other contraband. A few Middle Eastern groups (including the Palestinian Authority, PA) enjoying state sponsorship, and others such as Al Qaeda, LTTE, KLA, ASG, and MILF, have contracted or acquired ships that can navigate over long distances. For instance, Karine A, a 4,028 dwt Tongan-flagged ship with fifty tons of rockets, mortars, and explosives was seized by Israeli commandos in international waters in the Red Sea in January 2002. Registered to an Iraqi national, the ship was used by the PA to smuggle weapons from Iran. Some terrorist groups have expressed an interest in using their ships as a weapon, rigging them as bombs. Others have expressed an interest in shipping containers laden with explosives to target either ships or ports. After Norwegian intelligence uncovered in December 2001 that Al Qaeda owned or controlled twenty-three ships, a number of ships were searched by U.S. Special Forces and other military forces. Prior to 9/11, Western intelligence agencies only monitored (as opposed to interdicted) terrorist ships, as they were believed to pose limited or no threat to Western interests.

Although both commercial and military maritime industries have invested significantly in security, terrorist groups have also expressed a greater interest in exploiting the maritime environment. Within three weeks of the USS *Cole* attacks, both Hamas and the LTTE mounted maritime suicide operations against Israeli and Sri Lankan naval craft. Terrorist success, industry fear, and public alarm generated after the *Cole* attack drove several terrorist groups to consider developing maritime capabilities. The threat to the maritime industry has continued to escalate, with terrorists planning to develop mini-submarines, use explosives-laden ships as weapons to attack port cities in the aftermath of 9/11, attack warships in the Indian Ocean by crashing commercial airliners on them in early 2002, and plant explosives in cargo containers. With heightened security, the trend is for maritime terrorist attacks to be few but more lethal.

Just as terrorist groups continue to exchange land and aerial technologies, they exchange maritime technologies, techniques, and tactics. Initially the terrorist knowledge base of maritime terrorist technologies improved when state actors provided them with specialized training and resources. CIA-trained Cuban exile groups in the United States staged the largest number of terrorist attacks against Cuban and Soviet maritime targets during the 1960s; several Latin American and Middle Eastern groups received similar training from Soviet bloc countries. India and several other countries developed underwater demolition techniques for foreign terrorist groups. Maritime conflicts between states have also raised the threshold for maritime terrorism. During the post–Cold War period, state-to-state conflicts in the maritime environment declined. There are a few exceptions: a North Korean ship sinking a South Korean ship killed four people and injured eighteen others on June 28, 2002. Although a few terrorist groups innovate their own terrorist technologies, techniques, and tactics, most are copycats and receive or emulate know-how and resources from state actors.

Post-9/11 countermeasures include government hiring of additional immigration and investigative personnel; development of machine-readable, tamper-resistant visas and other travel and entry documents using biometric identifiers; advanced notification of all cargo, vessels, crew, passenger, and other personnel arrival and departure information; and civil penalties to those who fail to conform. In addition to arrangements with foreign governments to search and seal U.S.-bound cargo in their ports, it became mandatory for all vessels to inform governments ninety-six hours before entry to a port. Especially after the successful suicide bombing of the oldest Jewish synagogue in Djerba, Tunisia, using a liquid petroleum gas vehicle on April 11, 2002, there is fear that Al Qaeda will use a ship with dangerous cargo to attack a port. The threat posed by liquefied natural gas and petroleum tankers is likely to persist until ports create special areas to service such vessels. In light of the new threat, the United States has amended the definition of "certain dangerous cargo" to include any explosive materials, oxidizing materials, blasting agents, spontaneously combustible products in bulk packaging, highway route–controlled quantity radioactive material, controlled shipments of fissile material, and bulk cargoes such as butylenes oxide, chlorine, and elemental phosphorous.

Although countering conventional threats, the United States will also need to invest more in thermal, infrared, chemical, biological, and radiological detection systems. In addition to declaring all U.S. ports as security zones, the U.S. Coast Guard will develop passenger-profiling systems to screen all commercial vessels with the intention of identifying high-interest vessels for closer examination. With several tens of thousands of ships entering U.S. ports annually, and with as many as four thousand containers in one ship in some cases, the U.S. government will have no option but to invest in better-quality intelligence. Together with Lloyds Maritime Intelligence Group in London, the Maritime Intelligence Group in Washington, D.C., has developed the best vessel profiling system to date. The U.S. Coast Guard has also established protection zones for a distance of five hundred yards around all U.S. naval vessels in navigable waters of the United States. The U.S. government has stipulated that nonmilitary vessels are not allowed to enter within one hundred yards of a U.S. naval vessel, whether under way or moored, unless authorized by a U.S. Coast Guard or U.S. Navy patrol. Open ports like New York and New Jersey came under restrictions with revised traffic management plans, and vessels were barred from within 150 yards of Liberty and Ellis Islands. Furthermore, unauthorized vessels and persons are prohibited from approaching within 175 yards of the headquarters of the United Nations, on the East River in New York City, and vessels must remain at least twenty-five yards away from bridge piers and abutments, overhead power cables, and tunnel ventilations. Although clarifying and amending various other restrictions in the wake of 9/11, the United States also eliminated the requirement that deep-draft vessels enter the New York port via Ambrose or Sandy Hook Channels as well as the security zones around piers 90, 92, and 94 on the Hudson River. The security of cruise ships too came under greater scrutiny. The threat is likely to be greatest in zones where protection of U.S. naval vessels is shared by host navies, coast guard, and maritime police authorities. Port security will include cargo security, where containerized cargo will be identified, tracked, screened, and physically secured by standard seals and locks; personnel security; and foreign port assessments including screening containerized cargo, access restrictions, vessel security, certification of compliance with security measures, and security management.

The future security of U.S., allied, and coalition partner maritime assets will depend on the ability and the willingness of Western governments to work with the rest of the world to enhance maritime security worldwide.

# Terrorist Financing

Financing, the lifeblood of terrorist groups, has developed dramatically over the past thirty years. Only creative and innovative terrorist groups survived the transition from the Cold War to the post–Cold War. The dramatic loss or decline in state sponsorship led several groups to abandon violence as a means to political power. Post–Cold War terrorist groups are becoming dependent on organized crime for their survival. The trend is for sophisticated groups with an international reach to move from dirty-clean money routes to clean-clean money routes. Penetration of legitimate businesses, from manufacturing to trade and investment, is evident. Today, all the major terrorist groups enjoy a transboundary presence. With traditional state sponsors distancing themselves, several Middle Eastern, Asian African, and Latin American terrorist groups generate support for terrorism in North America, Europe, and Australasia. Political and economic conditions in liberal democracies allow foreign terrorist groups to establish support infrastructure far away from their theaters of conflict. Terrorist groups have become highly mobile during the 1990s and move rapidly in search of new opportunities. Only by host and target states both sharing the burden of counterterrorism can terrorism be reduced and suppressed. Target governments are dependent on host governments for intelligence, security, and judicial cooperation to combat externally supported terrorism.

Traditional law enforcement attacks on only the criminal activities of terrorist organizations have neither mitigated nor deterred terrorism because there has been no worldwide attack on noncriminal infrastructures that generate the lifeblood for terrorist groups. The international environment has permitted most terrorist groups to generate support in one theater and fight in another. The community of nations recognized the need for an international response to terrorism during the Cold War, but a well formulated, multipronged, multidimensional, and multinational response became feasible only after the end of the East-West confrontation. After recognizing this threat, the international community formulated a UN convention to suppress terrorist financing of terrorism—calling on governments to dismantle front, cover, and sympathetic organizations, especially of foreign terrorist groups operating on their soil. However, impediments to developing a global strategy that will suppress the financing of terrorism still remain. Host governments have been confronted with legal, political, and operational impediments against disrupting terrorist front, cover, and sympathetic organizations engaged in fund-raising. Most countries lack comprehensive legislation to regulate their financial and banking institutions. Legislation in some countries forbids operational agencies from mounting surveillance on any particular community contributing funds to a terrorist group. Some terrorist-infiltrated ethnic and religious communities exert pressure on their politicians to legitimize their cause in return for the ethnic and religious vote. Likewise, liberal democracies (e.g., Canada, United Kingdom, France, Switzerland, Germany, Scandinavia, Australia, and New Zealand) have permitted foreign terrorist groups to raise funds openly and even issue receipts to their contributors. The reality is that most host governments allow foreign terrorist groups to operate on their soil unless the terrorists directly threaten either host domestic or foreign interests.

Aside from preserving the core and penultimate leadership and ideologically indoctrinating the support base, building up the financial, supply, and logistical infrastructure is paramount for the success of any group. Sustained support (domestic, international, or both) has enabled the terrorist leadership to replenish losses and wastage in the rank and file. By creating innocuous front, cover, and sympathetic organizations, terrorists draw support from domestic and foreign governments, intergovernmental and nongovernmental organizations, and individuals. Registered charities in liberal democracies and in some emerging democracies generate support, evade taxation, and launder and transfer funds for procurement. Broad democratic latitudes help a number of Asian, African, Middle Eastern, and Latin American terrorist groups exploit the open society and liberal immigration laws. In response, the terrorists establish bases, gateways, or springboards to either stage or transit terrorist operations. By taking advantage of the liberal constitutions, a few hundred terrorists violate the right to life and human rights of several million citizens in other countries. Most terrorist groups move from diaspora-migrant "taxation" to investment in enterprise (trade and businesses) depending upon the host country's laws and regulations. Any host government that turns a blind eye to terrorist fundraising and structure for disseminating propaganda risks supporting terrorist training and procurement. The incremental escalation of support is intimately linked to the incremental escalation in violence. Disrupting the financial infrastructure of terrorist groups—constraining access to sophisticated weaponry, expertise, and other resources—can appreciably affect the sustainability of a terrorist group and its campaign.

The study of opportunities available and strategies adopted by terrorist groups to accumulate economic wealth reveals that the post–Cold War political climate facilitated terrorist groups in accruing significant international and domestic political, economic, and military support. Because international terrorist infrastructures are not subject to national jurisdiction, they are a greater threat to national and international security. International terrorist infrastructures disseminate propaganda, lobby foreign governments and potential supporters, raise funds, invest funds in trade or businesses, procure weapons and hire expertise, recruit and train personnel, and ship personnel, weapons, and other supplies to the theaters of conflict. Contemporary sources of terrorist finances are varied, as will be examined next.

## Domestic

All terrorist groups enjoy varying degrees of domestic or territorial financial support. However, only a few groups generate more funds domestically. Domestic support (both individual and corporate) can be voluntary or involuntary. Terrorist groups institute either a mandatory or an ad hoc tax to ensure a continuous financial flow.

## Diaspora-Migrant

The conflicts of the 1990s, along with the end of the Cold War and the ensuing phenomenon of globalization, generated unprecedented displacement and refugee flows. This in turn facilitated the formation of diaspora and ethnic networks that provide the rudimentary international infrastructure for insurgent/terrorist groups to operate overseas with relative ease. With external support, most insurgent/terrorist groups of the 1990s have been transformed from rag-tag assemblies to sophisticated groups. Groups that have vibrant external support networks are mostly ethnonationalist groups (Irish, Kurds, Sri Lankan Tamils, Kashmiris, Basques, Croats, Albanians, Armenians, etc). The insurgent/terrorist campaigns that are hardest to defeat are those empowered by ethnonationalist sentiments and emotions. They have the longest staying power; their struggles can be dampened more politically and less militarily. However, to make such groups more amenable to negotiation, they have to be militarily weakened and politically marginalized. For instance, had U.S.-U.K. security cooperation not disrupted the PIRA transatlantic pipeline, PIRA would not have reached a military stalemate with

British troops. Similarly, had Indo-Bangladesh cooperation not ended Indian support to the Chakmas in the Chittagong Hill Tracts, the Shanthi Bahini rebels would still be fighting the Bangladeshi troops. Multipronged political, military, economic, and diplomatic countermeasures are required to disrupt insurgent/terrorist support networks.

After 9/11, terrorist infrastructures tapping their overseas-based communities have become more clandestine, although terrorists continue to raise funds from their diaspora and migrants through individual and corporate contributions and coercive measures. Force, or the threat of force, may be used against family members in the homeland to make reluctant members of the diaspora-migrant communities pay; to prevent threats coming to the attention of the host law enforcement, implicit coercion is used rather than explicit coercion.

At a domestic level, countermeasures must be aimed at the country of origin of the insurgent/terrorist organization itself. It is important to meet the aspirations and grievances of the ethnonationalists before the insurgent/terrorist group gathers momentum. Because the diaspora represents the thinking of the domestic population, it is imperative for governments to focus first on altering the internal dynamics that have spawned rebellion. Many governments have lacked the skills and expertise to develop nonmilitary (political, socioeconomic, and international) dimensions of counterinsurgency. Many governments have failed to develop and implement sustained political and economic strategies to provide an alternative leadership to their minorities from "getting sucked into the gun culture." Therefore, to dampen popular support for insurgency/terrorism, political reform to give the marginalized and the deprived members of society more autonomy and enhanced security is essential.

When the insurgency/terrorist campaign persists, the groups can develop international infrastructures, some even independent or semi-independent of their diasporas. Procurement operations are sustained by finance generated both by diaspora collections and insurgent/terrorist investments. Therefore, the key to restraining procurement is to generate an effective counterpropaganda network. Most states have made some headway by launching coordinated counterpropaganda initiatives against insurgent/terrorist-infiltrated diaspora organizations. Most governments operate overseas through pro-state diaspora organizations and through their foreign missions. Effectively disseminating the "right" propaganda can strategically weaken the fundraising capability of an organization. The nongovernmental community has played a major role in curbing the activity of insurgent/terrorist fronts. Many NGOs have pressurized host governments to withdraw their support to, or even to ban, an organization. In the United States until October 1997 and in the United Kingdom until September 1998, it was not an offense for insurgent/terrorist groups to raise funds for perpetrating violence. In continental Europe and in Canada, several groups continue to publicly raise funds to procure weapons.

The key to regulating procurement and shipping per se is international and regional interagency and security cooperation. Some states have been successful in developing frontline intelligence on the international procurement and shipping operations of their insurgent/terrorist groups. There should also be a political commitment to embark on high-risk operations both overseas and on a domestic level. Many states have failed to thwart the external threat due to a lack of a comprehensive understanding of the international networks of their insurgent/terrorist groups. This understanding is a paramount requirement before developing a counterstrategy. At a domestic level, institutions should be created to ensure that there is cooperation and coordination, and not confrontation or competition, between government intelligence and investigative agencies. However, the problem of sharing intelligence and protecting sources will always arise.

## Co-ethnic and Co-religionists

Contributions from members of a kin ethnic background are referred to as *co-ethnic* support. In contrast, *co-religionist* support relates to contributions made from the members of the same faith and is driven by religious affinity. Islamic groups in particular have benefited from donations from wealthy Arabs in the Persian Gulf, Middle Eastern, and North African countries. Although there is no conclusive proof, it may be surmised that the habit of providing such donations originated when the Afghans were fighting the Soviets from 1979 to 1989.

## State Sponsorship

State sponsors (or patron states) provide active contributions to terrorist groups to attack inimical states. Usually foreign policy considerations drive states to sponsor terrorist groups in inimical countries. For instance, the government of India sponsors a number of Pakistani groups, and the government of Pakistan sponsors a number of Indian groups. The late 1990s witnessed a decline in state sponsorship. Because the international community now punishes state sponsors, many states have distanced themselves from sponsoring groups engaging in terrorism as opposed to guerrilla warfare. Finance is the key component of any terrorist support infrastructure. With the international community targeting terrorist state sponsors, the terrorist capacity independently to generate terrorist finance appears to be the key to their survival.

During the height of the Cold War, a large percentage of terrorist groups funded their existence and activities by receiving the active sponsorship of superpowers or their satellite states. The Soviet Union and its satellite states provided finance and weapons to the MPLA in Angola, SWAPO in Nambia, FRELIMO in Mozambique, ANC in South Africa, PLO in the Middle East, POLISARIO in Western Sahara, and the PKK in Turkey. The United States provided finance and weapons to groups in Angola (UNITA), Cambodia (Khmer Rouge), and Nicaragua (FDN: Contras) as well as to Cuban exile groups and the Afghan mujahedin. For instance, between 1980 and 1989, the CIA provided through the Inter-Services Intelligence (ISI) $2 billion in weapons and 80 percent of the CIA's covert budget to Afghan groups. The bulk of the weapons and finance went to Hezb-e-Islami, led by Gulbuddin Hekmatyar, who was vehemently opposed to the United States and who supported Al Qaeda, led by Osama bin Laden. Similar to other agencies that acted as conduits for weapon and financial transfers to guerrilla and terrorist groups, the ISI retained a bulk of the weapons and finance for use in subsequent campaigns, including to support the Taliban and Kashmiri mujahedin.

The CIA also supported the Sudanese Peoples Liberation Army (SPLA) against Dr. Hasan Al-Turabi's National Islamic Front, which worked closely with Al Qaeda. The CIA supported the Northern Iraqi opposition forces beginning in late October 1994. NATO members supported the KLA until the UN Security Council passed a binding resolution in March 1998 forbidding such activity. Turkey supported Chechen groups, and while Pakistan supported several Kashmiri and other Indian groups, India supported several Pakistani groups.

## Low-Level and Organized Crime

Organized crime differs from low-level, individual, and casual crime in the degree of scale and coordination. Whereas organized crime is conducted by an organization, low-level crime is done by disconnected individuals. Organized crime can be broadly divided into *fraud* (e.g., taking a percentage from prisoner welfare or social security; illegal logging; cultivating or refining narcotics; video, CD, and cassette piracy; taxi scams such as running unregistered taxis; not paying taxes), *smuggling* (cigarettes, alcohol, narcotics, humans), *racketeering* (extorting percentages from prostitution, human smugglers, narcotic trafficking, forgers of identity and travel documents, drinking clubs, and taxi services), *kidnapping for ransom*, and *armed robbery*. In addition to developing links with organized crime groups, terrorist groups engage directly in organized crime. For instance, in exchange for weapons, FARC provided cocaine to Russian organized crime groups.

With the end of the East-West confrontation, the porosity of borders enhanced terrorist mobility. The geographic range of terrorist organizations, especially in operations into Western countries, has increased. Contemporary groups can operate over long distances with relative ease. Today most terrorist groups engage in the narcotics trade, human trafficking, illicit weapon transfers, kidnapping, extortion, credit card fraud, and video, audio, and CD piracy. As such, they have a lesser need to depend on state sponsors. The international environment has also favored many of these groups establishing front, cover, and sympathetic organizations in Western European countries and North America. Appearing as human rights, humanitarian, cultural, and social organizations, these terrorist affiliates engage in organized crime. Often migrants from the conflict zone help terrorist groups establish such organizations and conduct such operations. As a result, there is an extensive organized crime infrastructure in Canada, Australia, New Zealand, France, Germany, Switzerland, Belgium, Austria, and Scandinavia (mostly Sweden and Norway). Today funds raised by terrorist groups operating in these host countries are comparable to (and in some cases more than) the contributions that they have received from state sponsors. Weapons, explosives, and dual technologies purchased from funds raised by terrorist groups through organized crime in Western liberal democracies have killed several thousand civilians and security force personnel around the globe.

The proceeds from organized crime constituted a small percentage of terrorist financing during the Cold War. Only the innovative terrorist groups, able to develop alternative sources of income, have survived. The decline of state sponsorship and the distancing of states from sponsorship is forcing terrorist groups to be dependent on organized crime. Today, many groups engage in or are linked to organized crime groups trafficking narcotics (FARC, ELN, AUS, IMU, PKK, LTTE, ASG, MILF, several Myanmar groups), weapons (almost all groups), and humans (PKK, LTTE, GIA). Although most groups depend on organized crime proceeds, the more sophisticated groups finance themselves by investing in legitimate businesses, thus reducing chances of getting caught "laundering." They want "clean money"; they don't want to "dirty their hands."

Traditionally, terrorists have used criminal funds or proceeds from organized crime to fund their existence and activities. However, the terrorist modus operandi for generating funds is undergoing a major change. With the transition from accruing vast profits through legitimate businesses, should investments and the profits of legitimate businesses owned by terrorists be considered criminal funds? Because the motivation of the terrorist group is to use clean money for illegitimate purposes, it is necessary to think of ways and means of criminalizing the generation of clean money for nefarious activities. With the sweeping changes in the post–Cold War international strategic environment, almost all major terrorist groups engage in organized crime or transact with organized crime groups. The access to criminal groups has strengthened many terrorist groups. In addition to attempts to procure CBRN material, Al Qaeda used the criminal groups operating in Europe to purchase weapons. For instance, when the Belgian Special Intervention Unit (Escadron Special d'Intervention) raided the apartment of an Al Qaeda suicide bomber named Nizar Ben Abdelaziz Trabelsi on September 13, 2001, they found among his clothes a machine-gun type Uzi N ERO 168302 Croatia with two big magazines, containing 9-millimeter para caliber cartridges.

With governments allocating significant resources to combat money laundering, it will become increasingly difficult for groups to rely on the proceeds of organized crime. To evade police tracing, the clever groups are likely to develop and maintain clean money sources. Irrespective of who does it, it is not a criminal offense in most countries to generate funds through businesses and to raise funds through charities. This again illustrates the need for international cooperation between law enforcement and intelligence agencies. Dirty money can be traced back to drug cartels, alien smuggling networks, and so on. The dirty money trail is obvious and relatively easy to trace. Clean money sources are not as easy to trace. In the future, terrorists are likely to be rag-tag groups using "dirty to clean" money routes and sophisticated groups using "clean to clean" money routes. This development in the terrorist environment should be viewed in light of the latest UN convention to suppress terrorist financing. The terrorists are probably a step ahead of the convention, segments of which are being integrated into domestic legislation by a number of states. It is worth remembering that many groups have accountants and lawyers working full-time to identify international and domestic legal loopholes and ways of hiding money in order to finance themselves and operate. The organized crime-terrorist nexus will ensure terrorist survival. With the decline in state and public support (sanctuary, recruitment, finance, and weapons), investment in crime will be essential to maintain a viable terrorist organization. Future terrorist existence and activities are dependent on a sustained and consistent flow of support from organized crime. Thus any successful counterterrorist agenda should include measures to combat organized crime also.

## Financial Crime

Several terrorist groups (especially groups operating outside their territorial borders) engage in financial crime using credit cards and checks. Using blank credit cards, a card embossing machine, a skimmer (mobile card data reader), a computer, a data reader/writer, and cables to connect devices, terrorist support cells operating throughout Europe counterfeited and cloned credit cards, raising millions of dollars annually. At restaurants, gas stations, garages, and stores, as a person swipes a genuine credit card through a skimmer, the terrorist cell downloads it to a computer, then saves it or e-mails it to a second cell, usually in another country. This data can be loaded onto the magnetic strip of any plastic card, or it may be edited and given a new name. Thus counterfeit cards are prepared for an individual who may have supporting identity documents in that name. Terrorist groups have overcome many countermeasures by obtaining genuine credit cards and replacing the magnetic information on the rear with details from skimmed cards. Visual examination, however, showing whether a card is genuine or not, still reduces risks of fraud.

Support members of terrorist groups using genuine (mostly stolen), forged, and adapted identifications have established accounts in reputed financial institutions and built strong credit histories by frequently depositing small sums. By putting in cash and taking it out, it builds up a turnover. After churning, building credit histories, and generating bank confidence, they take huge loans and overdrafts and disappear at times, making in excess of $100,000. Often a terrorist supporter will open a dozen accounts to build a legend around the false identities of the account holders, making his time and resources profitable; when one account is defrauded, there will be another dozen accounts available under multiple fictitious identities. In world capitals like London, Paris, and Amsterdam, some terrorist groups built financial networks to issue checks and amass several tens of thousands of dollars. The depth of activity includes a dozen members stockpiling checkbooks and issuing the checks all at once, backed by check guarantee cards. Terrorist modus operandi includes different types of bank fraud, including getting a loan and repaying it the first time, and then getting a bigger loan or issuing checks. Until recently, most banks did not aggressively investigate these frauds because insurance covered the losses. Since 9/11, bank managers have become more alert. However, because banks want to open as many accounts as possible, they are reluctant to run detailed credit checks on new customers. One of the biggest failures of governments, especially Western governments, in regulating financial crime is their failure to target the terrorist organization as opposed to criminal activity. By targeting criminal activity and the individuals engaging in it, the activities of the group become increasingly clandestine. Thus financial fraud is more an embarrassment than a loss for a bank. Bank frauds are rarely reported and are least likely to be detected. Among the many groups that engage in financial fraud are, for example, Al Qaeda, GIA, GSPC, LTTE, PKK, and BKI. Terrorist groups often favor operating in countries such as Latin America or South Africa, where there is a need for foreign investment, financial regulation mechanisms are weak, and officials can be bribed fairly easily.

## Investments and Legitimate Businesses

Although money laundering is investment to lose the dirty track and generate clean money, many contemporary groups invest money to generate high profit both in safe and high-risk ventures, including in trade and enterprise investments. Following the UN convention on the suppression of the financing of terrorism in January 2000, more terrorist groups are investing in legitimate businesses to become less reliant on individual contributions that can be easily monitored by government authorities. This is problematic for counterterrorist agencies, as special legal powers are needed to target *legitimate* businesses. However, an example of what can, and arguably should, be done is in the case of new laws being brought into Northern Ireland. According to the Northern Ireland Office, a support agency for the Secretary of State for Northern Ireland (http://www.nio.gov.uk), if there is adequate suspicion, instead of the courts or law-enforcement agencies having to prove the guilt of a suspected terrorist using a legitimate business as a front, the onus will be on companies and individuals to prove that they are indeed legitimate and have no involvement with the suspected illegal activities.

## Nongovernmental Organizations

Several well-endowed and respectable NGOs active in the political, religious, cultural, judicial, human rights, and humanitarian fields located in the northern hemisphere contribute vast sums of funds to poorer and needy organizations in the southern hemisphere. Usually, the terrorists or their political activists cultivate vulnerable individuals with either compatible ideologies or interests in the NGO sector to channel funds to front, cover, and sympathetic organizations of terrorist groups.

## Individual Financiers

The Afghanistan-based Saudi dissident Osama bin Laden is the best known of the individual terrorist financiers. Several less-known individual financiers living in the Persian Gulf region support terrorist-controlled welfare, social, and religious organizations.

## Community Organizations

By infiltrating or establishing community organizations, terrorist groups protect their identity and gain respectability. Organizations as well as individuals sympathetic to terrorists have little or no hesitation of interacting with community organizations that promote community interests, provide services and incentives, and care for the needs of a community. Some community organizations controlled by terrorist groups initiate grant applications under the guise of promoting community interests.

## Public and Private Donor and Other Benevolent Organizations

By operating through registered human rights, humanitarian, and other organizations committed to humanity, terrorist groups deceive their donors and benevolent organizations into making considerable public and private contributions. To accumulate and transfer wealth and to evade paying taxes, several terrorist groups seek charity status.

## Sale of Products

To generate funds, terrorist groups have produced newspapers, magazines, books, videos, audios, CDs, T-shirts, clocks, watches, radios, and other products that promote their aims and objectives, and have marketed them at sympathetic stores or terrorist-organized public and private events.

## Lobbying

Although not a source of financial support for terrorism, some terrorist groups with overseas infrastructure have developed a capability to affect the economic sustainability of some target states. If the target state is dependent on foreign sources of support, terrorist lobbying against country donors, travel agencies, and investors, as well as terrorist attacks on tourist infrastructure, has had an adverse impact on the national economy. Operating through terrorist front, cover, and sympathetic organizations, several terrorist groups attempted to influence country contributions at the Paris Aid Group, a meeting held annually to assist the countries of the developing world. Terrorist groups operating through human rights and humanitarian organizations, including some reputable nongovernmental organizations, have placed country consortiums under pressure. If the target state is hard-pressed for revenue to combat terrorism, overseas terrorist informational infrastructures have a capacity to damage government counterinsurgency procurement, training, recruitment, and infrastructure.

Terrorist groups are capable of organizing and maintaining highly sophisticated operational and support networks. In order to counter an international or transnational problem, there needs to be an international response. However, with this comes the immediate issues and problems of jurisdiction, sovereignty, and intelligence sharing. What is needed, though problematic, is more effective and rigorous monitoring of capital and transactions, and universalized banking standards. But *who* should take the lead in these problems and *how* are questions important to debate.

## Notes

1. See Bjorgo's definition of bounded and unbounded groups, *Racist and Right-Wing Violence in Scandinavia.*

2. The concept of "uneven development" (UD) is mainly used by Marxists to emphasize capitalism's unequal spread of global economic benefits. The spread of capitalism according to this theory resulted in the exploitation of colonies, and in the present period characterizes the world economy. See Viotti and Kauppi, *International Relations Theory* (New York: Macmillan, 1993), 596.

## References

"Algeria's Army Picks Its Man." 1999. *The Economist*, March 20, 53.

"Arms Availability and the Situation of Civilians and Armed Conflicts." 1999. Report of the International Committee of the Red Cross, July.

Bjorgo, T. 1997. *Racist and Right-Wing Violence in Scandinavia*. Oslo: Tano Aschehoug.

Bowyer Bell, J. 1998. *The Dynamics of the Armed Struggle*. London: Frank Cass.

Buzan, B. 1991. *People, States, and Fear: An Agenda for International Security Studies in the Post–Cold War Era*. London: Harvester Wheatsheaf.

Claridge, David. 2000. "Exploding the Myths of Super-Terrorism." *The Future of Terrorism.* London: Frank Cass.

Clark, R. 1983. "Patterns in the Lives of ETA Members." *Terrorism* 6, no. 3: 423–454.

Douglas J., Burgess, A., and Ressler, R. 1997. *FBI Crime Classification Manual.* San Francisco: Jossey-Bass.

Douglas, J., and Olshaker, M. 1997. *Mindhunter.* London: Arrow.

———. 1998. *Obsession.* London: Pocket.

Gellner, E. 1985. *Islamic Dilemmas: Reformers, Nationalists, and Industrialization.* New York: Mouton.

Hoffman, B. 1999. *Inside Terrorism.* London: Indigo.

Jamieson, A. 1989. *The Heart Attacked.* London: Marion Boyars.

*Journal of Prohibited and Concealed Weapons* 3, 12 (Autumn 2000).

Kobrin, S. J. 1998. "The MAI and the Clash of Globalizations." *Foreign Policy* 112 (fall): 97–109.

McGartland, M. 1998. *Fifty Dead Men Walking.* London: Blake.

———. 2000. *Dead Man Running.* London: Mainstream.

Nkrumah, K. 1965. *Neo-Colonialism: The Last Stage of Capitalism.* New York: International Publishers.

O'Callaghan, S. 1999. *The Informer.* London: Corgi.

Pelton, Robert Young. "Dangerous Places." http://www.comebackalive.com/df/dplaces/algeria/index.htm.

Pilger, J. 1998. *Hidden Agendas.* London: Vintage Publications.

Post, J. 1996. "Terrorist Psycho-logic." In *Origins of Terrorism,* ed. Walter Reich. Cambridge: Cambridge University Press.

Reich, W., ed. 1996. *Origins of Terrorism.* Cambridge: Cambridge University Press.

Sheehan, M. 1996. "A Regional Perspective on the Globalization Process." *Korean Journal of Defence Analysis* 8, no. 2 (winter): 53–74.

Sprinzak, E. 1998. "The Great Superterrorism Scare." *Foreign Policy* 112 (Fall): 110–124.

Stohl, M. 1990. "Demystifying the Mystery of International Terrorism." In *International Terrorism,* ed. C. W. Kegley Jr. New York: St. Martin's.

Taylor, Max, and John Horgan. 2000. *The Future of Terrorism.* London: Frank Cass.

Viotti, Paul, and Mark Kauppi. 1993. *International Relations Theory.* New York: Macmillan.

Wilkinson, P. 2001. *Terrorism Versus Democracy.* London: Frank Cass.

# 2

# Counterterrorism: Perspectives, Issues, and Solutions

## Moral and Legal Issues

Terrorists commit acts of great atrocity and inhumanity, and many affected by such acts may be tempted to take "an eye for an eye" approach, but it is important that any response or emergency powers follow democratic principles. By retaliating harshly, the state runs the risk not only of looking like an "oppressive bullying regime" (according to terrorist propaganda, anyway) but also of alienating the public, thus perhaps causing sympathy for the terrorists and making it harder for the state to refuse their demands.

With the capture in March 2003 of the Al Qaeda number-three man, Khalid Sheik Mohammed, who was widely thought to have masterminded 9/11, a question was raised about whether more extreme measures of interrogation and torture should be used in order to capture other Al Qaeda members planning further attacks, to prevent such attacks and casualties, weaken Al Qaeda, and bring those responsible to justice. Would torturing a person already responsible for taking the lives of thousands, and planning more, be morally and legally justifiable if it resulted in preventing further loss of life and bringing to justice the perpetrators of such past and future acts? *Utilitarians*, who believe that "the greatest happiness of the greatest number should be the basis of all (political) action" (see, for example, works by J. S. Mills), feel that given majority interests this would be justified; in contrast, *Universalists*, who believe that there are some moral truths that are universal, not ambiguous, and that such rules should apply to all without exception (see, for example, works by Immanuel Kant), consider this unacceptable. A problem with the utilitarian approach is that once started, where does one stop? Who decides how important the situation has to be to allow such acts/behavior by the state and its agencies? Could the state then be accused of terrorism? Israel takes a utilitarian approach and has been accused regularly of human rights abuses, state terrorism, and murder. But doesn't such action erode public confidence and undercut the social contract whereby the state protects the citizen? (On the notion of a social contract between state and citizen, see works by Hobbes, Locke, and Rousseau.) It is ironic when the state resorts to more invasive, intrusive measures that affect the population in the name of protecting the population. On the subject of morality in counterterrorist actions one could argue that it is the politicians, as elected representatives with the interests of the electorate in mind, who must make the decision, and that a different type of morality exists for them due to their position. It is hard to imagine a president or prime minister who would not allow extreme emergency measures to be undertaken if a city or nation were at risk. This may be a more Machiavellian approach, but many argue that it is more realistic. In any event, what is needed is a way to make such measures under emergency circumstances more accountable and less open to abuse.

The counterterrorist approach/capability needs to have a preventive (before), responsive (during), and "post" or "after" approach to deal with incidents and eventualities afterward. If conflict prevention and deterrence fails (prophylaxis), then there must be an effective law-enforcement, military, and emergency/contingency services combination to react to events and a strong accountable and clear criminal justice system to punish perpetrators fairly afterward.

## Models for a Counterterrorism Response

In combatting terrorism, the *criminal justice model* (CJM) prioritizes the preservation of democratic principles as being the fundamental premise in the fight against terror, even at the expense of reduced effectiveness of counterterrorist measures.

*The war model* (WM) places a stronger emphasis on restraining or countering terrorism rather than upholding liberal democratic rights. Viewing terrorism as an act of revolutionary warfare, the onus for response is placed on the military, ranging from using elite special forces, retaliatory strikes, and large troop deployment. The reasoning behind this is that because terrorists are "waging war," the state must deploy its war-fighting capability in order to counter the problem effectively. But this raises several civil liberties problems, such as what are the legal ramifications of soldiers taking over a policing role, given that they are trained to kill rather than to use minimum force and to know the law and its application.

Many academics think these two models are mutually exclusive. However, most democracies use a hybrid of the CJM and WM. Indeed, an "expanded criminal justice model" (ECJM) would be a useful analytical tool, covering the "gray areas" between the other two models and dealing with theoretical, moral, and legal considerations. Paul Wilkinson, a leading expert on terrorism and counterterrorism, argues that the need for flexibility and the ability to use and combine all measures to suit specific cases are paramount in countering terrorism effectively.

The ECJM and the WM belong to the school of utilitarianism, where any efforts or actions are justified if they are in the interests of the "greater good" or serve the interests of the majority. The CJM, in contrast, belongs more to the philosophical school of universalism, where one rule should apply to all without exception, such as "one should do to others as you would have done to yourself." Under utilitarianism a person giving his life to save others would be justified, whereas it would not under universalism.

Many political decisions in countering terrorism are viewed as controversial or quasi-legal—the choice of the "lesser of many evils." It is noteworthy that the meaning of the word *politics* derives from the Greek *politik,* which roughly translates as the search for the good life, the greater good, or the action that best serves the majority of the population. Counterrorism response depends on two criteria: *effectiveness* and *acceptability*. It is important to note that the most effective measures against terrorism may not be acceptable; thus, counterterrorism response involves finding the balance between the two. It is thus important to examine the ethical dimensions of counterterrorism response to help explain the difference between, and the justification for, the various models of response (Crelinsten and Schmid 1993, 307–341).

# Counterterrorism Measures

When referring to *counterterrorism measures* we mean both defensive measures, to reduce vulnerability to terrorist acts, and offensive measures, to prevent, deter, and respond to terrorism, along with any contingency measures preparing for and having the ability to respond to a terrorist attack/incident.

There are a number of different measures that can be used in the fight against terrorism. Remember that because terrorists operate at a number of different levels and dimensions (political, economic, illegal, military, national, international), one needs a capability to counter the terrorist at each level. Many of these measures are listed on the UN Web site "Classification of Counter-Terrorism Measures" (http://www.undcp.org/terrorism_measures.html).

# Political Measures

A number of political measures can be used to counter terrorism and to try to ameliorate or resolve its causal factors. States need thus to address the terrorists' specific political, economic, or social grievances by changing policy to accommodate the terrorists or by offering some kind of concessions. But concessions send out the message that terrorism works; concessions often encourage other groups, or those that might become more hard-line, to try to achieve their demands. However, by addressing a group's legitimate grievances, the state shows that it has done something in response; then, if the group persists, it may lose support and credibility. The state can also appease the general populace. For example, if grievances are social or economic, engaging in measures that are seen to redress grievances (employment schemes, antidiscrimination measures, poverty-reduction schemes like land redistribution, and opening legal economic alternatives to black-market activities) can work.

Conflict resolution measures such as public dialogue, secret mediation, or negotiations to try and initiate peace processes can also be used, although many groups may only consider them if they are either at a position of stalemate or are losing (perhaps with casualties or arrests too high) and need time to regroup and rearm; the group needs to feel it cannot win, increase its position, or afford (in terms of resources, personnel, finance, support, etc.) to continue using violent means. When dialogue or negotiations and a cease-fire are acceptable, it is important to be sure that the group does not use the time to regroup, reorganize, and rearm itself. Intelligence is key here. Provided the group shows its commitment to democratic means (through public announcement and cease-fire, for example), a further option is to allow it to participate in elections. To counter a group's actual and potential support base, information pertaining to any atrocities committed by the group that shows its undesirability for political involvement can be leaked to the press to minimize support. Steps can be taken to encourage opposition groups or to develop alliances with opponents of terrorist groups in order to further decrease the appeal of the group.

Amnesties can be used to weaken the group and its cause. But in Northern Ireland many terrorists walked free and as a result attracted severe criticism. Although amnesty may work to some extent, there is still a strong argument, especially from proponents of the Criminal Justice Model, that terrorists should be punished for the crimes they commit and not their beliefs. At the opposite end of the scale, banning membership of such groups and their front organizations can work, and declaring the political and military wings illegal can also be effective. It is important, however, not just to ban the groups but to ban their sponsors also. With the use of diplomatic pressure and punitive measures, one should use both positive and negative means and always leave a face-saving option for the country if terrorists respond and wish to cooperate. Diplomacy and foreign liaison between intelligence and counterterrorist agencies are extremely important, as a great deal of intelligence comes from such practices. Diplomatic pressure can be used to lever state sponsors to decrease their support by expelling diplomats from states supporting terrorist organizations, by breaking off diplomatic relations with sponsors of terrorist organizations, and by listing and thus ostracizing states and other entities that sponsor terrorists. The gathering of intelligence and evidence is vital here.

More of an international approach to countering terrorism is essential, given that most groups have international operational and support structures; yet, many countries continue to proscribe groups that only pose threats to themselves. If there are areas where terrorists can operate or reside legally, for example, they will shift operations there; if places to go become harder to find, groups will find it harder not only to operate but also to survive. Examples of international political measures include the G7 and G8 declarations over extradition and intention for cooperation, the Paris summit in 1996, The Hague convention, and the ten recent UN conventions. Such multilateral initiatives are beneficial as they help provide an international framework for making demands and implementing responses, as well as reinforcing international opinion against terrorism and providing common standards that facilitate cooperation on issues such as terrorism

## Punitive Measures

A key aspect of counterterrorism is the severing of a group's means of financing, such as by banning fund-raising and the transfer of funds from potential front organizations of terrorist groups. This must be done nationally and internationally. Other measures listed by the UN include the boycotting or placing of sanctions on state sponsors or supporters of terrorists; freezing assets; banning trade, travel, arms sales, and the sale of dual use and precursor substances; and placing sanctions on companies that invest in countries alleged to be state sponsors of terrorism. Tracing terrorist funds is very important but difficult, as many groups have become very skillful in covering their tracks. Popular suggestions have included trying to reduce bank secrecy, but this is problematic when dealing with the unregulated Hawallah system (an informal financial system based on trust), for example, and is almost useless when one realizes that many groups invest in legitimate businesses. Facilitating the exchange of information between states on the movement of funds suspected of supporting terrorism can help, but practical problems appear when states and agencies are reluctant to share information and compromise sources, especially if it means that someone else may gain credit for any resulting captures or prosecutions. Offering financial rewards for information leading to the arrest of terrorists is another measure that can be effective, but many are deterred from doing so because group reprisals on informers are extremely severe. In areas where kidnapping is rife, a long-term deterrent can be to freeze the assets of families of kidnap victims to prevent a ransom payment; this is a very unpopular and controversial strategy, but some argue that the terrorists would *eventually* get the message if they realized that families could not pay ransoms.

Punitive measures can include *economic sanctions,* such as those on Iraq, Iran, or Cuba, arms embargoes, freezing assets, and diplomatic boycotts. Blocking the assets of state sponsors can become bargaining tools over policy/actions later. However, to be effective, the international community must agree and adhere to the measures. There have been cases in the past when one state has continued to trade and reduced the effectiveness of such measures.

## Judicial Measures

International judicial measures for countering terrorism include the signing and ratification of *international conventions and protocols,* such as the ten UN conventions and some regional agreements. There has been an expansion of extradition treaties and efforts to increase compliance with well-founded extradition requests for suspected terrorists on states' territories, efforts to enhance mutual legal assistance with other states, and an exchange of information with judiciaries in other countries.

There are many obstacles to overcome in using *extradition* measures. Whether to extradite or prosecute terrorists domestically is one problem. The lack of universal levels of judicial response is another. If a terrorist is caught in one country, the authorities who hold him may not want to extradite him to the country where he is wanted if he would face the death penalty. However, they may not want to prosecute the terrorist themselves for fear of retaliation from the terrorist group. For effective international judicial measures, there would need to be an effective and enforced international criminal court.

Another problem is *proving* the link between terrorist and act. Due to the international and sophisticated nature of many terrorist networks and their ability to cover their tracks, it is hard to prove that money from a legitimate business or registered charity in London, for example, paid for arms and explosives in the Balkans that ended up in Sri Lanka. A further example is the Omagh bombing in Northern Ireland, where it is widely believed that the authorities know exactly who planned and committed it but lack the evidence required to convict them, or cannot give evidence that would compromise source(s) that provided the intelligence. This sends a message to other terrorists that they can get away with such acts.

*Prosecution* is another area riddled with problems for countering terrorism. First, terrorism is hard to define (many different definitions are used by different academics, agencies, and countries) so that legal authorities have problems convicting terrorists. Terrorists benefit when discrepancies or ambiguities give their lawyers loopholes. Judges often have no experience or little understanding of terrorism. Intelligence agencies are reluctant to identify sources in court, and there are poor witness protection schemes for sources who are identified in court or for repentant terrorists (O'Callaghan 1999; McGartland 2000). Lawyers, judges, and jury members need better protection, given ways in which groups protect their secrets and their members. The judicial process is lengthy and costly. The slow nature of the court system often means that terrorist actions arise before there is legislation over them, such as terrorist use of encryption. Measures to rectify some of these problems include trying to increase the speed of the judicial process against terrorism, introducing special courts to deal with terrorist crimes, and holding trials *in absentia*. In each case the value of a prosecution must also be weighed against the possible opportunities to learn of, and prevent, further terrorist activity, as intelligence sources often "dry up" after investigations and prosecutions (Pillar 2001, 84).

What happens after the court case, in terms of the actual sentence or punishment? If the sentence is death, there is the problem of *finality* (the need for there to be no doubt). There is also the risk of creating martyrs and inciting retaliation. Bobby Sands, the IRA hunger striker, has near-legendary status because he died for his cause; many believe that Sinn Fein sprang from the Dublin insurrection and hangings that created martyrs and the cause. But if a prison sentence is given, how should one separate and treat prisoners? Political prisons need to be avoided, as they can and usually turn into terrorist training schools. The experiences of authorities in Northern Ireland and Israel have shown that if terrorists are allowed political or prisoner of war status and not isolated, they keep their organizations intact while in prison, and that anyone not a terrorist on entry would be one on leaving. Prison systems are not properly adapted to hold large numbers of terrorists, especially when they demand to be treated as prisoners of war and use hunger strikes and other tactics to gain concessions. There should be more research to develop measures to inhibit the formation and perpetuation of terrorist networks in prison.

Extending judicial powers, either in accordance with the war or expanded criminal justice models, is inherently risky because any "extrajudicial powers" are often incompatible with the fundamental principles of the law. In Italy people were convicted by association and found guilty until proven innocent; in Israel people can be held on suspicion for years. Miscarriages of justice due to "faceless courts" in Colombia and Northern Irish efforts for "internment without trial" alienated most of their populations and resulted in greatly increased support for the terrorists. To avoid this the state must try to fully and widely explain that any measures that affect the public are in their best interest. If measures are not explained, and the public does not understand the reasons for them, how long they will be for, who they are targeting, and their effects, the public is more likely to side with the terrorists. Although countries should avoid examples of failed initiatives by other states, they should likewise learn from their successes by reviewing and updating emergency legislation and monitoring and adopting successful measures/legislation from other countries.

Wilkinson argues that the criminal justice model can work, citing such successes as the Italian *Pentiti* (repentant) laws used in the 1980s. These were very effective, as the courts were given the ability to discreetly bargain with terrorists to reduce sentences provided they gave significant information and cooperation. A certain degree of flexibility and discretion is advantageous to empower the courts to adjust (either to increase or decrease) sentences for terrorist crimes where deemed appropriate. However, there remain issues over who should hold such a decision and at what level. Given that many judges do not have sufficient experience or understanding of terrorism, should the decision be made at the ministerial (government) level or at a specialized terrorism court? Further questions arise, such as how to justify such decisions and make them accountable so they are not abused.

# The Military

In the fight against terrorism there are two main uses of the military: the MACP—*military aid to the civilian power* (in the CJM and ECJM), and the *retaliatory response* (WM). Examples of MACP include military units with specialist expertise that police units may not have sufficient resources for or experience in (bomb disposal, surveillance, hostage rescue, "snatch-squads," or units that detect and deal with CBRN threats/incidents). In many cases, highly skilled special forces trained to be used surgically to achieve a limited goal, for example, are extremely valuable assets. The use of such units does not mean that the war model is suddenly in play, as they can be incorporated into the civil system with the government ultimately holding on to its power. In the United Kingdom, for example, the Special Air Services (SAS), often used for hostage rescue and police support such as in Northern Ireland, are controlled by COBRA, a 24-hour emergency unit (named for the cabinet office briefing room where the unit meets) and the Joint Operations Command (JOC). They are also accountable to the law because after each operation they have to hand over their weapons for forensic investigation, provide detailed accounts of what happened, and so on. The military can be incorporated into the civil system and perform peace-keeping duties, erecting roadblocks to prevent clashes (as in Northern Ireland), setting up vehicle checkpoints, helping the police by patrolling areas and searching for weapons, and assisting in cross-training. Through the use of military skills, resources, and experience, civil powers can avoid spending money to duplicate and develop similar capabilities in other agencies and services.

When examining the various uses of special forces, the "willingness to take the fight to the terrorists; to meet them on their own ground rather than passively wait for them to strike," has led to major counterterrorist successes (Adams 1989, 81–82). In relation to international cooperation against terrorism, although cooperation may be lacking at an official, political level, special forces in the West have shared information and run exchange programs so that officers and men have had access to extensive debriefings following an operation and learned from it. Also, if any country mounts a major counterterrorist operation, most of the major Western countries will usually send a special forces representative to observe the action and report back what is learned. Other examples of military use include protecting facilities such as those forming the critical infrastructure, such as nuclear power plants, electricity grids, oil depots and rigs, data flow switchboards, water-storage tanks, and propane gas tanks.

The use of the military for *retaliatory response* insinuates the adoption of the war model and implies the suspension of a civilian legal system being replaced with martial law. However, this fuels terrorists and often alienates the public, as well as possibly creating more sympathy and support for the terrorists. In the international context it has serious implications, as any international response to a substate group that operates or resides in a state could be seen as an act of war. Furthermore, the various missile strikes against Bin Laden in Afghanistan gave him folk-hero status, as "the might of the West," with all its resources and expertise, could not (so far) manage to kill or catch bin Laden. The strikes on the pharmaceutical factory in Sudan were controversial, as it was never made publicly clear whether the factory was being used for NBC production. Collateral damage in such situations where intelligence has been lacking can also decrease international will for cooperation. Such responses can do more harm than good; thus, only the most significant, credible, and unambiguous targets should be engaged. The attempts to justify the motives for an invasion of Iraq in order to topple Saddam Hussein's regime by the United States (pointing to links between Iraq and Al Qaeda) were widely perceived as tenuous and have caused international rifts in relations in the U.S./U.K. partnership and with countries such as Russia, France, and China. These events have also raised serious questions about the effectiveness and credibility of the United Nations. With retaliation there are also issues over legality and legitimacy, whether it is a just war, justified under UN Charter Article 51 (self-defense). Such justification is usually argued on the basis of either:

- *Jus ad bellum* (justice of the cause), for example, self-defense against aggression or helping victims of aggression, after exhausting peaceful means, and with reasonable hope of achieving legitimate objectives
- *Jus in bello* (justice of the conduct), for example, that the means employed are proportional to the ends sought, and actions taken with the right intention to accomplish legitimate military objectives and to minimize collateral death and destruction.

A main danger of a militarized response is that it can lead to war, which is more of an evil than terrorism because it usually causes more deaths and incites further retaliatory acts of terrorism (Wilkinson 2001). Although we have mentioned the outcry and controversy involved in international retaliatory responses, as well as the fear felt by liberal democracies over losing public support if they fight terrorism with strong and proactive countermeasures, what we have yet to see, however, is whether the public might favor stronger counterterrorist measures in the face of the emerging threat of the terrorist use of nuclear, biological, and chemical weapons.

There are examples where the use of stronger, proactive countermeasures have arguably been taken too far; in Peru, Prime Minister Fujimori found that liberal democratic constraints were restricting the response to terrorism, so, supported by the military, he took more of a dictatorship approach. In Northern Ireland in the 1970s and 1980s there were allegations of the British Special Forces operating under a shoot-to-kill policy and of the military intelligence Force Research Unit (FRU) colluding with loyalist terrorists to aid the locating, targeting, and killing of PIRA members and supporters. The latter example blurs the distinction between the war model and the CJM and perhaps illustrates the need for further discussion over an expanded model that would make emergency measures more accountable. It is important that any complaints of alleged abuses of powers by security forces are investigated by an independent body, and that any agencies involved be held accountable. This not only reassures the public that the state and its agencies do not abuse their power, but also can help counter any possible terrorist propaganda. The use of military force should also be timely and appropriate, have public support and a high probability of success, and be used as a last resort (Weinberger in Jenkins 1985, 34).

The contribution that can be made from the military in counterterrorism, such as the specialized tasks mentioned, cross-training, and establishing links for cooperation both domestically and internationally, all help formulate a valuable counterterrorism capability. Although it is understood that exceptional circumstances might warrant exceptional measures, they must at least be clear and accountable and perhaps have a specific time frame so that they will correspond as far as possible with the principles of liberal democratic and human rights. A high standard of proof should also be evident before military force is employed against those believed responsible for terrorist acts (Pillar 2001, 101).

# Intelligence Agencies

Before the Madrid bombings of March 2004, a leading Spanish specialist on terrorism, Fernando Reinares, once suggested that "the resort to oppressive responses reflects, in part, inefficiency (such as poor intelligence) and, in part, a lack of government control over its security agencies" (Reinares 2001).

The role of intelligence agencies is paramount in the fight against terrorism. Valuable information that can be turned into intelligence can be acquired and gathered through signals (SIGINT), electronic communications (ELINT), and human sources and agents (HUMINT), as well as through open and closed sources, surveillance, and a variety of other means. The United States has spent millions on technical and technological superiority but seems to falter in terms of human expertise. What is equally, if not more, important is to ensure that intelligence agencies have plenty of personnel with diverse experience; agents and analysts need to have cultural, linguistic, and regional expertise in all the geographic areas. Such people are needed for a variety of reasons—to infiltrate terrorist cells, recruit agents/informers, and acquire information—to understand the nature of terrorist objectives and plans, their political motivations, and alignment; the leadership and membership; the logistics and financial resources; the links, if any, with other terrorist groups, terrorist states, and international organized crime; and ultimately to help prevent terrorist acts. Such personnel also make good analysts if they understand the language, as well as the culture, so that they can make balanced judgments on any intelligence acquired and not fall foul of cultural misunderstandings such as the notorious remark by Soviet prime minister Nikita Khrushchev at the height of the Cold War: interpreted by U.S. analysts as a threat against the United States, "We shall bury you" was "merely a folksy way of predicting that communism would outlast capitalism" (Cohen 1996, 114).

As with the use of the military, it is important that all emergency measures are accountable and under government regulation; as far as possible they must be in accordance with the principles of liberal democratic and human rights. There are examples where intelligence agencies either have been allowed to become laws unto themselves due to lack of control or regulation by the government, *or* have been tasked by the government to execute extreme duties. In the earlier section on the role of the military, the example of Northern Ireland and the FRU, with allegations of security forces colluding with loyalists to kill terrorists, illustrated the theory that if loyalist targeting of PIRA terrorists was so effective then potential PIRA recruits would be deterred and PIRA would have to think about peaceful negotiations as opposed to bombings and murders. A further example is that of the Defense Information Service (Servizio Informazioni Difesa, SID) in Italy colluding with neofascists over the "strategy of tension." Here the SID aimed to create and exploit an atmosphere of extreme civil unrest throughout the country with the expectation that this would induce public demand for increased law and order measures against the Red Brigades (Brigate Rosse—BR). This is thus an example where an intelligence agency almost orchestrated a coup d'etat that threatened liberal democracy. There is also the example of the "dirty war" in Spain where antiterrorist death squads called GAL operated. This example shows a violation of several principles: of using minimum force to apprehend suspects, of being innocent before guilty, and of the right to a fair trial. Although due to the nature of the work, intelligence agencies must retain levels of secrecy, it is important that they do not become laws unto themselves and thus need to be accountable and under the control of their government. One option for this is an intelligence committee composed of former intelligence members as well as politicians who are familiar with the requirements and nature of intelligence operations/activities, as opposed to a body of people with no experience or knowledge of the nature of such activities having involvement in what should and should not be done. The use of intelligence or military agencies to assassinate leaders/members is often counterproductive as it is undemocratic, usually creates martyrs and encourages other and potential terrorists as it plays into the propaganda of the group, and can cause doubt or lack of confidence in the state from the population; it should not be used unless it appears accidental and would seriously disrupt the group.

The role of intelligence agencies also includes the planning, acquisition, processing, and dissemination of intelligence. L. K. Johnson notes that the *planning phase* must identify the correct targets/threats and direct adequate resources against them; the *collection phase* must be riveted on tracking the terrorists and must employ the right mix of intelligence-gathering techniques and agencies; and the *processing phase* must move faster and with greater skill to determine what's important and what's not—analysts must possess a deep understanding of foreign countries that harbor terrorist cells, as well as a solid comprehension of what makes terrorists tick. In the *dissemination phase,* intelligence officers must provide policymakers with information that is pertinent, on time, reliable, all-source, and unbiased, as opposed to information that supports the president's political agenda rather than reflects the often unpleasant reality that an administration's policy has failed. Equally, policymakers must hear the truth rather than brush it aside if it does not fit with their political agenda (Kegley 2003, 239–252).

Intelligence can also be disseminated to sister agencies, affected parties/entities, and increasingly to intelligence/security agencies abroad. Although there have been calls for a multilateral intelligence agency in the fight against terrorism and organized crime, Wilkinson (2001, 196) illustrates the problems associated with the example of Interpol, where "[some of] the states engaged in sponsoring terrorism belong to Interpol, and hence other states are reluctant to allow highly sensitive information into the Interpol network." This lack of control of information that can find its way back to the wrong hands and compromise sources shows why bilateral intelligence sharing has been more productive. Examples of the type of information that can be shared internationally are records or databases containing information on all suspected and actual terrorists that can be accessed by intelligence agencies as well as customs and excise agencies, airport security, and border control police.

## Movement Restriction

Economic globalization, the reduction of trading barriers and borders, initiatives such as the Schengen agreement, and the ensuing freedom of movement have benefited terrorists and allowed them to move not only themselves but funds, materials, and equipment more easily. A substantial problem associated with this phenomenon is that there are extremely diverse security and border controls throughout the world. Security varies greatly from port to port, airport to airport, border to border, city to city, and country to country.

Therefore, more effective travel and immigration measures should be introduced, as listed on the UN Web site—the tightening of visa restrictions and harmonization of visa policies with neighboring countries; the tightening of border controls, and the use of spot checks; profiling; deportation, banishment, and expulsion; the introduction of counterfeit-proof passports; and the maintaining, updating, and sharing of a database of suspected terrorists/criminals, as well as more efforts to prevent the abuse of asylum. Further efforts to standardize border control, aviation/airport security, maritime and port security, and so on, should also be made in order to prevent terrorists accessing areas with good security from areas with poor security.

# The Police

The main role of the police in counterterrorism is to ensure that the law and its principles are upheld and maintained, along with gathering and preparing evidence for use in law courts ranging from forensics to eyewitness accounts.

Other police roles associated with counterterrorism include protective security and the hardening of possible, probable, and high-risk targets (high-profile persons and events they attend, as well as components of critical infrastructure like communications, power grids, and nuclear/energy plants) in order to deter and prevent attacks. The police also engage in preparedness exercises and contingency planning for, i.e., an NBC attack or hostage-taking, as well as in cross-training such as joint simulation exercises with the military and other agencies and emergency services.

The police also have their own intelligence capability, run their own undercover agents, use informers, and organize witness protection and relocation schemes. Attempts at controlling infiltration of the police are sometimes made through external checks on police officers by internal affairs departments or intelligence agencies. The police also try to enhance national and international police cooperation by stationing liaison officers abroad, organize connections with other organizations involved in similar duties (intelligence agencies and the military), and participate in multinational and regional initiatives or conferences.

A common problem in terms of the police and counterterrorism is that the necessary specialized expertise is fragmented regionally. In the United Kingdom, counterterrorism expertise is centralized in a few urban areas; what is needed is a more effective nationwide response capability. Further difficulties arise from competing rivalries and turf wars over jurisdiction, funding, and so on. A more coordinated response is required in order to be more effective.

It is important that a state agency does not act as a law unto itself. Because the police uphold and maintain the law and its principles, questions arise over *quis custodiet ipsos custodies:* "who will guard the guards themselves?" Procedures thus are needed to ensure an independent investigation of any charges of police brutality, and the regulation of the use of deadly force, to ensure that the police are also accountable, regulated, and under the control of the government, and also that they uphold and operate within the principles of liberal democratic and human rights.

# Counterpropaganda

The importance of propaganda and publicity to the terrorist is paramount; thus the importance of countering such propaganda, from a counterterrorism perspective, is both extremely valuable and beneficial.

*Conflict resolution techniques*—encouraging and facilitating dialogue, mediation, and negotiation—are important in breaking down negative stereotypes of opposing factions that may perpetuate the use of violence. One tactic is to target those involved with the conflict or terrorist campaign by trying to establish and ultimately build on a common theme, belief, or value base with political opponents (a value of dignified life, prosperity, treating others as you would like to be treated, not becoming a victim). This is most applicable to cases where the conflict is linked to and mainly occurs in a geographic location between communities, such as in Northern Ireland. Another tactic is to provide a forum for free speech by finding and providing a public space where any conflicts between affected/involved parties can be discussed openly, in an academic forum, for example, on neutral territory.

Any initiatives toward dialogue should also include victim support; this not only helps deconstruct negative stereotypes and animosity but can also lead to the gathering of valuable information from postincident debriefing. Victim-support organizations can also provide platforms for political opposition against violence/terrorism. These organizations can also encourage potential and actual repentant terrorists to leave the group if there are counseling, rehabilitation, and reintegration services that offer victims a sense of purpose and an opportunity to voice political opinion and opposition to the group, the campaign, or the conflict (as seen in Chapter 1 in the section examining factors motivating entry to and exit from terrorist groups).

A counterterrorism public relations campaign should include a variety of initiatives, such as those listed by the UN—measures to initiate or strengthen public awareness programs and activities on the illegitimacy of terrorism, as well as the human and economic costs of terrorism. The media might condemn terrorist acts, perhaps using highly respected people and celebrities, former victims of terrorism, and former (repentant) terrorists to speak out against terrorism. Other measures might include the use of "wanted" posters showing terrorists and listing their crimes (in full detail), as used so successfully in Germany in the late 1970s.

To *delegitimize* the group, it is important to convey and emphasize the inhumanity and immorality of the terrorists' activities while emphasizing that the actual impact (death, injuries, etc.) is relatively small (McEwen 1984, 10). However, "a balance must be struck between the 'delegitimation' of terrorism in political life, typical of offensive [psychological/media] operations, and leaving the door open to those who wish to come back [but felt there was no return from terrorism], typical of defensive [psychological/media] operations" (Schmid and Crelinsten 1993, 329). These techniques help reduce the support/sympathy base as well as detracting from any propaganda successes through sensationalized media reporting. As the use of other counterterrorism measures causes "disruption of the infrastructure [it] thus deals a blow to terrorist capabilities, by sowing various forms of doubt [through counterpropaganda] among those not rousted" (Pillar 2001, 119). It also affects terrorist intentions, as the group can become confused or paranoid over informers and disloyalty. Furthermore, moderate terrorists will be more likely to leave the group after realizing the actual atrocities caused, leaving hard-line terrorists to which a hard-line response can be more surgically applied. This prevents the hardening of any moderate resolve through a hard-line response to the whole group.

# The Media

The relationship and importance of the media to terrorism and counterterrorism warrant further examination. The media can convey the terrorists' message, spreading terror and fear. This is significant when one realizes that "the public's fear of terrorism and sense of insecurity influence political, social, and economic decisions regionally and internationally. One may therefore 'win the battle' against terrorism by thwarting terror attacks, but 'lose the war' when the threat of terrorism succeeds in disrupting the daily life of civilians" (http://www.ict.org.il/).

As one of the leading American specialists on terrorism, David Rapoport (1996) notes, "The relationship between publicity and terror is paradoxical. Publicity focuses attention on a group, strengthening its morale and helping to attract recruits and sympathizers. But it also helps an outraged public to mobilize its vast resources and produces information that the public needs to pierce the veil of secrecy all terrorist groups require."

What we know as "the media" includes newspapers, radio, television, books, magazines, movies, theater, and word of mouth. Terrorists—from medieval Muslim sects to nineteenth-century groups in Russia and the Balkans—have used word of mouth in marketplaces and houses of worship to relay news of their attacks (Wilkinson 2001, 174). It was no coincidence that in 1968 with the first TV satellite being launched, the first terrorists began to hijack airliners, resulting in the birth of what we now refer to as international terrorism (Hoffman 1998, ch. 3). The media benefit from terrorism in terms of ratings and units sold. As Wilkinson observes, the media do not create terrorists, but they convey the terrorists' cause; the relationship becomes symbiotic because terrorism by nature is a psychological weapon dependent on communication to a wider society. Terrorists use the media to:

- Convey propaganda of deed and create fear in a target group
- Mobilize wider support for and attempt to legitimize their cause in the general population and in the international community
- Frustrate and disrupt the response of government and security forces
- Mobilize a constituency of actual and potential supporters (and thereby boost recruitment and funding)

Margaret Thatcher once stated that "Terrorists crave publicity: it gives them purpose, spreads their message, and is their 'oxygen' for survival" (Apple 1985). The nature of broadcast journalism, in particular, to air a story first means that more sensational stories are often taken, with less time for editing, thus leading to more reckless reporting as opposed to portraying a balanced analysis of the situation. In the rush for the "scoop" and high ratings, little thought is given to the possible consequences. Accuracy is often sacrificed for speed or emotional impact, but television runs on financial impetus, not moral principles. There is a theory referred to as the "Heisenberg principle," whereby the media are supposed to be independent and neutral but by covering something, actually change or influence the situation.

Reckless reporting has challenged counterterrorism policy and endangered operations several times. In Somalia the footage of one marine dragged through the streets caused an actual reversal of U.S. foreign policy. A media circus over the TWA flight in 1985 with heart-rending personal accounts put immense pressure on government negotiations. News *reporters* are thus becoming *news makers*. In such a situation "does an American president stick unswervingly to his principles and philosophies or does he react to daily opinion polls and listen to spin doctors in formulation of policy?" (Adams 1999). When thousands of Americans cancelled flights to Europe after the Lockerbie crash, the press did not put the risk into perspective (one was more likely to be killed by a dog in 1989 than a terrorist) and caused the travel industry to suffer unduly. Bruce Hoffman (1999, 149) once stated that "arresting footage or pithy phrases/sound-bites are [now] valued above considered analysis." Some argue that the objectives and concerns of law-enforcement agencies in terrorist situations are intrinsically in conflict with the media. Media action has also endangered counterterrorism operations: at the 1972 Munich Olympics, terrorists watched live footage of where armed police were positioning themselves; during the Iranian Embassy siege in 1980, one TV crew continued filming and could have jeopardized the whole operation if the terrorists had had access to TV; when the international media surrounded the Kuwaiti airliner in Cyprus with Hezbullah members aboard and used infrared equipment, it prevented any hostage rescue operation from being mounted; and in England, media printed material caused a judge to declare a mistrial, thus freeing five IRA members.

The media also help feed propaganda because there is less time to research and balance stories with objective analysis due to the rush to get on the air or in print before other corporations do. Television journalists in particular fail to look at the wider picture; for example, in the context of the PLO against Israel, the media rarely mention that the PLO deliberately uses stones against Israeli guns, so it looks like the Israelis are overreacting when they respond. Equally, the media focus on the unusually high numbers of children both demonstrating and being injured, often failing to mention that in the occupied territories, over 50 percent of the population is under age seventeen. The fact that terrorist groups often have press spokesmen illustrates the importance of the relationship, as bad publicity can affect levels of support and funding for the group. U.S. Attorney-General John Ashcroft banned the media from interviewing Oklahoma City bomber Timothy McVeigh before his impending execution because the interview could serve the interests of McVeigh and his comrades. As Margaret Thatcher observed, "The news media should consider whether those who, like terrorists, use freedom to destroy freedom, should have so much publicity for their work" (Apple 1985).

Although the media can benefit the terrorist and impede counterterrorism efforts, it can also benefit the government and democracy, serving as a check on government power by informing citizens of the implications of government policies and abuses of government. Through coverage of terrorist acts and atrocities, the media also harden public resolve against terrorists, dispelling myths of "Robin Hood"–type images or reputations of terrorists by showing the savagery of their nature and activities. The media can help create heightened public awareness or vigilance, provide public warnings, and advise how to react in emergencies. Investigative journalism often provides information and leads on foreign movements, personalities, and descriptions of personnel. The media can also provide a forum for discussing counterterrorism policy formulation and remind the government of the need to adhere to democratic norms.

Although the contributions of the media outweigh the disadvantages, there is room for improvement. Free press is a vital aspect of democracy. Currently, as noted by Wilkinson, a laissez-faire approach is likely to leave current problems unsolved and to encourage spectacular attacks, as well as more challenges to policy and counterterrorism efforts. Censorship, in contrast, is undemocratic and can cause distrust of the government and the media, and creates a vulnerability to terrorist propaganda. "If the freedom of the media is sacrificed in the name of combating terrorism, one has allowed small groups of terrorists to undermine the democratic values, institutions, and processes and rule of law" (Wilkinson 2001, 220). The best way forward is arguably for the media to exercise *voluntary self-restraint*, trying to avoid live coverage, using experts on terrorism, obeying the police, and working closely with security forces. Journalists also need training about responsible coverage of terrorist events and the harmful effects of premature or full disclosure of information on terrorist activity. The capacity of the mass media to convey terrorist propaganda needs to be more widely understood in order to prevent the media from becoming unwitting accomplices to the political goals of terrorists. In serious crime cases in both the United States and the United Kingdom, the police, the FBI, and forensic psychologists already work closely with the media and have seen real benefits result from close cooperation and liaison.

# Problems of Transnational Response

A useful tool for analyzing causes of terrorism is Buzan's definition of security:

> Generally speaking, *military security* concerns the two-level interplay of the armed offensive and defensive capabilities of states, and states' perceptions of each other's intentions. *Political security* concerns the organisational stability of states, systems of government and the ideologies that give them legitimacy. *Economic security* concerns access to the resources, finance and markets necessary to sustain acceptable levels of welfare and state power. *Societal security* concerns the sustainability, within acceptable conditions for evolution, of traditional patterns of language, culture and religious and national identity and custom. *Environmental security* concerns the maintenance of the local and the planetary biosphere as the essential support system on which all other human enterprises depend. These five sectors do not operate in isolation from each other. Each defines a focal point within the security problematique, and a way of ordering priorities, but all are

woven together in a strong web of linkages. (Buzan 1991, 19–20)

This definition is important, as "intra-state" problems should not be viewed in isolation but in the context of the state within which they exist.

Looking briefly at Latin America, for example, we can see that in many areas several "sectors of security" are denied to large portions of the population. Political security does not exist in many areas or is either not legitimate or nonrepresentative of substantial factions of the population. Similarly, economic security does not exist partly because of the lack of resources and industry, but also because money and resources are available to a select (corrupt) few. Various Latin American leftist terrorist groups use this information in their propaganda. Many groups are also "anti-globalization," viewing large multinational corporations (MNCs) as international parasites that come into the country, suck the resources dry, and allow only corrupt elites and MNC members to benefit. Corruption encourages people to turn to crime, especially when their standard of living is so poor and they have few or no alternatives. The lack of societal security is another causal factor, although to a lesser extent; people sometimes turn to terrorism if they feel their culture or way of life is threatened and there is no alternative. For the most part, the main causal factors for terrorism are political and economic, with environmental issues playing a minor part when resources are not widespread or shared fairly in order to promote a better standard of living for the masses.

Economically, many countries are facing domestic difficulties and are becoming increasingly dependent on external or foreign financial investment. It then becomes harder for institutions to refuse foreign currency, even when sources are illegal or under question. Corruption is likely to continue and increase in regions like Latin America and other developing/undeveloped countries, and illegal groups and activities are more likely to move into and increase their operations in these areas.

Where generally poor standards of living, poor economic prospects, and the increase of illegal activities exist, the phenomena of a "culture of crime" is also likely to increase as more individuals turn to illegal activities to feed themselves and their families.

Countering terrorism in such areas is not easy. It is well known that in "lawless areas," organized crime syndicates are "first in," taking advantage and setting up new operations due to their entrepreneurial nature and from having savvy businessmen involved in planning. As seen in the Balkans, Afghanistan, and elsewhere, this occurs mainly because of the lack of rapid and effective action by any international force, such as the United Nations. Whereas international forces take time (as is often the nature of bureaucracy and democracy) to decide, agree, and mobilize, organized crime syndicates do so quickly, and by the time any international action is taken these syndicates have become so deeply entrenched that it is extremely difficult to do anything effective about them. Similarly, terrorist organizations are not merely groups of people who "make and then plant bombs," but often huge sophisticated transnational organizations with involvement and contacts in a number of areas that require an equal or greater degree of sophistication, organization, and response to counter them. In areas where country borders are close, the question of sovereignty also comes into question as groups pick areas where they can shift operations into the neighboring country quickly.

To prevent terrorism, one cannot merely prevent the placing and detonation of bombs but must also prevent financing, procuring, recruiting, researching, networking, and mobility. Furthermore, by targeting operations in one place, the structure (cells) and mobility mean that if that cell does not relocate, another one will pop up elsewhere. Thus, to counter international terrorism we need an international response and a full set of counterterrorism measures; it is almost a certainty that if there is a loophole or weakness, the organization will find and exploit it. The same can be said of organized crime due to its huge and diverse international operations; only an international response can counter such entities.

# Response

The response needed is a multidimensional counterterrorism capability—including preventative economic, military, legal, political, punitive, social, psychological, and communication measures. These measures must deal with every possible aspect of terrorism and means to counter it. A mechanic would not respond to a call of a car breakdown with only a wrench, but would take a whole toolbox in preparedness for any situation or possibility causing the problem.

Implementing counterterrorist measures at any level is often extremely difficult. A local, regional, or national response has its own problems and obstacles; with an international response, problems multiply and become much more complex (especially in sensitive areas of internal security and law and order) when sovereign states are involved. Lack of a clear (independent) single forum for Western democratic cooperation compounds this problem. Furthermore, many states are afraid of attracting revenge attacks through international cooperation.

"Areas of lawlessness" illustrate some of the obstacles to international counterterrorism. Many areas in developing and undeveloped countries are showing trends of growing instability, weak policing and financial laws, corruption, and transnational criminal and insurgent operations, as well as growing involvement of international criminal and terrorist organizations. Colombia is one of many examples of "safe havens" where terrorist and paramilitary groups are becoming involved in the drug-trafficking business and are forging links with organized crime syndicates as well as other terrorist groups and "rogue states" due to the needs and nature of their organisations and activities. If left unchecked, this could develop into a serious security problem of international scope. In some areas it already is extremely serious, but nothing significant has been done to counter it effectively. Another concerning example is the "triborder area" between the cities of Puerto Iguazu, Foz do Iguazu, and Ciudad del Este, where the borders of Argentina, Brazil, and Paraguay meet, and where arms dealers, drug traffickers, contrabandists, and terrorists have met and partaken in illegal activities worth billions of dollars.

# Countering Terrorist Activities

Some of the practical problems in countering terrorist activities become apparent when one views some examples of activities in more detail. The U.S. State Department notes that Paraguay, for example, is a major transit country for cocaine. U.S. government experts estimate that approximately 1,500 kilograms of "HCl" traverse Paraguay's territory every month, primarily from Bolivia en route to Argentina, Brazil, the United States, Europe, and Africa. The cocaine trade benefits from Paraguay's central location in the heart of Latin America, its extensive river network, its lengthy and undeveloped land borders, numerous unpoliced airstrips (both registered and unregistered), and persistent official corruption. In addition, election-year politics lessen the Paraguayan government's and opposition parties' political will to confront the politically influential and economically powerful frontier commercial and contraband interests (U.S. State Department 1998). Such problems are in danger of becoming increasingly thematic of Latin America in general.

Banking sources confirm that significant money laundering occurs, but they claim it is fueled primarily by the regional contraband trade, tax evasion, and capital flight rather than by narcotics trafficking. Recent intelligence reports suggest that most South American countries, with clandestine financial networks based on drug trafficking, have become a favorite location for Osama bin Laden and his associates to stack their resources beyond regulatory scrutiny. The main hindrances to money-laundering investigations are the lack of police investigators in this field and the reluctance of banking institutions to cooperate with police. A law to facilitate police/bank cooperation was not applied to any public official in 1997 due to the involvement of government, police, and other officials in the illicit production or distribution of drugs or controlled substances, or the laundering of proceeds from illegal drug transactions (U.S. State Department 1998). Illegal drugs and money-laundering problems are widespread and compounded by borders, sovereignty, and other issues. Sufficient measures to prevent or punish officials engaged in corruption, specifically with respect to drug trafficking, have not been taken. For example, judicial corruption was suspected in the release of four traffickers caught in possession of over twenty-six kilograms of cocaine, as well as in the rejection of a request from France to extradite a suspected French trafficker. The judge who released the four suspects was sanctioned only with one month's suspension and a letter of reprimand. Judges and prosecutors continue to work also under outdated criminal and criminal procedure codes.

Both the ease and range of such activities have attracted terrorist organizations for several reasons; for funding their operations by involvement in such activities, for support structure bases in order to procure weapons and launder money, and as a staging post for terrorist cells to rest or prepare before and/or after an attack. Many activities are interlinked, both in terms of the growing network formed by those who take part in them and in terms of the linking of each activity in the same process. Furthermore, terrorists and criminals know that it is relatively easy to enter Latin American countries, as entry visas are often issued without sufficient checks, border controls are inefficient, customs are often corrupt or disorganized, police corporations are weak and mostly corrupt, identification papers such as passports and driving licenses are easy to counterfeit, civil servants can be bribed to obtain real identification documents, and lack of effective state cooperation among these countries facilitates their movements. Some countries are also used to "naturalize" or procure false identity documents as, for example, Argentina has no verifiable registry of births. It has been alleged by Richard Tomlinson, the rogue SIS/MI6 agent, that the SIS (and Eastern Bloc agents during the Cold War) have used this loophole to provide their agents with false passports and identities for some time (Tomlinson 2000, 109). Once inside these countries, it is very easy to hide or escape due to the close borders with different countries, and especially where there are diaspora communities to blend in with and utilize existing contacts. In terms of Islamist terrorism, this is significant when one realizes that approximately six million people of Muslim descent live in Latin America: 1.5 million in Brazil; 700,000 in Argentina, and large communities of strong Muslim faith in Venezuela, Colombia, Paraguay, Chile, Peru, Honduras, and Bolivia (Andersen 2001, 20). In sum, all these characteristics help terrorists and criminals to move easily and operate clandestinely in Latin America.

Perhaps the most significant and primary concern of so many different organizations operating in such small areas is the danger of hitherto independent or isolationist criminal or terrorist organizations developing links with others or effectively joining forces or pooling their resources to further their campaigns. Such a problem is not unlikely when one realizes that in the past, organized crime groups tended to try to control *all* activities in a particular territory. Recently, however, many groups have realized that it is easier, and indeed often more profitable, to specialize in one or a few activities and then hire their services to others. This is a worrying feature, as many terrorist groups are well known for their ability and willingness to adapt, diversify, and embrace new technology, links, and operations. This could cause immense problems for those countering such groups due to obstacles associated with multilateral intelligence sharing and cooperation. This is especially so when one considers the international scale of certain terrorist or crime organizations. In Latin America alone, Osama bin Laden launders money through banks and financial institutions in Colombia, Ecuador, Peru, Bolivia, Chile, Argentina, Uruguay, Paraguay, Brazil, French Guiana, Surinam, Guyana, and Venezuela, along with the British Virgin Islands, Cayman Islands, and the Bahamas. These are only the areas in Latin America that are *known.*

Continue with the Latin American example and look at the case of the triborder region between Argentina, Paraguay, and Brazil. It has been extremely hard to determine exactly how many groups and organizations either operated in or used the area and the nature of their involvement, strength, and possible links; the best we can do is speculate. More effort should go into investigating and countering such links and activities, as the "worst-case scenario" is truly a bad one: the possibility of these groups forming closer links has serious international implications. For instance, it is interesting to look back to Revolutionary Armed Forces of Colombia (FARC) links with Hezbollah and Iranian intelligence and speculate about linkages and cooperation. It is believed that FARC has links with the Russian mafia, PIRA, ETA, ELN, EPL, ARG, and Cuba, to name but a few, and FARC operates in Venezuela, Panama, Ecuador, Peru, Brazil, and Paraguay (for rest and recuperation, procurement, drug trafficking, etc.). In 2000 the Peruvian government investigated allegations that a small group of Peruvian military officers sold a substantial quantity of small arms to FARC. Paraguayan counternarcotics police in October 2000 arrested an individual believed to be representing FARC for possible involvement in a guns-for-cocaine ring between Paraguay and FARC. Despite these counterterrorism successes, an ineffective judicial system and pervasive corruption facilitate criminal activity supporting terrorist groups and hamper most counterterrorism efforts. If left unchecked, the possibilities for terrorist and organized crime organizations are endless and extremely disadvantageous to those targeted by terrorists and to groups that oppose or work against terrorists and organized crime.

A number of possible countermeasures can be used to respond to these problems, including developing an international registration mechanism for firearms, ammunition, explosives, and other related materials; regional, national, and international agreements dealing with each of the problems mentioned; and stricter enforcement of immigration laws to crack down on the use of falsified entry documents. However, regardless of such initiatives, there still remain many diverse and multilevel problems that impede such measures.

Latin American governments must increase cooperation and coordination at all levels, particularly among security, police, and intelligence agencies. The lack of cooperation between some countries in the region has permitted terrorists to cross their borders with impunity. Like many developing regions worldwide, Latin America has poor antimoney laundering and terrorist financing laws. In some countries those laws simply do not exist. Where they do exist, the law enforcement is so weak and/or corrupt that the law is not applied. Drug trafficking in the region, from Mexico to Brazil, proved this. In Mexico, for example, 2,817 suspicious financial transactions were reported in 2001, generating thirty-one apprehensions. However, none of the thirty-one received any sentence (Becerra 2003).

## Problems of Response

"No single state, no matter how powerful, can make an effective response to the problems of global terrorism" (Sederberg, in Kegley 2003, 282). In terms of responding to, or dealing with such problems, obstacles appear through limitations and lack of will and resources in many, if not all, of the sections mentioned throughout this chapter:

- Political measures
- Punitive measures
- The judicial/legal aystem
- The military
- Intelligence agencies
- Movement restriction
- The police
- Counterpropaganda

Even if a government takes a proactive role trying to counter global terrorism, corruption, practical policing problems, and a lack of resources and infrastructure in bordering countries oftentimes impedes what little there is in the way of enforcement, border control, or police presence, thus illustrating the need for transnational approaches or solutions to transnational problems.

Obviously more of an international approach is needed because not only do terrorist organizations have transnational operations, but also many of the countries in and around these lawless areas lack both the resources and incentives to curb illegal activity. Corruption is so rife at so many levels that countries "turn a blind eye" (especially as it is so lucrative to do so). In terms of an *international response*, the problems/obstacles also include:

- Lack of political will (and weight of public opinion) for solutions that cost money
- Lack of economic resources (and MNCs' lack of adherence to economic sanctions)
- Lack of military and police resources/expertise
- Practical coordinating problems (different modus operandi, different national interests, different political views and sympathies, intelligence concerns for secrecy and protecting sources, etc.)
- Domestic constitutional/legal problems (e.g., extradition)
- Sovereignty—how do you pursue terrorists/criminals in another country?
- Who oversees it?—(UN, NATO, WEU, OSCE, INTERPOL, etc.)

This further demonstrates the importance of multilevel, multilateral approaches incorporating and coordinating political, social, economic, legal, and military measures in order to predict, preempt, prevent, and respond. Otherwise, the terrorists and criminals will always remain several steps ahead.

The situation in lawless areas illustrates the permeability of borders and the dangers of lax controls and weak enforcement. If one country fails to control terrorist activity, the whole subregion will likely feel the effects, thus a preemptive, as well as reactive, multinational response is needed. All the causal factors of terrorism must be addressed, as must be the factors allowing such activity to occur. The transnational problems of terrorism can only be countered by carrying out a policy of prevention, cooperation, and control, which puts aside national pride and resentment and unites forces against a common enemy: organized crime and international terrorism (Montoya 2001). As Montoya further notes, it is necessary to use human and material resources jointly; the task of removing corruption from institutions actively involved in social life can be difficult, especially when those institutions are suspected of having taken part directly or via alliances with foreign crime. The juridical-political system must also be adjusted to deal with new types of criminality that often have a technical and economic capacity greater than the state. Ordinary criminality and organized crime can form part of a sociocultural and political phenomena typical of the area, and they have connections with foreign organizations that are more powerful and more experienced than local authorities. This further demonstrates the need for a multilevel, multilateral approach incorporating and coordinating political, social, economic, legal, and military measures. However, in terms of multilateral international response, further obstacles arise from getting states to agree on definitions, laws, policies, and actions, as when countries join forces they are often reluctant to relinquish sovereignty to any single driving state or supranational body.

# Conclusion

Sederberg (in Kegley 2003, ch. 21) drew the following conclusions for countering terrorism:

- The more limited the support for the adversary, the more likely coercive or repressive tactics will prove effective
- Conciliatory strategies increase in relevance as the base of support for the adversary expands
- The more diffuse and decentralized the terrorist organization, the more emphasis will need to be placed on intelligence and interdiction
- Sincerely held, totalistic ideologies preclude conciliation and compromise (extremist/religious groups are more likely to see their struggle in totalistic terms, and thus will be less likely to be open to negotiations and concessions—Hoffman, RAND 1988)
- Insincerely held ideologies open opportunities to promote pragmatic transformation
- Inconsistently held ideologies create opportunities to promote disintegration through defections (although they may be worth keeping in the group if they turn into informers)

- Ideological appeals reflecting concrete objectives (e.g., greater autonomy, representation, etc.) create opportunities for compromise
- Given the number of factors that can affect groups (internal cohesion, competition with other groups, nature of groups leadership, etc.), increasingly complex organizations create opportunities to pursue either their transformation or disintegration through conciliatory measures
- The more substantive the concessions proposed by the regime, the greater will be the internal political resistance to a strategy of accommodation
- Conciliatory strategies that encourage defection of moderates tend to increase violence from remaining radicals—this is fine, as hard-line measures can then be directed against hard-liners (those with less support) Otherwise, if direct measures are taken against all elements of the organization, this will likely encourage moderates to stay in and perhaps become more violent
- Any negotiations are likely to be frustrated by the challenger's desire to expand the agenda and the regime's desire to narrow it

Any measures that aim to *appease* the terrorist, such as reform legislation that makes concessions to the legitimate concerns and demands of moderates, can reduce levels of terrorist violence, but residual terrorist violence by an irreconcilable minority is likely to persist. Emergency measures to *combat* the terrorist are hard to justify continuing when violence or terrorist activity decline, and there is a danger of becoming dependent on emergency powers. Quasi-legal or extrajudicial measures are often incompatible with the fundamental principles of law, and it is also important to have compensation procedures for any grievances under emergency powers. A state must be careful of whom any measures affects and how, and it must keep in mind that suspending democratic rights puts the government on the same moral plane as the terrorist. Examples of proactive emergency measures like the "terror from above" campaigns demonstrate that such actions delegitimize the state and legitimize the terrorists.

There must be adequate checks and balances to prevent the abuse of power; the response to terrorism must be firm, but not taken too far; and there must be safeguards to legitimize and generate public acceptance of the state's use of coercive violence in the exercise of criminal justice. Any response has to have a commitment to uphold and maintain constitutional principles of law and order (Chalk 1998):

- Any response needs to be *limited*, well defined, and should only be directed against the terrorists themselves. There should be no question of extending the antiterrorist campaign to the families or sympathizers of terrorists, as this alienates the government from the people and encourages moderates to join extremist organizations
- Any response needs to be *credible* (in the eyes of the general population)
- All counterterrorist measures need to be made subject to constant parliamentary supervision and judicial oversight (*accountability*)

Any emergency powers should also be clearly and simply drafted, published as widely as possible, and administered impartially. Taken together, the three principles of limitation, credibility, and accountability detailed above can help to ensure that the state's response to terrorism is well defined, controlled, and exercised in a manner that is consistent with the imperatives of due process. The best way to achieve legislative and judicial control of antiterrorism operations is to ensure that they take place within a clear framework of legal controls. Scrutiny of the criminal justice system should not be left to the judiciary, as self-regulation does not work. Independent scrutiny is therefore needed to prevent or weaken any terrorist propaganda campaigns regarding corruption.

Furthermore:

- The *effectiveness* of the liberal democratic state's *response* to terrorism depends on its *acceptability*
- Any solution must bear in mind the long-term impact that it will have on the wider process of liberal democratic life
- Counterterrorism policies that disregard democratic norms are a symptomatic treatment (that is, the problem is still inherent) (Chalk 1998)

It is important to address the causes of terrorism while also countering its symptoms. For this there need to be effective measures that both deter and prevent terrorism, along with appropriate legislation and the other mechanisms discussed earlier. Every mechanism needs to be used (or have the capability to be used) and coordinated together to work successfully. Consideration must be given to applying the mechanisms most appropriate to each case, treating each case as unique and tailoring different policies to different challenges (as there are different motivations for terrorism as well as varying aims). As certain measures may take some time to organize/mobilize, it is important to have interim "quick" measures until the other measures are in place. One cannot generalize over terrorism due to the diversity of factors involved, thus tailor-made policies are often more effective than legislation, which is better suited to general rules than specific applications (Pillar 2001, 224). A pressing question for U.S. counterterrorism efforts will be whether the new Homeland Security initiative will be able to effectively coordinate the various agencies and overcome the problems such as rivalries and turf wars in the fight against terrorism.

In terms of the debate over the theoretical models, the war model predominantly uses the military, and the criminal justice model predominantly uses the police, but the reality today is that most cases are a hybrid, with joint operations using all tools. An expanded criminal justice model could be a good method or theoretical framework for analysis and for laying foundations for political, legal, and moral accountability in those occasions when democracies *need* to invoke emergency powers, while keeping in mind Wilkinson's warnings and guidelines with regard to emergency measures.

Terrorism is not new, and it will not go away. It is impossible to completely eradicate; thus, more needs to be done in order to prevent, manage, and minimize its effects. Repression and conciliation are not mutually exclusive counterterrorism tactics (the attractiveness of conciliatory carrots depends on the threat of repressive sticks), and neither repression nor conciliation obviates the need for lessened vulnerability (defense), interdiction of planned attacks (intelligence), or emergency preparedness (recovery) (Kegley 2003, 279). In concert with contemporary conflict resolution theory and practice, what is needed is a multidimensional, multilevel, comprehensive approach to terrorism. It takes a multitude of different actors working at different levels to try to attain peace, increase understanding and tolerance, and develop credible and feasible pathways out of terrorism at all levels while addressing causal factors. This should not be done at the expense of other counterterrorism measures—intelligence gathering, prophylaxis, and a strong criminal justice system—but in combination with them. There must be a multidimensional, multilevel coordinated capability to counter terrorism. Cross-training, cooperation, and liaison are all integral parts. The role of each arm of the state is important, and as we have seen from the importance of counterpropaganda, effective liaison with the media is equally important. One important method to promote such approaches can be interagency working committees, where there is a framework to both discuss threats, scenarios, and responses as well as to implement any decisions. As the varying parties (military, law enforcement, etc.) will favor and push their own methods to respond, it is best to have such a committee in order to ascertain the many means of response and how best to approach each specific situation. Counterterrorism policy should also not be viewed in isolation, but along with any major domestic and foreign policy decisions.

# References

Adams, J. 1989. *Secret Armies.* London: Pan.

———. 1999. *The Next World War.* London: Arrow.

Andersen, M. E. 2001. "Al Qaeda across the Americas." *Insight on the News* 17, 44 (November 26): 20.

Apple, R. W., Jr. 1985. "Meese Suggests Press Code on Terrorism." *New York Times,* 18 July.

Buzan, B. 1991. *People, States, and Fear: An Agenda for International Security Studies in the Post–Cold War Era.* London: Harvester Wheatsheaf.

Chalk, P. 1998. "The Response to Terrorism as a Threat to Liberal Democracy." *The Australian Journal of Politics and History* 44, 3 (September): 373.

Cohen, Raymond. 1996. "Cultural Aspects of Mediation." In *Resolving International Conflicts,* ed. R. Bercovitch. London: Lynne Rienner.

Doran, James. 2001. "Global Search for bin Laden Blood Money." *The Times* (London), Business section, September 20.

Hoffman, B. 1999. *Inside Terrorism.* London: Indigo.

Jenkins, B. M. 1985. "The U.S. Response to Terrorism: A Policy Dilemma." *Armed Forces Journal* (April).

Johnson, L. K. 2003. "Strategic Intelligence: The Weakest Link in the War against Terrorism." In *The New Global Terrorism*, ed. C. W. Kegley Jr. Upper Saddle River, NJ: Prentice Hall.

Kegley C. W., Jr., ed. 2003. *The New Global Terrorism*. Upper Saddle River, NJ: Prentice Hall.

McEwen, M. 1984. "Intelligence and PSYOP in Terrorism Counteraction." *Military Intelligence* (January–March).

McGartland, M. 1998. *Fifty Dead Men Walking*. London: Blake.

———. 2000. *Dead Man Running*. London: Mainstream.

Montoya, Mario Daniel. 2001. "War on Terrorism Reaches Paraguay's Triple Border." *Jane's Intelligence Review* (December 1).

O'Callaghan, S. 1999. *The Informer*. London: Corgi.

Pillar, P. R. 2001. *Terrorism and U.S. Foreign Policy*. Washington, DC: Brookings Institution Press.

Ranstorp, Magnus, and Pedazhur, Ami. 2001. "The Expanded Criminal Justice Model." *Terrorism and Political Violence* 13, 2: 1–26.

Rapoport, David. 1996 "Editorial: The Media and Terrorism; Implications of the Unabomber Case." *Terrorism and Political Violence* 8, 1 (Spring): viii.

Reinares, Fernando. 2001. *European Democracies against Terrorism, Governmental Policies and Intergovernmental Cooperation*. Brookfield, VT: Ashgate.

Schmid, A, and Crelinsten, R. 1993. *Western Responses to Terrorism*. London: Frank Cass.

Tomlinson, R. 2000. *The Big Breach*. Moscow: Narodny Variant.

U.S. State Department. 1998. International Narcotics Control Strategy Report, 1997. Released by the Bureau for International Narcotics and Law Enforcement Affairs. Washington, DC: U.S. Department of State, March. Available at http://www.state.gov/www/global/narcotics_law/1997_narc_report/samer97_part2.html (accessed May 10, 2004).

Wilkinson, P. 2001. *Terrorism Versus Democracy*. London: Frank Cass.

# 3

# Chronology

**1968**   *July 22.* PFLP hijacking of (Israeli) El Al plane B-707 to Algiers in order to coerce Israel to release prisoners (following the June 1967 "Six Day War," the Palestinians realized their situation was desperate and needed to change tactics).

**1969**   *August 29.* PFLP hijacking of (U.S.) TWA B-707 in order to coerce Israel to release prisoners.

**1970**   *September 6–12.* PFLP members hijack three planes and fly to Jordan, release hostages, and then blow up all three aircraft, along with a Pan Am B-747 that is blown up in Cairo. Jordanian authorities retaliate against Palestinians resulting in many lost lives. Palestinians respond by forming the terrorist group Black September.

**1972**   *July 21.* A PIRA bomb kills eleven and wounds 130 in Belfast.

*September 5.* At the Munich Olympics, eight Palestinian Black September members take eleven Israeli athletes hostage (shooting and killing two) and demand the release of two hundred imprisoned Palestinians. Advice from Israel is ignored (as were warnings that an attack was likely and that security was inadequate). West German police volunteers with no specialized rescue

| | |
|---|---|
| 1972<br>(*cont.*) | training attempt rescue but fail, resulting in the death of the remaining nine hostages and five terrorists, partly because the terrorists are able to watch the rescue attempt live on TVs in the hotel rooms as the world's media filmed. This event leads governments to set up hostage rescue commando units and counterterrorist exchange programs between international units (SAS, GSG9, GIGN, etc.). |
| 1976 | *February 3–4.* The Front de la Côte des Somalis (FLCS) hijacks a school bus near Djibouti with thirty children on board, demanding the immediate independence of the French territory of Afars and Issas; otherwise, they would cut the children's throats. Groupe d'Intervention de la Gendarmerie Nationale (GIGN) snipers kill four terrorists, but a fifth manages to kill one child before being shot. The remaining twenty-nine child hostages are safely freed. |
| | *June 27–July 3.* Israeli counterterrorism operation at Entebbe, Uganda, rescuing 258 passengers of a hijacked airliner kidnapped by PFLP and Baader-Meinhoff Group members. |
| 1977 | *May 23.* Nine Moluccan terrorists seize about fifty hostages onboard a train in Holland while simultaneously 105 children and six teachers are taken hostage at a school in Bovensmilde, Holland. In the train, the terrorists released children and the elderly. Dutch marines stormed the train and freed the remainig hostages while killing six terrorists. Some of the hostages at the school are released due to a stomach illness, after which the terrorists are caught unawares by an assault that results in their capture. All the hostages are unharmed. |
| | *October 13.* A German GSG9 counterterrorism operation (with the assistance of two SAS members) at Mogadishu, Somalia, results in the rescue of passengers of a hijacked airliner (Lufthansa Flight LH181). |

1978      *March 16.* Prime Minister Aldo Moro of Italy is kidnapped by the Brigate Rosse (Red Brigades). He is executed fifty-five days later.

1979      *November 4.* Iranian extremists seize sixty-six diplomats in the U.S. Embassy in Tehran. Iran gives no protection or help to the embassy, and Ayatollah Khomeini, Iran's religious leader, openly sanctions the siege. A U.S. military rescue operation fails with heavy U.S. military casualties. Many hostages are not released until January 1981.

     *November 20.* Two hundred Islamic terrorists seize the Grand Mosque in Mecca, Saudi Arabia, taking thousands of pilgrims hostage. Joint Saudi and French teams retake the shrine after 250 are killed and 600 injured.

1980      *April 30.* Princes Gate Siege—six anti-Khomeini terrorists take twenty-six hostages at the Iranian Embassy in London. The SAS (U.K.) storms the building, carrying out one of the most effective hostage rescues ever. The operation demonstrates the increasingly effective response of counterterrorist organizations and acts as a deterrent to terrorists from using such tactics (thereby causing the terrorists to evolve and develop different tactics).

1981      *October 6.* The president of Egypt, Anwar Sadat, is assassinated while inspecting troops. Since then, on such presidential inspections, no soldiers are allowed to have either live ammunition or loaded weapons on their person.

1983      *April 18.* Lebanese Hezbollah suicide bomber detonates (by ramming) a 400-pound truck-bomb at the U.S. Embassy in Beirut, Lebanon, killing sixty-three and injuring 120.

1983
(cont.)

*October 23.* Lebanese Hezbollah use same tactics but with 12,000 pounds of explosive against U.S. Marine barracks in Beirut, killing 242, and also against French barracks, killing fifty-eight.

**1984**

*April 12.* Hezbollah targets U.S. Air Force personnel and civilians at a restaurant near their base at Torrejon, Spain. Explosives kill eighteen and injure eighty-three.

*June 5.* Sikh separatists seize the Golden Temple in Amritsar, India. Hundreds are injured or killed in the daylong gun battle that ensues when Indian forces launch an operation to restore order and retake the temple. Among those killed is the Sikh leader, Jarnail Singh Bhindranwale. The government's response sparks a violent backlash by militant Sikhs.

*October 12.* PIRA attempts to kill the entire British government cabinet at the Grand Hotel in Brighton, England, with a bomb that had been built into the hotel during construction work earlier. PIRA famously stated afterward, "Today we were unlucky, but remember we have only to be lucky once; you will have to be lucky always." Such an act, were it successful, would have paralleled the Gunpowder Plot of November 5, 1605, wherein Guy Fawkes conspired to blow up the Houses of Parliament. Prime Minister Margaret Thatcher allegedly responds with a "shoot to kill" policy in Northern Ireland and more severe restraining of terrorist activity.

*October 31.* Indian Prime Minister Indira Gandhi is killed by her Sikh bodyguards. Her assassination is in retaliation of her order to seize the Golden Triangle, the most holy site of the Sikh religion.

**1985**

*June 23.* Babbar Khalsa International plants and detonates a bomb onboard an Air India B-747, killing the 329 passengers and crew. The India-bound flight is above Ireland when the bomb explodes.

*September 30.* Sunni terrorists kidnap four Soviet diplomats in Beirut and kill one, causing the Soviets to respond by kidnapping relatives of the terrorists and mutilating them. The terrorists release the three remaining diplomats shortly afterward.

*October 7.* Palestinian terrorists seize the *Achille Lauro* cruise ship in the Mediterranean, taking seven hundred hostages. After they kill a sixty-nine-year-old wheelchair-bound U.S. citizen named Leon Klinghoffer, an Egyptian government negotiator promises safe passage home if the terrorists cease the siege. U.S. intelligence organizes an ambush of the EgyptAir flight taking the terrorists home and uses U.S. warplanes to force the plane to land in Italy, at which point Italian authorities take the terrorists into custody.

**1986**    *April 5.* Libyan terrorists target off-duty U.S. servicemen in a discotheque in West Berlin. A bomb in the nightclub kills two and injures as many as two hundred people.

*May 9.* Members of the Abu Nidal Organization hijack Pan Am Flight 73 in Pakistan, taking 374 passengers and fifteen crew members hostage for sixteen hours. On the second night, the power runs out on the plane, causing the terrorists to panic (thinking a hostage rescue operation is about to be launched) and begin firing, resulting in twenty-one hostages being killed and sixty injured.

**1987**    *November 8.* PIRA bombs a Remembrance Day gathering at the war memorial in Enniskillen, County Fermanagh, Ireland, killing eleven people and injuring sixty-three.

**1988**    *December 21.* Libyan sabotage of Pan Am 103—the biggest terrorist act in the United Kingdom—killing 259 passengers and crew and an additional eleven people on the ground in Lockerbie, Scotland.

1992      *March 17.* Hezbollah bombs the Israeli Embassy in Buenos Aires, Argentina, resulting in twenty-nine dead and 242 injured; the embassy building is completely destroyed.

1993      *February 26.* The World Trade Center (New York) bombing. Al Qaeda detonates a car bomb in one of the underground levels, killing six and injuring more than one thousand.

     *April.* PIRA detonates a huge truck bomb (a month after the Warrington bombing) in London at Bishopsgate, killing two, injuring forty-four, and causing approximately £350m (US$ 635m) of damage. The government responds by instituting a "ring of steel" around the city.

     *April 16.* The first suicide bombing by Hamas. A driver in a stolen van packed with explosive devices plunges into a roadside cafeteria near Mehola. The blast kills the driver, an Arab worker, and injurs nine other people. The bombing shows clear evidence of cooperation with Hezbollah.

1994      *February 25.* Jewish right-wing extremist (and U.S. citizen) Baruch Goldstein fires an automatic weapon at Muslims attending a mosque in Hebron, the West Bank, killing twenty-nine Palestinians and injuring 150 before being overpowered and beaten to death.

     *December 24.* GIA members hijack Air France Flight AF8969 in Algiers, killing three passengers in the process. They fly to Marseilles, France, and then threaten to fly and destroy the plane over the city of Paris. Upon receiving this news, the GIGN on December 26 are authorized to storm the plane, resulting in all terrorists being killed and the remaining 170 passengers and crew being rescued.

**1995**     *March 20*. Aum Shinrikyo launches an attack on the Tokyo underground using the nerve agent Sarin, killing twelve and injuring up to five thousand. This watershed moment causes mass fears of a new trend of superterrorism and prompts leaders such as U.S. president Bill Clinton to order cities to conduct emergency exercises. The ensuing hysteria also encourages more terrorist groups to acquire chemical/biological weapons capabilities.

*April 19*. Right-wing U.S. extremists Timothy McVeigh and Terry Nichols detonate a truck-bomb that destroys the Federal Building in Oklahoma City, Oklahoma, killing 166 and injuring hundreds. Believed to be a response to the Waco siege of April 19, 1993, this event shocks the United States, inducing the fear of the "enemy within." The event has implications for gun laws and results in increased budgets for counterterrorism agencies nationwide.

*September 19*. The *Washington Post* prints the complete 46-page manifesto of the U.S. "Unabomber."

*November 4*. Israeli prime minister Yitzhak Rabin is assassinated by a Jewish fanatic.

**1996**     *January 5*. An Israeli cell-phone bomb that kills a Palestinian Hamas operative leads to retaliatory suicide bombings by Hamas and the Islamic jihad, which results in an election turnaround of Benjamin Netanyahu being elected prime minister of Israel over the favorite, Shimon Peres (the message being that terrorism works).

*January 31*. LTTE members detonate a truck-bomb by ramming it into the Central Bank in Colombo, Sri Lanka, killing 91 and injuring 1,400.

*February 9*. PIRA bombs the Canary Wharf in London, signifying a continuing trend of larger-scale attacks and a shift in targeting of "soft" economic targets. Two

1996
(cont.)
people are killed in the blast, and a large number are injured; damage is valued in the millions.

*February 26.* A Hamas suicide bomber boards a bus in Jerusalem and detonates a bomb that kills twenty-six and injures eighty.

*June 15.* PIRA detonates a truck-bomb in Manchester City, England, injuring 206 people and resulting in damage to the city center that takes years to repair.

*June 25.* U.S. servicemen are targeted when a bomb in a fuel truck is detonated outside Khobar Towers in Dhahran, Saudi Arabia, killing nineteen and injuring around four hundred.

*June 27–29.* The G8 Summit and follow-up ministerial meetings on terrorism.

*July 27.* Atlanta Olympics bombing; believed links to U.S. white supremacist groups.

*December 17.* The Tupac Amaru Revolutionary Movement (MRTA) seizes the Japanese ambassador's residence in Lima, Peru, taking hundreds hostage, including many foreign diplomats, and demanding the release of three hundred jailed MRTA members. After negotiations lasting months that result in the release all but seventy-two hostages, a rescue operation is launched. All the terrorists are killed, along with one hostage and two rescue team members; the remaining hostages are freed.

**1998**
*August 7.* Al Qaeda bombings of U.S. embassies in Nairobi and Dar-es-Salaam leave over 270 dead and over five thousand injured. The United States responds with cruise missiles, targeting training camps in Afghanistan and a pharmaceutical factory in Sudan.

*August 15.* PIRA detonates a 500-pound car bomb in the center of Omagh, Northern Ireland, killing twenty-nine and injuring more than 300.

1999    Hijacking of a plane from Afghanistan to Russia, then on to the United Kingdom for claimed asylum raises implications for asylum laws in the United Kingdom and elsewhere.

2000    *October 12.* Al Qaeda suicide attack of the USS *Cole* while in port in Aden, Yemen, kills seventeen servicemen and injures forty.

2001    *Planned for February 11–14.* Planned sarin attacks on the London underground are thwarted by U.K. security forces. It is believed that the Islamic terrorists (mostly Algerian and Al Qaeda members) based in Britain were also planning a sarin attack on the European Parliament building in Strasbourg as part of the operation: they planned to kill all 625 Euro-MPs, as well as officials in the vicinity, by releasing the nerve agent into the building. The attack was to be the first in a series of assaults against prominent buildings across Europe. The London cell, apparently funded directly by Osama bin Laden, worked with other cells in Milan, Italy, and Frankfurt, Germany.

*September 11.* The unprecedented hijacking of four large passenger aircraft in the United States results in devastation at the World Trade Center in New York City (both Twin Towers are completely destroyed) and the Pentagon in Washington, D.C.; one of the aircraft was thought to be on its way to the U.S. Capitol building but crashed in a field in Pennsylvania. More than three thousand people were killed, and direct and indirect damage estimated at billions of dollars.

2001
*(cont.)*

The events of this day, now obliquely referred to as "9/11," also precipitate mass trauma in the United States and throughout the world, which responds with increased international cooperation against terrorism, the reprioritizing of national security with terrorism as the top threat, and huge budgetary increases of counterterrorism and intelligence agencies.

*October 12.* The bombing of a Bali nightclub kills nearly two hundred people and injures over three hundred (many young Australian tourists included). Jemaah Islamiyah is believed responsible.

*October 23.* A group of mainly Chechen terrorists (approximately thirty males and twenty females) seizes a Moscow theater with automatic weapons and large suicide bombs, holding hostage the audience and production crew of approximately seven hundred. Some hostages (mainly Muslims) are released in return for airtime on television to convey the terrorists' message. The Russian counterterrorism Alpha Team uses gas to render those inside unconscious in order to minimize collateral damage from a firefight and then launches a rescue mission. More than one hundred hostages die as a result of the effects of the gas and inadequate medical treatment afterward when officials refuse to identify the gas for medical staff so that the victims could be given the appropriate treatment. Many others are permanently injured.

*November 28.* Simultaneous attacks in Kenya: three suicide bombers kill sixteen people at the Israeli-owned Paradise Hotel near Mombasa, and two SAMs are fired at an "Arkia" B-757 carrying 261 passengers. The plane lands safely at Ben Gurion Airport in Tel Aviv, Israel, shortly after takeoff.

2003     *May 12.* Nearly two hundred people are injured and thirty others killed in an Al Qaeda suicide attack on a residential compound housing mostly foreign workers in Riyadh, Saudi Arabia.

*May 16.* Suicide bombings in Casablanca, Morocco, involve twelve bombers, eighty-seven collaborators, and five physical targets (Western and Jewish), resulting in forty-five dead. The attacks are attributed to the hard-line Islamic groups Salafia Jihadia and Al-Assirat al-Moustaquim. Both have suspected Al Qaeda links.

For a comprehensive list of all terrorist events worldwide, it is advisable to view the RAND-MIPT database of events at http://db.mipt.org/mipt_rand.cfm.

# 4

# Profiles of Terrorist and Counterterrorist Leaders and Organizations

In terms of countering or understanding terrorism it is often not enough to develop a "profile." It is also important to consider the position of the terrorist in the hierarchy within the organization. For example, one should differentiate between the roles in the hierarchies of terrorist organizations, as Allison (2003) notes regarding the bomb designer, bomb maker, and bomb layer (the person placing, arming, or initiating the device). The latter will generally be an expendable person who only has a very basic knowledge of the workings of the device, which will have been imparted from the bomb maker, to allow the layer to fulfill his or her mission. The bomb maker is more valuable, with more advanced knowledge/expertise received from either a senior bomb maker or the bomb designer, and thus is a group asset and therefore unlikely to be tasked with dangerous operational missions that may result in the loss of his or her life and expertise. The bomb designer is a valuable group asset who provides the group with new and innovative methods of IED attack in response to security force countermeasures. Bomb designers will usually have a particular skill or university qualification in a subject transferable to IED design/production.

There will be differing motivations and personalities for the persons undertaking the different roles. Almost all terrorist training manuals (e.g., the *Afghan Jihad Encyclopedia*, the *Terrorist*

*Handbook,* and the "Declaration of Jihad against the Country's Tyrants") emphasize the need to identify a correct type of person to undergo the highly specialized explosives course: someone calm, quiet, and intelligent, not a hothead who might kill himself/herself or others. A different personality profile may likely be required for a suicide bomber.

In terms of profiling terrorists one can thus begin to see the problems inherent given the different roles. Equally, people involved in the financing or *support* aspects of terrorism (e.g., lawyers, business people, petty criminals) will have different "profiles" to those involved in the *operational* aspects of terrorism. It is thus important to not look for a "one-size-fits-all" profile of a terrorist, but treat each case uniquely, or at least use general characteristics.

As regards leadership backgrounds and profiles, it is impossible to portray a standard profile as there are so many different types of factors that motivate a person to become a terrorist, as seen in Chapter 1, as well as the various and diverse range of aims of each group, which can all affect the membership and profiles of groups as well as their leaders. Although the following list illustrates some of the common characteristics of leaders, there are obviously different personalities, backgrounds, experiences, intellects, and different levels of success in their respective aims and campaigns. Thus one should not generalize and should only use it as a general guide.

General Terrorist Leader Profile:

- Often educated to university level, often in subjects that have terrorist applications, such as engineering, business, architecture, or sciences (thus giving them natural leadership through expertise or advanced knowledge)
- Often organized planners, sometimes with some military training/experience, and able to plan operations as well as train members in certain operational aspects
- Usually are the brains behind operations or targeting and so have the most detailed knowledge of their group's workings and intentions; it is thus important for them to not be noticed by the authorities. For these reasons they will often appear to be law-abiding persons of normal disposition with the ability to mix and interact

- Often charismatic, having the ability to convince and manipulate individuals to join their cause, as well as being able to conceptualize an idea and turn it into a real-time mission, as well as articulate it
- Truly believe their cause is right and just, and the killing of combatants and civilians is both justified and incorporated into the mission for psychological effects
- Sometimes may get involved in personal risk-taking endeavors such as monitoring or executing the mission, but will usually try to distance themselves from all aspects so as to avoid capture and prosecution and maintain plausible deniability in order to survive and continue (Olivares 2001)

Although one will see from the following profiles that many of these points are evident in terrorist leaderships, not all of these factors need to be present for a terrorist to be a leader, and indeed there will sometimes be leaders who display none or few of these characteristics. Types of leadership also vary from group to group; some groups have single leaders whereas groups like PIRA take their direction from a seven-member "Army Council," as well as from their political leadership, Sinn Fein. For these reasons it is important to look at the roles and importance of group leaders in the context of the organization and to examine and counter each case according to its own specific circumstances.

Due to the vast number of terrorist groups and leaders, it is beneficial to examine a select *few* in more depth in order to illustrate the complexity and sophistication of such entities rather than list basic (widely available) data about *many* groups.

# Profiles of Terrorist Leaders

## Al Qaeda—"The Base"

### Osama bin Laden
**Position:** Head of Al Qaeda

**Significance:** Figurehead and symbol of Islamic resistance and hatred against the West (wanted for the murder of U.S. nationals outside the United States, conspiracy to murder U.S.

nationals outside the United States, and attack on a federal facility resulting in death).

**Aliases:** The Emir, Hajj, the Director, the Prince, Abu Abdallah, Mujahid Shaykh, Shaykh Usama bin Laden, Usama bin Muhammad bin Laden

**Date and Place of Birth:** Believed to be July 30, 1957, Riyadh, Saudi Arabia (it was not compulsory to register births in Saudi at that time).

**Description:** Height—6'4" to 6'6"; weight—approximately 160 pounds, thin build; language—Arabic (probably Pashtu)

> A tall, thin man weighing about 160 pounds with a full beard, bin Laden walks with a cane. He wears long, flowing Arab robes fringed with gold, and wraps his head in a traditional red-and-white checkered headdress. He is said to be soft-spoken, extremely courteous, and even humble. He is described in some sources as ordinary and shy. He speaks only Arabic. Bin Laden has been linked to a number of Islamic extremist groups and individuals with vehement anti-American and anti-Israel ideologies. His name has been connected to many of the world's most deadly terrorist operations, and he is named by the U.S. Department of State as having financial and operational connections with terrorism. Because he has dared to stand up to two superpowers, bin Laden has become an almost mythic figure in the Islamic world. Thanks to the ineffectual U.S. cruise missile attack against his camps in Afghanistan following the bombings in Kenya and Tanzania in August 1998, thousands of Arabs and Muslims, seeing him as a hero under attack by the Great Satan, have volunteered their service. (Hudson 1999, 170–176)

**Background:** Osama bin Laden's father, Muhammed bin Awdah bin Laden, and his family moved from southern Yemen to Saudi Arabia, where Muhammed distinguished himself as a construction magnate. After Muhammed renovated the holy cities of Mecca and Medina, the bin Laden family came to be highly respected by both the Saudi house royalty and the public. They were the richest nonroyalty in Saudi Arabia. Muhammed's approximately sixty-five children rarely saw their father, and when they did, it was not an individual one-on-one meeting but as a group, and very brief. As such, none of the children, including Osama, were close to the father. Muhammed's death left his family a financial empire believed to be worth $10 billion. (The Saudi bin Laden Group is now run by Osama's family, who publicly condemn terrorist activities and claim to have no contact with him.) Osama invested the bulk of his inherited wealth overseas. The intelligence community is divided over exactly how much Osama inherited. The Australian government believes it is over $250 million. The British estimate $280 million–$300 million. Swiss intelligence, with access to superior banking information, provides a figure of $250 million–$500 million.

Osama's Syrian mother, Hamida, is still alive and maintains contact with him. Although Osama's mother travels to Europe—mostly to Paris and London—and to the Middle East, she lives in Saudi Arabia. Osama had no other immediate brothers (from his mother), only sisters, including one who married Mohammad Jamal Khalifa. All his half-brothers were sent to boarding schools in Lebanon, Syria, and Egypt except for two of his half-brothers: Ali and Abdullah. Like Osama, they stayed in Jeddah and studied at Saudi schools. Osama married a Syrian, a relative of his mother, and attended King Abd Al-Aziz University, where he studied economics and management with the intention of joining the family construction and contracting company. He was an average student who often traveled to Beirut, Lebanon, to frequent nightclubs, casinos, and bars. He left university during his third year of study. (Contrary to several other writings, he neither studied engineering nor completed his degree.) After leaving university, Osama worked in his father's construction business. It was at this time that Osama not only became deeply religious but also began preaching the necessity of armed struggle and worldwide monotheism. He credits Dr. Abdullah Azzam, a Palestinian of Jordanian origin and an influential figure in the Muslim Brotherhood, with forming his worldview.

His exact date of arrival in Pakistan or Afghanistan remains disputed, but some Western intelligence agencies place the date in the early 1980s. Bin Laden's early mentors were Azzam, today regarded as the historical leader of Hamas, and Prince Turki ibn Faisal ibn Abdelaziz, chief of security of Saudi Arabia. Subsequently, Dr. Ayman Zawahiri started to fill the role of religious mentor. Between 1982 and 1984, Azzam founded Maktab al Khidimat il mujahidin al Arab (MaK), known commonly as the Afghan Bureau, Office Bureau, or Service Bureau. As MaK's principal financier, bin Laden was considered the deputy to Azzam, the emir of MaK. At the height of the foreign Arab and Muslim influx into Pakistan-Afghanistan from 1984–1986, bin Laden spent more time traveling widely and raising funds in the Arab world. In addition to recruiting, ideologically and physically training several thousand Arab and Muslim youth from around the world to fight the Soviets, MaK channeled several billions of dollars of Western governmental financial and material resources for the Afghan jihad. Bin Laden transformed it into an international network, recruiting Islamic fundamentalists with special expertise, such as engineers, medical doctors, and drug smugglers; he also volunteered the services of the family construction firm to blast elaborate tunnels and new roads through the mountains. MaK worked closely with Pakistan, especially the Inter-Services-Intelligence (ISI), Pakistan's formidable military intelligence organization; the wealthy Saudi government and its philanthropists; the Egyptian government, the leader of the Arab world; and the vast Muslim Brotherhood network in the Arab world.

The ISI was both the CIA's conduit for arms transfers and source of training for the Afghan and foreign mujahedin. The CIA configured special weapons and provided state-of-the-art technologies from Stingers to satellite imagery to the mujahedin. Both the fighting and relief efforts were assisted by two banks; the Dar al Mal al Islami, founded by Turki's brother, Prince Mohammad Faisal, in 1981, and Dalla al Baraka, founded by King Fahd's brother-in-law in 1982. The two banks channeled funds to twenty NGOs, the most famous of which was the International Islamic Relief Organization (IIRO). Both IIRO and the Islamic Relief Agency functioned under the umbrella of the World Islamic League, led by Mufti Abdul Aziz bin Baz. In addition to benefiting from the vast resources and expertise of governments channeled through domestic and foreign sources, MaK developed an independent global reach. Several mosques and charities, including the Kiffah refugee center in Brooklyn, New York, and its mosque, served as MaK outreach offices in the United States.

As a philanthropist, Osama bin Laden became popular in Afghanistan. Although he came from one of the richest families in the Arabian Peninsula, his commitment to the jihad, his qualities of humility and simplicity, and his ability to befriend and communicate with the fighters on the ground appealed to the muja-hedin. A fellow mujahedin claimed that not only had bin Laden given them his money, but he also gave himself. They said that the bin Laden way was to renounce his wealth and status and come and live with the Afghan peasants and the Arab fighters. Many spoke of how bin Laden cooked, ate, and dug trenches with them. While living in the Afghanistan-Pakistan border area, bin Laden became increasingly religious and built close relationships with several religious personalities, including the spiritual leader of the Egyptian Islamic Group Omar Abdel Rahman, the Blind Sheikh, during his first visit to Pakistan in 1985. Although bin Laden played more of a support role than a combat role, he par-ticipated as a frontline fighter in the battles fought in the late stages of the campaign. In 1986 he joined the Afghan Arabs and participated in the battles for Jalalabad. In 1987 the mujahedin mounted a daring and spectacular attack against a powerful So-viet offensive involving land and air power. It was one of the most famous battles during the whole war and, due to the high risk encountered, it was known as "The Lion's Den Operation of Afghanistan." Many notable mujahedin personalities partici-pated in this operation, including Abu Zubair al-Madani and Shaykh Tameem Dnani. Shaykh Abdullah Azzam was in the sec-ond line of the front. Bin Laden was exposed to poisonous gas during an attack and also suffered minor physical injuries. Bin Laden again joined the mujahedin in a decisive battle. His per-sonal participation in battle made him a hero in the eyes of many. By winning one battle against the Soviets, he demonstrated and argued that the Soviet military machine could be defeated. His wealth, influence, and fearlessness made him a natural leader for the Arab mujahedin contingent in the second half of the 1980s.

At the end of the anti-Soviet campaign, bin Laden returned to Saudi Arabia. While there, he helped create the first jihad group in south Yemen, under the leadership of Tariq al Fadli. His

Although Soviet troops withdrew from Afghanistan in 1989, the Soviets installed Najibullah, a procommunist leader, in Kabul. As such, MaK continued to strengthen the organization to fight the Najibullah regime and channel resources to other interna-tional campaigns where Muslims were perceived as victims. In addition to benefiting from MaK's pan-Islamic (as opposed to the pan-Arab) ideology, Al Qaeda drew from the vast financial re-sources and technical expertise mobilized during the decade-long anti-Soviet campaign.

support for the Saudi-based Islamists of Yemen continued well after the end of the Afghan jihad, until the ousting of the communists of south Yemen. Although very little is known about his role, bin Laden was one of the key players in the fight against the communists in Yemen for nearly two decades.

After the Iraqi invasion of Kuwait, the United States became involved in the Persian Gulf War. At the request of Saudi Arabia, the United States based its troops in Saudi Arabia. A disturbed bin Laden, who did not want armed non-Muslims on the land of the two holy mosques, expressed his displeasure to Prince Turki. The failure of the Saudi royalty to honor the U.S. pledge to withdraw foreign troops as soon as the Iraqi threat diminished led bin Laden to initiate a campaign against the Saudi rulers. In his eyes they were infidels. He claimed that the Saudi rulers were false Muslims and that it was necessary to install a true Islamic state in Saudi Arabia. Meanwhile, the National Islamic Front, led by Hasan al Turabi and which came to power in Sudan, sent a delegation to Pakistan. Within three years of the departure of the Soviets from Afghanistan, bin Laden started to relocate a part of the Al Qaeda infrastructure of well-trained and well-experienced fighters from Pakistan and Afghanistan to Sudan. Beginning in 1991 he started to use Khartoum, Sudan, as Al Qaeda's headquarters. He established about thirty companies in Sudan, including high-tech labs engaged in genetic research, and funded the construction of a road from Khartoum to Port Sudan.

According to Hudson (1999, 170–176), "Osama also financed and help set up at least three terrorist training camps in cooperation with the Sudanese regime, and his construction company worked directly with Sudanese military officials to transport and supply terrorists training in such camps. During the 1992–96 period, he built and equipped 23 training camps for Mujahidin. While in Sudan, he also established a supposedly detection-proof financial system to support Islamic terrorist activities worldwide." In 1992 he focused his efforts against Egypt and also claimed responsibility for attempting to bomb U.S. soldiers in Yemen. In 1993 he again attacked U.S. soldiers, this time in Somalia, and that winter he traveled to the Philippines to show his support for the terrorist network that would launch major operations in that country and the United States. Convinced that the House of al-Saud was no longer legitimate, bin Laden began actively supporting Islamic extremists in Saudi Arabia also that year, prompting Saudi authorities to revoke his Saudi citizenship on April 7, 1994, for "irresponsible behavior," and he was officially expelled from the country. As Hudson (1999, 170–176) details, bin Laden "subsequently established a new residence and base of operations in the London suburb of Wembley, but was forced to return to Sudan after a few months to avoid being extradited to Saudi Arabia." In early 1995 he instructed Al Qaeda to increase activities against Egypt and Saudi Arabia. The following year, the Saudi government began to pressure Sudan to exert some form of control over bin Laden, at which point he and his family returned to Afghanistan on board his unmarked transport plane.

Bin Laden established a mountain fortress near the city of Kandahar, southwest of Jalalabad, under the protection of the Afghan government. Between 1996 and 1998 he issued three *fatwas* (religious rulings), each threatening a jihad against U.S. forces in Saudi Arabia and the Holy Lands, and each calling for Muslims to concentrate on "destroying, fighting and killing the enemy."

Bin Laden appears to use marriage as a binding tactic, similar to the concept of the Italian mafia family. At one of his son's marriages in Afghanistan several years ago, he invited the regional chiefs of Al Qaeda, as well as leaders of Islamic terrorist groups from around the world. Osama's son Muhammad, born in 1985, "rarely leaves his father's side. Muhammad has already received extensive military and terrorist training and carries his own AK-47. He serves as his father's vigilant personal bodyguard" (Hudson 1999, 170–176).

**Ideological Influence:** Toward the end of the anti-Soviet Afghan campaign, bin Laden's relationship with Azzam began to suffer. Throughout the second half of 1988 and in 1989, he and Azzam disagreed over several issues. Despite these differences, they maintained public appearances and worked together. Although bin Laden and Azzam agreed on the principal issue of continuing to support Muslims in distress worldwide and on the creation of Al Qaeda, they disagreed on the future tactics to be adopted. The tension between them came to head over an Egyptian proposal to train the mujahedin in terrorist tactics. The Egyptians were keen to train a force that would use these tactics back home in Egypt, but Azzam insisted that the funds were only for use in Afghanistan. Having lived in Egypt, Azzam knew the futility, danger, and limits of starting a terrorist campaign there. As the Egyptian Islamic Group wished to invest in terrorism, Azzam issued a fatwa stating that using the money to train in terrorist tactics would be a violation of Islamic law. On the killing of noncombatants, Azzam's writings clearly reflect the finer points of fighting combatants as well as his position on jihad to aid the suffering Muslims. One of the final disputes was over Azzam's support for Masood, the leader of the Russian-backed Northern Alliance fighting the Taliban. Bin Laden always preferred Hekmatiyar, who was both anticommunist and anti-West. During the anti-Soviet campaign, when Hekmatiyar visited the UN headquarters in New York, the Afghan mujahedin spurned an invitation to meet the U.S. president. However, bin Laden never openly expressed any hatred toward the United States while living in Afghanistan or Pakistan. When the Soviets decided to withdraw from Afghanistan, bin Laden decided to form his own group for the purpose of making a *khalifa*, uniting the whole Muslim world into a single entity. He wanted to establish Islamic states where there were non-Islamic rulers in power. Despite their differences, Azzam and bin Laden worked together until Azzam was mysteriously assassinated on November 24, 1989, along with his sons Ibrahim and Mohommad by a 20-kilogram TNT device activated by remote control while he was driving to Friday (jummah) prayer. Since then, bin Laden has never criticized Azzam in public and in his writings only praised him. Nonetheless, it is very likely that bin Laden, a genius in deception, was behind Azzam's murder. Nearly a decade later, an Al Qaeda Palestinian member (Mohammed Saddiq Odeh alias Mohammed Sadiq Howeida) was arrested in Pakistan and told his interrogators that bin Laden personally ordered the killing of Azzam.

In many ways, Azzam had controlled bin Laden. With Azzam's death, bin Laden reached his full potential as a radical under the religious mentoring of Dr. Ayman Muhammad Rabi Al-Zawahiri. Ten years younger than Azzam, Al-Zawahiri came from one of the most influential families in Al-Sharqiyyah, Egypt, and was the leader of the Egyptian Islamic Jihad. Largely due to Al-Zawahiri's influence, bin Laden was perceived as favoring the two Egyptian terrorist organizations—the Egyptian Islamic Jihad and the Egyptian Islamic Group. Bin Laden was so impressed by

Al-Zawahiri that many believed that he was supporting Egyptians more than Al Qaeda members and their families. Gradually, he resolved many of the differences between the two Egyptian groups, which pertained to the religious issue of dealing with excusing ignorance as well as the leadership structure and the *shura*, or consultation body. As the Egyptian Islamic Group leader, Rifa Taha Ali (alias Rifai Ahmad Taha) disagreed on the organizational structure and the appointment of Sheikh Omar Abdel Rahman, the Blind Sheik, as the new international group leader. However, Al-Zawahiri and Taha agreed to preserve their organizational structures, retain their group leaderships, and cooperate under bin Laden's leadership.

Many insiders including, Al-Zawahiri's former lawyer, Muntasir Al-Zayyat, have argued that bin Laden was transformed from a guerrilla into a terrorist by Al-Zawahiri. What is clear is the extent of influence Al-Zawahiri wields over bin Laden. In almost all the media and public appearances after bin Laden moved to Afghanistan, Al-Zawahiri has been by his side. Al-Zayyat has stated that Al-Zawahiri is bin Laden's "brain" that controls and determines his actions and reactions. Al Qaeda's first military commander, Ali Al-Rashidi (alias Abu-Ubaydah al-Banshiri), an Al-Zawahiri loyalist, may well have been bin Laden's "heart." When he drowned in Lake Victoria in Kenya in 1996, he was not only Al Qaeda's military commander but also its emir. His deputy and successor, Subhi Abd-al-Aziz Abu-Sittah (alias Muhammad Atef), was also an Al-Zawahiri loyalist. Muhammed Atef always sat next to bin Laden during his public appearances, suggesting that Atef held the post of military commander and emir in Al Qaeda. The U.S. bombing of Afghanistan in November 2001 killed Atef.

In many ways, both Zawahiri and bin Laden fit the bill of the new generation of terrorists. Unlike the leaders of the terrorist groups during the Cold War, the rank and file of contemporary terrorist groups come from wealthy, educated, and well-to-do families. It is a clear demonstration that the terrorist ideologies equally appeal to all classes and strata of society. Both the Al Qaeda leader and the deputy leader came from privileged families. Bin Laden came from the wealthiest non-royal Saudi family in Saudi Arabia. Al-Zawahiri came from one of the most educated families in Egypt. Although Al-Zawahiri did not hold an important administrative or military position in

Al Qaeda at its formative stage, he was very much present from the inception. In addition to attending all the important Al Qaeda meetings starting in 1989, Al-Zawahiri influenced the thinking both of bin Laden and the organization. Al-Zawahiri was head of the religious committee, one of the key Al Qaeda committees that issued fatawa, or legal rulings, and the consultative council "the Shura." Under Al-Zawahiri's influence, bin Laden began to assign a high priority to the military structure of his organization. Bin Laden appointed the Al Qaeda military commander also as emir of Al Qaeda. Successive military commanders dominated the meetings and the decision-making. In all public appearances, the military commander sat next to Bin Laden. After Al Banshiri's death, Atef was always with Bin Laden and Al-Zawahiri.

Both Al-Zawahiri and bin Laden are followers of the Salafi school of Islam and not the Wahabi school, as stated by many experts and in many publications. The Wahabi school is a part of the Salafi school. The followers of the Salafi school are called "the pious pioneers of Islam." The Salafi Dawah is Islam in its totality. It addresses all humanity irrespective of culture, race, or color. It is this aspect that has enabled bin Laden's message to reach beyond Sunni Muslims and to the Shias and to establish links with Shia groups such as Hezbollah. The Salafi school aims to return the entire Islamic nation to the sublime Koran and to the Prophet's authentic Sunnah. It also strives to revive Islamic thought within the boundaries of Islamic principles, meaning the presentation of realistic Islamic solutions to contemporary problems and to establish a true Islamic society governed by Allah's laws. It is pure and free from any additions, deletions, or alterations. As such, for the Al Qaeda member, the Salafi school is complete, perfect in the methodology of understanding Islam, and acting according to its teachings. Members also believe that the Prophet has deemed the Salaf the best generation of muslims, and all who follow them are guaranteed success, victory, and salvation from hell. For the current generation of Al Qaeda members, bin Laden is considered a Salafi.

### Khalid Shaikh Mohommad
**Position:** Third in command of Al Qaeda (captured as of March 1, 2003)
   **Significance:** Masterminded 9/11

**Aliases:** In the 1990s, law enforcement, security, and intelligence agencies have identified *at least* fifty aliases for Khalid. Among them are Walid Muhammad Salih Ba Attas, Khalid Al-Shaikh, Mohammad Khaled, Salim Ali, Ali Salem, Muhammed Khalid Al-Mana, M Almana, Ashraf Refaat Nabith Henin, Nabih Hanin, Fahd bin Abdallah bin Khaled, Muhammad Muhannadi, Ashraf Ahmed, Ahmed Refaat, Khalid Abdul Wadood, Khalid the Kuwaiti, Babu Hamza, Mukhtar, Al-Mukh, Muhammad Ali Al Balushi, Mukhtar Al-Baluchi, Abdul Rahman Abdullah Al-Ghamdi, Khalid Mohammad Mohammad, Khalid Abdul Wadood, and Khalid Saeed Muhammad.

**Date and Place of Birth:** Although he appears to be older, he used the birthdates of April 14, 1965, and March 1, 1964, Kuwait.

**Description:** Khalid frequently altered his appearance. He is portly, light brown in complexion, with brown eyes and thinning dark hair, and has a long round face. He has been described as "relatively short" and "slightly overweight" by Al Qaeda detainees in U.S. custody. He is 5 foot 5 inches (1.55 meters) tall and weighs 160 pounds (72 kilograms). He often sported a closely trimmed beard and mustache and wore glasses. He tinted his hair, the color ranging from dark brown to black. He wore Western clothes, speaks very good English, and traveled frequently.

**Background:** Khalid's origin remains in dispute. U.S. government reports initially stated that Khalid's father was the first imam of Al-Ahmadi Mosque in Kuwait and was stripped of his citizenship after a dispute with a leading Kuwaiti family. Born as Khalid Al-Shaikh Muhammad Ali Dustin Al-Blushi in Kuwait, Khalid spent his early years in Fahaheel, south of Kuwait City. After Khalid was identified as the mastermind of 9/11, the U.S. intelligence community stated that he was a Kuwaiti national; however, being born in Kuwait does not automatically qualify someone as a citizen. After the European Union issued in December 2001 a terrorist list citing Khalid as a Kuwaiti, the Kuwaiti information ministry stated that neither Khalid nor his father were Kuwaitis. The Kuwaiti intelligence service checked all its records, and its Ministry of Foreign Affairs through its missions overseas clarified to governments worldwide that the "said person in question is not a Kuwaiti national and does not hold a Kuwaiti passport." In fact, he acquired Pakistani citizenship and obtained a Pakistani passport from the Pakistani Embassy in Kuwait on December 6, 1982, after which he left Kuwait for the United States. He studied at Chowan College in northeastern North Carolina for one semester in 1984, then transferred to another university in North Carolina where he obtained a degree in mechanical engineering. Thereafter, he moved to Pakistan and served as the secretary of Abdul-Rab Rasool Sayyaf, leader of Ittehad-e-Islami, one of seven large groups that fought against the Soviet troops and Najibullah in Afghanistan. Sayyaf was well disposed toward bin Laden and to Abdul Rajak Janjalani, the founding leader of the Abu Sayyaf Group. As there were many Arabs in the ranks of Ittehad-e-Islami, Khalid established a wide network during the second half of the 1980s.

While in Pakistan, he engaged in anti-Shia operations in Pakistan, including the assassination of prominent Shia leaders and bombing of Shia shrines, and trying to assassinate Benazir Bhutto, Pakistan's pro-West prime minister. He also expanded his network by recruiting and enlisting many followers from Kuwait. From Fahaheel, where a significant percentage of Palestinians lived, many Arabs and Pakistanis joined, supported, or sympathized with Al Qaeda. Among them were Ramzi Ahmed Yousef; Abdul Shakur, the attempted assassin of Benazir Bhutto; Wadi Al Hage, secretary to bin Laden; Abdul Hakim Murad, the first Al Qaeda pilot; and Murad's associate Nasir Mubarak, also a pilot who had trained at the same U.S. flight school. Once again, this demonstrated that Al Qaeda recruited from familial and social networks.

Khalid visited the Philippines and lived there in 1994. Until Yousef's cell was exposed, Khalid lived mostly on the top floor of Manila's Dona Josefa Apartments, where Yousef experimented with explosives to destroy U.S. airliners. The apartment was Al Qaeda's operational center until a fire erupted. In fact, Khalid arrived at Yousef's apartment just as it caught fire, but he managed to escape. After the detection of the Yousef cell in Manila, Yousef fled to Pakistan, where he was arrested. Khalid, who had known Yousef since childhood, was affected by his arrest but remained in the Philippines. Due to the security measures he adopted, Khalid was confident that he would not be arrested. According to an FBI officer, he was observed visiting the VIP Restaurant in the Harrison Plaza Complex in Manila almost everyday at around the same time. After Yousef fled Manila, the FBI mounted an operation together with its Philippine counterpart to arrest Khalid at the Bandido (Bandit) restaurant in

Manila, which he had begun to frequent. The operation was unsuccessful (due to the visibility of FBI and other agents), and Khalid immediately left Manila for Doha, Qatar. There he lived at the estate of Abdullah bin Khalid, an influential Islamist who supported Al Qaeda and had hosted bin Laden twice in the mid-1990s, and worked at the Public Works Ministry. When the FBI and CIA tracked Khalid to an apartment in Doha and was about to arrest him, the U.S. government believes that a senior Qatari official tipped him off. Although Qatar government officials were willing to hand him over to the United States, the process of getting permission to arrest him took time. Together with an associate, Khalid fled Qatar using forged passports. In the fall of 1996, Khalid surfaced in Brazil. The CIA arranged through its liaison with Brazil's security service to arrest him, but he again slipped away. Khalid reappeared in the Middle East and Europe in 1997 and 1998, building a network for the purpose of attacking U.S. targets.

Unlike most other Al Qaeda terrorists and leaders, Khalid's motivation was not religion but retribution, retaliation, and revenge. He appeared to be driven by pure vengeance—a single mission to punish the United States of America and its friends. Khalid was not an operative but an organizer of terrorist attacks. As he did not directly conduct terrorist attacks, his identity remained illusive and his personality largely unknown to the intelligence community until mid-2002. After Khalid was identified as a foreign terrorist in the mid-1990s, he remained on the run. However, he demonstrated his ability to function effectively over long periods of time under extreme pressure. Despite being placed on nearly one hundred watch lists and tracked by two-dozen governments even before 9/11, he managed to both organize and operate across the world, portraying himself as either a rich businessman from Doha, Qatar, or a trader of holy water from Medina, Saudi Arabia.

Khalid belongs to the rare category of highly experienced organizers of terrorist attacks across international borders. As an important functionary and thereafter the head of Al Qaeda's military committee, Khalid was the key planner of several Al Qaeda landmark operations: As far back as 1992, he developed a plan together with his nephew and protégé Ramzi Ahmed Yousef to bomb the World Trade Center in New York, topple one tower onto the other, and kill several tens of thousands of people. The resulting operation in February 1993 killed six people, injured more than a thousand others, and caused extensive damage to the structure. He also was the architect of the assassination attempt on Benazir Bhutto (1993), the Oplan Bojinka (a complicated plan to destroy a dozen U.S. airliners over the Pacific, assassinate President Bill Clinton and Pope John Paul II, and crash commercial airliners into CIA headquarters and the Pentagon in 1994–1995), and Operation HOLY TUESDAY (to be discussed in detail below).

There are several other operations where his hand has not been exposed but is suspected, such as the slaying of two American officials in Karachi, Pakistan, in March 1995, and four American oil workers slain in Karachi in November 1997, both in retaliation for Pakistan's extradition and U.S. sentencing of Mir Aimal Kansi, a Pakistani responsible for the murder of two and injury to three CIA employees outside CIA headquarters in Langley, Virginia, in January 1993. (Although Kansi did not belong to Al Qaeda, like Khalid he was a Baluchi from Quetta, the capital of the Balochistan Province of Pakistan, which borders Afghanistan.) Most infamously, Khalid organized "Holy Tuesday," the operation to strike America's most outstanding landmarks on September 11, 2001, the single biggest terrorist attack the world has ever witnessed. As the mastermind of Holy Tuesday—the Al Qaeda term for 9/11—Khalid became the world's most hunted terrorist.

Furthermore, although Ahmad Saeed Omar Sheikh of Jayash-e-Mohomad, an associate group of Al Qaeda, is accused of committing the murder of journalist Daniel Pearl, it was an Al Qaeda operation. Pearl's research of Richard Reid, the shoe bomber, led him to Karachi, also the forward headquarters of Khalid. Sensing the threat, the Pakistani intelligence community believes that Khalid ordered Pearl's death. As Yosri Fouda of *Al Jazeera*, who interviewed Khalid in Karachi in June 2002, was leaving the safe house where the interview had taken place, Khalid gave him a copy of the Daniel Pearl slaying video and a 112-page manifesto justifying the 9/11 operation.

Khalid was responsible for introducing two principles to Al Qaeda: first, its "losing and learning" doctrine. If Al Qaeda fails in an operation or suffers human and material losses, it is not considered a strategic loss provided the group learns, improves, and vows not to repeat its mistake again. As such Al Qaeda could revisit its failed operations and engage in retargeting the same old targets using improved or better tactics; Al Qaeda failed to destroy the World Trade Center in February 1993, but it succeeded on September 11, 2001. The second principle is that Al Qaeda should be goal-oriented rather than rule-oriented; for instance, when plans to attack government, diplomatic, and other hard targets were disrupted in Southeast Asia, Khalid approved a proposal by his Southeast Asian representative, Hambali, to attack population, economic, and other soft targets. The bombing of nightclubs, cafés, and other establishments frequented by Westerners in Southeast Asia—including the Bali attack on October 12, 2002—received the blessings of the Al Qaeda leadership.

Among the fraternity of terrorists, Khalid was one of the few surviving leaders still able to conceptualize grand designs, prepare a blueprint, and carry out his plans effectively and efficiently. To quote an Al Qaeda member, "Khalid thinks big . . . he engages in systematic and meticulous planning of spectacular or theatrical terrorist operations. He is a creative genius." To quote a former intelligence chief of the Philippines National Police, Colonel Rodolfo Mendoza: "He behaves like he's an intelligence officer. He appears and disappears. He has safe houses. He is very, very clever." In his capacity as the head of the military committee, Khalid dealt with a wide range of personnel both within and outside his committee. In addition to consulting with bin Laden and Al-Zawahiri, he regularly interacted with Al Qaeda experts who were young and impressionable. At the time of their capture, Abu Zubeidah, head of external operations, was thirty-one years old; Mohommad Mansour Jabara, coordinator of the suicide attacks in Southeast Asia, was twenty-two; Ramzi Bin Al Shibh, chief logistics officer of 9/11, was thirty; and Hambali, head of operations for Southeast Asia, was thirty-six.

Instead of communicating over the phone or by e-mail, Khalid dispatched couriers and operatives with guidelines and instructions. Although he remained in touch with his field organizers and operatives, quite early on in his profession Khalid mastered the art of protecting himself by positioning "cut-outs" between front-end organizers and operatives. Khalid used several layers of protection—even if one was breached, there was another, and behind that a third. As an extremely cautious and security-conscious terrorist, Khalid could afford to operate near the center of action but at the same time remain untouched. The security measures taken by Khalid prevented several governments investigating terrorist attacks throughout the 1990s from identifying bin Laden as the financier and himself as the organizer. Thanks to countermeasures enacted by Khalid following 9/11, the United States and other governments took eight months to identify Khalid as the key planner of Holy Tuesday. The U.S. government identified Khalid as the mastermind of 9/11 only after Abu Zubaydah, Al Qaeda's head of foreign operations, was arrested after a gunfight in Pakistan in March 2002. Although Abu Zubaydah identified Khalid as the mastermind of 9/11, the U.S. intelligence community did not believe him. For three months, FBI and CIA operatives worked to corroborate Abu Zubaydah's statement. Indeed, Holy Tuesday was so well compartmentalized that the U.S. authorities came to know of the details of 9/11 only after the arrest of Al Shibh, exactly one year after the event. The revelations of Al Shibh after his arrest in Karachi on September 11, 2002, enabled the U.S. government to conclusively identify Khalid as the mastermind of 9/11. Considering his past, Khalid was fortunate to evade capture for so long. For conspiring to hijack and bomb several transatlantic flights heading for the United States in January 1995, U.S. federal prosecutors in New York indicted Khalid in January 1996. Although the FBI offered $2 million for information leading to his capture, there was little effort to specifically target him until October 2001. In December 2001, the FBI placed him on the list of the twenty-two most-wanted terrorists and offered $25 million, the same reward offered for information leading to the capture of Osama bin Laden.

Khalid filled a void in the operational community by taking an idea and turning it into a reality with the vast global network he built over the years. As much as he had access to youth willing to kill and die, Khalid had sufficient funds. Whenever he needed funds, Khalid discreetly approached businessman, politicians, and charity workers he had cultivated over the years. Rarely did anyone decline or refuse a request for assistance from Khalid. What Al Qaeda lacked were trusted individuals located in the West with sufficient knowledge of the West to receive, protect, and guide the suicide terrorists to their enemy targets. Recruiting and positioning Al Qaeda members and supporters strategically in forward and rear bases for immediate and subsequent exploitation was Khalid's specialty. It was Khalid who always communicated with these assets and not the other way around. Although he knew the weaknesses and limitations of technologies in conducting terrorist operations, he intelligently exploited the technologies available to him. In July 2002, his four-bedroom apartment in Karachi, Pakistan, had three laptops and five mobile phones. His roles varied depending on the operation and circumstances—directly participating in the bombing of a Philippines Airline flight from Cebu to Tokyo that killed a Japanese executive and injured others in December 1994, chairing the planning meetings of Holy Tuesday, and wiring money to Yousef for Oplan Bojinka and to 9/11 hijackers. With experience, his operations were complex, often involving assets and operatives across many countries. For instance, Holy Tuesday involved operational planning in Afghanistan, Pakistan, Malaysia, Germany, Spain, the United Arab Emirates, the United Kingdom, and the United States. With his unrivaled and unmatched career, he presented a clear and present danger to the international system.

**The Planning of 9/11:** Al Qaeda's watershed operation to wage a terrorist attack on U.S. soil took two and a half years of planning and preparation. It began after Al Qaeda established links with an Islamist cell in to Hamburg, Germany, in early 1999. Khalid met with Ramzi bin Al Shibh and Mohommad Atta (alias Mohamed El-Emir), the nucleus of the Al Qaeda cell in Hamburg. Beginning in mid-1999, Khalid dispatched four reconnaissance units to the United States in pairs or singles over the space of five to six months to mount surveillance on the intended targets. Due to navigation reasons, the White House was taken off the list and replaced with the U.S. Capitol building. The operation was originally referred to as "the Manhattan and Washington Raids." Al Qaeda used the Arabic word *ghazwah*, which refers to a raid against enemies of the Prophet. Al Qaeda leader Osama bin Laden's intention was to force the United States to withdraw from Saudi Arabia and disengage itself from the Middle East; the intention of the 9/11 operational team was to inflict maximum social and economic damage as well as to humiliate the United States.

In the autumn of 1999, Atta—who hated high-rise buildings—traveled to Kandahar and met with Khalid at Al-Ghumad House in Afghanistan. The house, where they planned Holy Tuesday, was named after the Saudi Al Ghamdi clan—four of whose young members would be the musclemen in the hijackings. The Holy Tuesday operational team, chaired by Khalid, configured into a consultative council. In addition to the pilots Mohommad Atta, Marwan al Shehhi, Hani Hanjor, and Ziad Jarrah, the council consisted of Khalid Al-Mihdar, Nawaf Al-Hazemi (Atta's deputy), Said Bahaji, and Ramzi bin Al-Shibh, all of whom had left Hamburg in late 1999 or early 2000 and trained in Afghanistan. If Atta was arrested or killed, Al-Hazemi was designated to lead the operation. As their passports had Pakistani visas and to prevent them from being subjected to suspicion when they applied for their U.S. visas, immediately after Atta, Al-Shehhi, and Jarrah returned to Germany, they reported that their passports were stolen. Believing that it would be a risk for the members of the operational team to return to Afghanistan, they decided to hold the first planning meeting in Malaysia in January 2000. Twelve Al Qaeda members arrived at the meeting; of those, the CIA identified Khalid Al-Mihdar and Nawaf Al-Hazemi. Except for Hani Hanjor, who was living in the United States prior to launching the operation, Al-Mihdar and Al-Hazemi were the first 9/11 operatives to enter the United States, from Bangkok, on January 15, 2000. Al-Midhar obtained a multiple entry visa to enter the United States, yet the CIA failed to ensure he be placed on a State Department Watch List to prevent him from coming to the country. Al-Midhar and Al-Hamzi were not placed on U.S. Watch Lists until August 23, 2001. Both Al-Mihdar and Al-Hazemi traveled to Thailand with the assistance of Hambali, who organized the Malaysia meeting. Both Tawfiq Al-Attash (alias Khallad from Yemen), chief planner of the USS *Cole* bombing, and Hambali paid the hijackers. For the 9/11 operation, Khalid wanted to personally lead it, but his request was turned down. (This demonstrated Khalid's fearlessness to enter the very heartland of his enemy in order to strike and destroy its landmarks.) When Atta arrived in New York in June 2000, he carried with him a report of potential targets made by Al Qaeda reconnaissance teams in mid-1999. Atta and Al-Shehhi enrolled in a flying course at Huffman Aviation in Venice, Florida; Jarrah enrolled in the nearby Florida Flight Training Center. Hanjour, already living in the United States and a trained pilot, underwent further training in Arizona.

Atta, Al-Hazemi, and other pilots studied security arrangements at airports and aircraft. The hijackers determined the best time to attack the cockpit was fifteen minutes after takeoff. Five months before 9/11, Khalid chose a dozen Saudis from the Martyrs Department of Al Qaeda as musclemen. After they were trained in the spring of 2001, Al Qaeda recorded their last will. Although they knew that they were going to die, they did not know how, when, and where until the last moment. They entered the United States by July 2001, demonstrating Al Qaeda's ability to infiltrate the nation without much difficulty. From an agent in

Afghanistan, Egyptian intelligence quickly knew that twenty Al-Qaeda members—four of them Cessna-trained—had entered the United States. Although the Egyptian service informed the CIA, there was no response.

In mid-July 2001, Atta flew to Madrid, Spain, and drove five hundred miles to Cambrils, the Spanish coastal holiday resort near Tarragona, for a second planning meeting. In keeping with Khalid's wish of giving operational leverage to Atta, the field operational commander decided on the choice and timing of the operation. Atta brought for Al-Shibh books and documents about the United States that would strengthen Al Qaeda's knowledge to conduct future airborne suicide operations inside the United States. He also brought the annual flight schedules for airlines and other information that enabled the Al Qaeda operational leadership that met in Europe to meticulously plan the hijacking of the airliners. This was necessary because Al Qaeda code forbade Atta from discussing the overall plan with any one of the nineteen hijackers. In preparation for the assault, the final reconnaissance of targets was conducted from the ground and the air, with the Al Qaeda pilots traveling as passengers or renting planes and flying over the intended targets at close range but without evoking suspicion. The spirit of the hijackers was reinforced by multiple techniques. They were even named and referred to after Islamic heroes: Ziad Jarrah as Abu Tareq, alias Tareq bin Ziad, the conqueror of Andalusia (Spain); Marwan Al-Shehhi as Abul Qaqaa, alias Abu Qaqaa, the conqueror of the Persians; and Khalid Al-Mihdar as Sinan, a reference to the great Islamic architect of Istanbul. Similarly, they each received an "Instructions and Prayers" manual that kept them on course.

Throughout the operation, Al Qaeda remained undetected in the United States by adhering to the strictest principles of security. When Atta in the United States and Al Shibh in Germany communicated by e-mail in German through the Internet chat rooms in July and August 2001, Atta pretended he was a young man in America talking to Jenny, his girlfriend in Germany. "The first semester starts in three weeks. . . . Nothing has changed. Everything is fine. There are good signs and encouraging ideas. Two high schools and two universities. Everything is going according to plan. This summer will surely be hot. I would like to talk to you about a few details. Nineteen certificates [reference to the 19 hijackers] for private study and four exams [reference to the four missions]. Regards to the professor. Goodbye." In keeping with his operating procedure, Khalid, perhaps the professor, communicated with Al-Shibh and not with Atta until the last moment. Atef's last phone call to Khalid on September 10, 2001, was monitored by the U.S. National Security Agency (NSA), but it was translated from Arabic to English only after the attacks. In code, Khalid approved the operation for the four teams to strike. (Similarly, Nizar Naouar, the Al Qaeda suicide bomber who targeted German tourists visiting the Jewish synagogue in Djerba, Tunisia, on April 11, 2002, placed three calls three hours before the bombing, of which one was to Khalid.)

Khalid ordered key Al Qaeda operatives to withdraw from Europe and North America immediately prior to 9/11. For instance, Al-Shibh dispatched his flat mate Said Bahaji, a German Moroccan, to Karachi, Pakistan. Although some operatives have since been identified by government intelligence agencies, others have not. It is likely that Al Qaeda may task these operatives to return to the West using false, forged, and adopted identifications to plan, prepare, and execute further operations. After gathering his belongings, Al-Shibh cleared the Marienstrasse apartment of any evidence before arriving in Pakistan to inform bin Laden, through a messenger, only of the date of Al Qaeda's watershed operation.

Khalid's capacity to conceptualize, plan, and actualize low-cost, high-impact operations was consistently underestimated by the international intelligence and security community. As Khalid made things happen, arguably more so than bin Laden, intelligence analysts increasingly developed the opinion that targeting Khalid was a priority. When Khalid met with *Al Jazeera* journalist Fouda in June 2002, he said that initially Al Qaeda "considered attacking U.S. nuclear facilities but decided against it" due to the risk of failure. To quote Khalid, "We decided not to consider this for *now*" (emphasis added). Khalid told Fouda that Al Qaeda "hope[s] to accomplish a thousand more assaults similar to September 11," meaning that Al Qaeda has not given up the fight. As an individual terrorist, Khalid posed one of the single biggest threats to domestic, regional, and international security.

### Ramzi Ahmed Yousef

**Significance:** Mastermind of the World Trade Center bombing on February 26, 1993.

**Aliases:** Real Name: Abdul Basit Mahamoud Addul Karim. Reportedly operated under forty aliases.

**Date and Place of Birth:** April 27, 1968, Kuwait

**Description:** Often described as slender, Yousef is six feet tall, weighs 180 pounds, and is considered white, with an olive complexion. Sometimes clean-shaven, he wears a beard in his FBI wanted poster. Ramzi got married and settled in Quetta in Pakistan where he bought a house. He has two daughters from this marriage.

**Background:** Ramzi Ahmed Yousef was born in Kuwait where his father Muhammad Abdul Karim moved from Pakistan to work as an engineer for the Kuwaiti airlines and married one of the Palestinian refugees. Ramzi, drawing his Palestinian origin from his mother's side, considers himself a Palestinian. Like other expatriates, he nourished the feeling that the Kuwaitis were treating him and his family as second-class citizens. This laid the foundations on which Ramzi's radical beliefs developed when he came under the influence of Sunni Wahhabi and Sufi preachers. Yousef completed his schooling in Kuwait, was an above-average student excelling in all subjects, especially chemistry, and was also very popular. In 1986, the Karim family migrated to Turbat, a village in the remote province of Baluchistan in Pakistan near the border of Iran and Afghanistan. Lack of policing and lawlessness made the area a haven for smugglers and traffickers of drugs and illegal weapons. The local tribesmen occasionally joined Afghan Mujahidins to attack the Soviets forces.

In 1986 Yousef went to Britain for his college education. He spent several months in Oxford studying English as a foreign language, and in 1987 he joined West Glamorgan Institute of Higher Education in Swansea University studying computer-aided electrical engineering. His major project was applying computer design to geometric Islamic patterns, but he also took a course in microelectronics, which the FBI believe almost certainly gave him the expertise to develop miniature nitroglycerin bombs. While at the university he mixed freely with students and locals and indulged in luxury (despite his internal hatred against the West that was building). He joined the Swansea branch of the outlawed Egyptian Muslim Brotherhood (Ikhwan al- Muslimin), which he found to be inadequately committed to the Islamic revolutionary cause.

In 1988 Yousef went to Pakistan and spent several months in training camps at Peshawar, funded by Al Qaeda, where he both learned bomb-making skills and taught electronics to other terrorists. There he met Zahid al-Shaikh, his maternal uncle and a senior functionary in Mercy International, a Saudi Charity providing assistance to Afghan veterans and refugees. He also met and be-friended Mahamud Abouhalima, an Afghan war veteran who later worked with Ramzi on the World Trade Center bombing in 1993. Yousef graduated from Swansea University in 1989 with a degree in engineering.

When Iraq invaded Kuwait in August 1990, Yousef was in Kuwait and allegedly became a collaborator with the Iraqi forces, not surprising given his known antipathy toward the Kuwaiti regime. In 1991, Ramzi went back to Pakistan where he forged links with the radical Sunni group Sipah-e-Sahaba, of which his father was a member.

While in Peshawar, Ramzi met Abdurajak Abubakar Jan-jalani, the founding leader of the Abu Sayyaf group in the Philippines and on Osama's request returned with him to the Philippines in December 1991. A Libyan missionary named Mohammed Abu Bakr, leader of the Mullah Forces in Libya, also accompanied Ramzi. Yousef stayed until May 1992, providing training together with Abdul Hakim Murad and Wali Khan Amin Shah (who were close bin Laden associates) to Abu Sayyaf guerrillas in the Madin camp in Basilan in the southern Philippines where he acquired the nickname "the Chemist" for his bomb-making skills.

Ramzi acquired forged travel documents in the Philippines and traveled to Pakistan on his way to New York. He arrived at New York's John F. Kennedy Airport on September 1, 1992, carrying an Iraqi passport in the name of Ramzi Ahmed Yousef and claimed political asylum on the plea that the Iraqi army had persecuted him. Passport control officers at John F. Kennedy Airport detained his Palestinian friend and fellow terrorist, Ahmad Ajaj, who was traveling with Yousef on September 1, 1992, for carrying a false Swedish passport. Ajaj was carrying papers containing formulas for bomb-making material, which prosecutors said were to be used to destroy bridges and tunnels in New York.

Yousef was allowed to stay in the United States while his political asylum case was being considered. U.S. immigration officials apparently accepted his false claim that he was a victim of the Gulf War who had been beaten by Iraqi soldiers because the Iraqis suspected that he had worked for Kuwaiti resistance. Yousef went to stay at the apartment of Musab Yasin, an Iraqi living in Jersey City where Abdul Rahman Yasin, Musab's younger brother, arrived from Iraq. In November, Yousef began to prepare the World Trade Center bomb.

On November 9, 1992, just after finalizing the bombing

plans, Yousef reported to Jersey City police that he had lost his passport. He claimed to be Abdul Basit Mahmud Abdul Karim, a Pakistani born and reared in Kuwait. Then, between December 3 and December 27, Yousef made a number of calls to Baluchistan. On December 31, 1992, Yousef went to the Pakistani consulate in New York with photocopies of Abdul Basit's current and previous passports. Consistent with his story told to police in Jersey City, he claimed to have lost his passport and asked for a new one. The consulate did not give him a new passport, but provided him with a six-month, temporary passport.

In mid-November, Yousef and the group started making the bomb, as appeared to be the case from many calls that he made to the chemical and supply companies. Meanwhile, two other local fundamentalists were recruited into the plot, Nidal Ayyad and Mahmud Abu Halima. In January 1993, Yousef and Salameh moved into another Jersey City apartment, where the bomb was actually built. Set well back from the street, the building provided seclusion. On February 21 a twenty-one-year-old Palestinian named Eyyad Ismail arrived from Dallas. Ismail is charged with having driven the bomb-laden van. On February 23, Salameh went to the Ryder rental agency to rent the van that carried the bomb. Yousef placed the bombs he made using mainly chemicals such as nitroglycerin in four canisters in the basement parking lot of the World Trade Center on February 26, 1993. The explosion killed six, about 1,000 were injured, and the damage to property ran into millions of dollars. That evening Salameh drove Yousef and Ismail to John F. Kennedy Airport. Yousef escaped to Pakistan on falsified travel documents, but Mahamud Abouhalima and Muhammad Salameh and Alah Jobrony were arrested. Yousef arrived in Pakistan and lived in his home in Quetta and an Al Qaeda safe house in Peshawar. There—together with Abdul Hakim Murad and Abdul Shakar, both from Kuwait—Yousef planned to assassinate Benazir Bhutto, who was then running for election as prime minister, but the bomb exploded prematurely and injured Yousef's left eye.

With Murad's help, Yousef returned to the Philippines in 1994. This time Yousef planned something big—code-named Opan Bojinka—reportedly in retaliation for the arrests of his co-conspirators in the World Trade Center bombing. Yousef, Murad, and Wali Amin Shah rented an apartment in Manila and made several plans: to assassinate Pope John Paul II and President Clinton during their visit to Manila, to assassinate President Fidel V.

Ramos, two senior government officials, several foreign ambassadors to the Philippines, other diplomats, military and police officials; to bomb commercial centers, department stores, the U.S. embassy, an international school, Catholic churches, and vital government installations; to kidnap prominent personalities for ransom, hold up banks and financial institutions, and rob commercial establishments such as department stores; to assassinate U.S. and Israeli nationals; and most important of all, to bomb eleven U.S. passenger aircraft flying over the Asia-Pacific region.

The audacious plan involved five operatives planning to bomb eleven aircraft, all belonging to American Airlines. One of the operatives, Mirqas, was to plant a bomb on a United Airlines flight from Manila to San Francisco, timed to explode in midair after it departed Seoul. Mirqas was to go to Seoul to plant another bomb on a Delta flight from Seoul to Taipei, timing the bomb to explode en route to Bangkok. Another operative, Markoa, was to plant a bomb on a Northwest flight from Manila to Chicago through Tokyo, where Markoa was to get out to plant a bomb in another Northwest flight from Tokyo to New York through Hong Kong. Both the bombs were to be timed to go off over the Pacific Ocean. Markoa, who was to disembark at Hong Kong, was to plant another bomb, set to explode a day later over the Pacific Ocean.

The operative, Obald, was to plant a bomb on another Northwest flight from Singapore to Los Angeles through Hong Kong, where Obald was to board a United flight from Hong Kong to Singapore and plant a bomb that was to explode on its return flight to Hong Kong. On another United flight from Taipei to Los Angeles through Tokyo, Malbos was to plant the bomb, then get out at Tokyo and board and plant another bomb on a United flight, timing it to explode twenty-four hours later as the plane was to fly from Tokyo to New York. Zyod was to plant a bomb on a United flight from Bangkok to Los Angeles through Tokyo, where he was to get out and plant another bomb, fly to Taipei, and place a bomb on a United flight to the United States.

The airline bombings were to use a virtually undetectable bomb that Ramzi had created converting Casio digital watches into timing switches that use lightbulb filaments to ignite cotton soaked in nitroglycerine explosive.

Yousef carried out a practice run on a Philippine Airlines flight 434 bound for Tokyo on December 9, 1994. A contact lens wearer, Yousef concealed the nitroglycerin compound in a bottle normally used to hold saline solution, left it taped under a seat, and disembarked in Cebu. The explosion blew a hole in the fuselage and killed one Japanese while eleven others were injured. The pilot safely descended the aircraft at Okinawa Airport.

The bombing in rapid succession would have caused untold deaths involving nationalities from all over the world, had it not been for a sudden accident in the flat where Yousef was staying: a fire broke out and Yousef was forced to escape. Police raided the apartment and seized the laptop computer left behind by Yousef (it survived the fire along with explosives); a map of the Pope's route, clerical robes, and a computer disk describing the plot against the Pope; as well as planned attacks against U.S. airlines. Yousef's fingerprints were on the material. The FBI decoded the complex data from the computer, which led to the arrest of Yousef, whose capture provided details of his plans..

Yousef, however, had escaped to Peshawar after ditching his Manila girlfriend Carol Santiago. For most of the three years before his capture in early 1995, Yousef reportedly resided at the bin Laden–financed Beit Ashuhada (House of Martyrs) guest house in Peshawar, Pakistan, and plotted to bomb the U.S. embassy in Bangkok as well as involve himself in the bombing of a Shia mosque in Iran.

On February 8, 1995, Yousef was picked up from the Su Casa guesthouse (also owned by a member of the bin Laden family) in Islamabad by the Pakistani authorities, who were tipped off by a former accomplice. He was arrested and extradited to the United States to face charges relating to the 1993 World Trade Center attack and his plans to destroy an American aircraft. Yousef had in his possession the outline of an even greater international terrorist campaign that he was planning, as well as bomb-making products, including two toy cars packed with explosives and flight schedules for United and Delta Airlines. His plans included using a suicide pilot to crash a light aircraft filled with powerful explosives into the CIA headquarters in Langley, Virginia, as well as blowing up eleven U.S. airliners simultaneously as they approached U.S. airports. Also found in his room was a letter threatening Filipino interests if comrades held in custody were not released. It claimed the "ability to make and use chemicals and poisonous gas . . . for use against vital institutions and residential populations and the sources of drinking water." On June 21, 1995,

Yousef told federal agents that he had planned and executed the World Trade Center bombing. On January 8, 1998, he was sentenced to 240 years in prison. He has remained incarcerated in the new "supermax" prison in Florence, Colorado.

# FARC—Fuerzas Armadas Revolucionarias de Colombia (Revolutionary Armed Forces of Colombia)

### Pedro Antonio Marín
**Position:** FARC founder and commander in chief

    **Significance:** Since its inception in May 1966, the FARC has operated under the leadership of Pedro Antonio Marín

    **Aliases:** Manuel Marulanda Vélez or Tirofijo ("Sure-Shot")

    **Date and Place of Birth:** May 1930 (according to Marín), or May 12/13, 1928 (according to his father), in Génova (a coffee-growing region in west-central Colombia), making him the world's oldest guerrilla leader

    **Description:** Five feet tall

    **Background:** Marín is the oldest of five brothers of a peasant family. His formal education consisted of only four years of elementary school, after which he began a series of jobs that included cutting wood and selling candy. His family supported the left-wing Liberal Party. When a civil war erupted in 1948 following the assassination of Liberal president Eliecer Gaitan, Marín and a few cousins took to the mountains to become guerrillas for the Liberal Party. Marín later fought with "peasant defense groups" and in 1964 became one of the founders of FARC. On becoming a guerrilla, Marín adopted the pseudonym or nomme de guerre of Manuel Marulanda Vélez in tribute to a trade unionist who died while opposing the dispatch of Colombian troops to the Korean War, but he is also known by other aliases.

    It is not known whether he ever married, but there are reports of numerous offspring from various women. According to journalist María Jimena Duzán, "Marulanda" lives simply, like a peasant, although he does smoke cigarettes.

    **Leadership:** Marulanda Vélez has been officially pronounced dead several times in army communiqués, but has always reappeared alive and active in guerrilla/terrorist actions.

He is described as a charismatic and determined guerrilla leader who has been personally involved in combat, inspiring confidence among his followers. He achieved the top leadership position after the death of Jacobo Arenas from a heart attack in 1990. He is reported to be a member of the Central Committee of the Communist Party of Colombia (Partido Comunista de Colombia—PCC), historically associated with FARC. Marulanda has been described as very astute with a great capacity for command and organization, and his peasant origins and his innate sense of military strategy have earned him nationwide recognition as a leader among politicians, leftists, and other guerrilla groups, although critics accuse him of putting his own quest for power above the needs of Colombia's poor. Marulanda represents the historical and agrarian line of FARC, which dreams of a rural utopian society and which "fears" the globalized world, even though FARC has its own Web page and releases communiqués through the Internet.

After helping Conservative Party presidential candidate Andres Pastrana win election in 1998 by implying that Pastrana endorsed Marulanda's peace plans, Marulanda persuaded Pastrana to grant FARC a safe haven the size of Switzerland in southern Colombia. Marulanda failed to make any concessions to the government in return and used the safe haven to expand FARC's reach into the lucrative drug industry. Operating in nearly half of Colombia, its 15,000-strong army continues to attack civilian, political, military, and economic targets rurally as well as in cities, towns, and military outposts.

### Jorge Briceño Suárez

**Position:** Second in command of the FARC; commander, Eastern Bloc of the FARC; member, FARC General Secretariat since April 1993

**Aliases:** Mono Jojoy

**Date and Place of Birth:** 1949, Duda region, Colombia

**Description:** Jovial-looking, heavily built, with a handlebar moustache; usually wears a simple green camouflage uniform with black beret

**Background:** His father was the legendary guerrilla Juan de la Cruz Varela, and his mother was a peasant woman, Romelia Suárez. He is known to have one brother, Germán Briceño Suárez "Grannobles," who later became a FARC front commander before being caught and charged in 1999. Briceño is reportedly a high school dropout and has spent his entire life as a guerrilla, where he grew up and learned to read and write within the FARC under the mentoring of Manuel Marulanda Vélez (nee Pedro Antonio Marín).

Briceño is another of the new second-generation FARC military chiefs who was born in the FARC. Both he and "Eliécer" created the FARC's highly effective school for "special attack tactics," which trains units to strike the enemy without suffering major casualties. He later decided that this limited the FARC's effectiveness, because the most it could muster were harassment attacks. Since then he appears willing to accept limited casualties in order to maximize pain and political leverage on the government, and has thus been known to mass several hundred guerrillas to attain decisive results at a time and place of his choosing. Mono Jojoy is credited with introducing specialized commando units by taking the best men from each front and assigning them high-risk missions.

Briceño is one of the most respected guerrilla leaders within FARC ranks, becoming second in command when Marulanda succeeded Jocobo Arenas in 1990, and now considered to be the FARC's chief military strategist. Some believe that due to his life as a guerilla/terrorist, he knows no other way of life and thus is most resistant/opposed to the peace process. Unlike most other university-educated FARC commanders, he rose through the ranks and learned everything about guerrilla warfare in the field. He easily moves among the departments of Boyacá, Cundinamarca, and Meta. He is said to know the Sumapaz region "like the palm of his hand." He is known as a courageous leader, with little emotion. His great military experience helps to compensate for his alleged low intellectual level. He is said to be unscrupulous and to advocate any form of warfare in pursuit of power, including using negotiations or peace processes to stall for time to regroup and rearm.

Under his command the Eastern Bloc has earned record amounts of cocaine-trafficking profits. In 1992, he arranged a large shipment of Soviet and Israeli-made weapons for the FARC from Central America, and he may have received advisers and/or training there as well, accounting for his ensuing battlefield successes circa 1996. He personally led the attack on Miraflores in August 1998. He is opposed to extradition of Colombians, including his brother, a FARC hard-liner who was charged on July

21, 1999, in the slayings of three U.S. Indian rights activists. He is contemptuous of the prospect of U.S. military intervention, stating that U.S. soldiers would not last three days in the jungle, but welcomes the idea of U.S. economic assistance to rural development projects, such as bridge building.

# HAMAS—"Zeal"/"Enthusiasm"/"Islamic Resistance Movement"

### Sheikh Ahmed Yassin

**Position:** Hamas founder and spiritual leader

**Date and Place of Birth:** 1937 or 1938, near Ashqelan (in the south of what was then Palestine under the British mandate). Sheik Ahmed Yassin was killed on March 22, 2004, after three missiles fired from an Israeli helicopter exploded outside the Gaza mosque that he had left minutes earlier after the Fajr prayer.

**Description:** Wheelchair-bound quadriplegic, blind and virtually deaf

**Background:** Ahmed Yassin lived as a refugee in the Shati camp in Gaza following the Israeli occupation in 1948. As with many others, his political motivation and aims derived from his growing up in an environment of inequality, discrimination, humiliation, and defeat for Palestinians. As a result of an accident in 1952, he became a quadriplegic and was confined to a wheelchair. His involvement with the Islamic fundamentalist Muslim Brotherhood organization began in the 1950s. After attending school in Gaza he worked as a teacher and preacher from 1958 to 1978. In 1973 Yassin founded the Islamic Center in Gaza. He studied Islam in Cairo at Al-Azhar University, where the Muslim Brotherhood originated. It was at this time that he adopted the view that Palestine was an Islamic land "consecrated for future Muslim generations until Judgment Day," and that no Arab leader had the right to give up any part of this territory. Inspired by the Islamic revolution in Iran in 1979, he set up and directed an Islamic Society in Gaza (Mujamma).

In 1984 he was jailed for ten months for security reasons and so had to relinquish his post as director of Mujamma. Up until the first Palestinian Intifada of 1987 (against Israeli occupation), Yassin had organized welfare and educational services through the Palestinian branch of the Muslim Brotherhood. In the same year he formed Hamas, which means "zeal" or "enthusiasm," and became the spiritual leader of the grassroots Palestinian organization. The military wing of Hamas, Izzedine al-Quassam, has been responsible for multiple attacks and suicide bombings against Israel. Hamas was against previous agreements between "Palestine" and Israel, and the following year it published a statement asserting that Israel was the enemy of Islam and as such, any actions against Israel were a religious duty. In May 1989, Yassin was arrested by the Israelis and sentenced to life imprisonment for ordering Hamas members to kidnap and kill two Palestinians alleged to have worked with the Israeli army. His popularity and importance as a symbol of resistance against Israeli oppression grew while he was in prison; however, Yasser Arafat remained more important and popular.

In October 1997, under a deal facilitated by the late King Hussein of Jordan, Yassin was released in exchange for the release of two Israeli Mossad agents arrested in Jordan after a failed assassination attempt against a Hamas leader there. On his release, Yassin returned to Gaza. Although Arafat was widely regarded as Yassin's rival, Yassin believed that the Palestinian leadership needed to be united, and so he started building relations with the Palestinian Authority and other Arab regimes. In 1998 he visited Saudi Arabia, Qatar, Iran, Yemen, Syria, Kuwait, Sudan, and the United Arab Republic to improve relations and procure funds. Saudi Arabia and Iran are believed to have donated between $50 million and $300 million for Hamas's military operations against Israel. He also received medical treatment in Egypt due to his deteriorating health, after which he returned to Gaza.

Yassin continued to hold substantial influence over Palestinians, disillusioned with peace process attempts that did nothing to improve their lives. He advocated violent activities, stating that the peace process did not constitute peace and was thus not a substitute for jihad and resistance. He advocated and inspired suicide-bombing as a tactic, stating that suicide bombers would achieve martyrdom. Attempts to reign in Yassin's activities had been violently resisted by his supporters, who responded with clashes with police and sustained suicide-bombing campaigns against Israel. Yassin led Hamas in building support by offering material help to Palestinians suffering from economic hardship and established charitable funds to establish schools, clinics, and hospitals that provide free services to families in distress. Such activities have attracted millions of dollars from the Persian Gulf area and around the world, as well as portraying a humanitarian dimension to a terrorist organization, and have done much to increase the credibility and legitimacy of their cause both locally and internationally. Yassin justified the use of violence through the concept of self-defense (including defending dignity and pride [Juergensmeyer 2001]) based on an interpretation of the Koran.

# LTTE—Liberation Tigers of Tamil Eelam (Tamil Tigers)

### Velupillai Prabhakaran

**Position:** LTTE leader

**Significance:** Mastermind of operations and campaigns and figurehead of resistance of "oppression of Tamil cause"

**Date and Place of Birth:** November 26, 1954, Velvettithurai, Sri Lanka (on the Jaffna Peninsula)

**Description:** Described as being of portly build, with black hair and moustache. He would only dress in military fatigues until the recent peace-process attempts, for which he adopted a more media-friendly attire of suit, shirt, and tie.

**Background:** Vellupillai Prabhakaran was the youngest child in his family (he has three older siblings) and is said to have been shy and introverted as a child. Although he did not excel at his studies, he developed an interest in reading as well as martial arts later on. His political motivation and aims for an independent Tamil homeland are believed to derive from his teenage years, where it is said that he was angered by inequalities and discrimination against Tamils in politics, employment, and education, and so began attending political meetings and became more politically active. From these early political beginnings he became instrumental in the foundation of the Tamil Tigers.

It is alleged that during some of his rare interviews, he listed his influences and heroes as including Napoleon, Alexander the Great, the Indian leaders Subhash Chandra Bose and Bhagat Singh (who were involved in the armed struggle for independence from Britain), and actor Clint Eastwood. He is married to Mathivathani Erambu, with at least one son and one daughter.

To pro-Tamils, Prabhakaran is a freedom fighter struggling for emancipation from Sinhalese oppression. To his rivals and enemies he is a terrorist megalomaniac with a brutal disregard for human life and property.

Obsessed by security, Prabhakaran rarely gives interviews and keeps his movements between jungle hideouts under the strictest secrecy after having narrowly avoided assassination and capture attempts several times. The many attempts at capture and assassination have caused him to become somewhat paranoid, and as a result he has murdered many of his trusted commanders for suspected treason. He is seldom seen in public except before battles or to host farewell banquets for any of the Black (suicide) Tiger divisions setting off on their missions. He wears a cyanide capsule around his neck, to be swallowed in the event of his capture. It is rumored that Tiger soldiers are expected to do the same. Prabhakaran has also been described as a military genius and charismatic leader, inspiring fanatical devotion from his "Tigers." He has a reputation for being fearless and ruthless, and under his command, the LTTE has become a highly disciplined and highly motivated terrorist group to be reckoned with. The LTTE operates substantial international networks and shows no sign of being defeated militarily by the Sri Lankan army, which arguably led to the recent peace-process attempts. Prabhakaran has repeatedly warned the Western nations providing military support to Sri Lanka that they are exposing their citizens to possible attacks.

Prabhakaran became heavily involved in the Tamil movement beginning in the 1970s. He was accused of being responsible for the murder of the mayor of Jaffna in 1975 (Prabhakaran remains the prime suspect), which was one of the first killings carried out by the Tamil movement. In Tamil Nadu, Prabhakaran gained the reputation and status of a folk hero due to his exploits, and he gradually assumed control of the Tamil uprising. In 1983 he married; since then, Tigers have been allowed to wed after five years of combat.

Prabhakaran is wanted on suspicion of involvement in a number of high-profile crimes. He has been accused by India of playing a key role in the murder of the former prime minister, Rajiv Gandhi, in 1991. The Indians allege that Gandhi was killed by a suicide bomber acting under direct orders from Prabhakaran in response to Ghandi's decision in the mid-1980s to deploy Indian peacekeeping troops in Sri Lanka. In 1998, warrants were issued for the arrest of Prabhakaran, LTTE military leader Pottu Amman, and eight others in connection with the killing of seventy-eight people and destroying the Central Bank Building by a bomb explosion in 1996, as well as other criminal acts between 1995 and 1996.

The success of the LTTE tactics and operations (such as the storming of Colombo airport), as well as the ineffectiveness of Sri Lankan counterefforts, causing a stalemate for so long, is believed to have been the key factor behind the recent attempts at a peace process. Due to Prabhakaran's strong leadership and influence it is believed that no attempts at peace will work unless they have his approval. The negotiations for a peace process broke down in early-mid 2003.

# Provisional Irish Republican Army (PIRA)

### Gerry Adams

**Position:** Head of Sinn Fein (elected political party member), alleged member of the PIRA Council

**Significance:** An alleged former active terrorist and now alleged member of the leadership of the terrorist group PIRA, while at the same time being an elected politician

**Date and Place of Birth:** October 6, 1948, West Belfast, Northern Ireland

**Description:** Dark hair with full beard, large square glasses. Average build.

**Background:** The oldest of ten children in a strongly republican family growing up in the working-class area of West Belfast (Ballymurphy estate), where he still lives with his wife and son.

Adams was interned by the British government in 1971 but was considered important enough to the republican movement, even at the young age of twenty-four, to be released in July 1972 to join the IRA delegation to take part in secret talks in London with then secretary of state William Whitelaw.

In security circles he is thought to have held senior positions in *all* branches of the republican movement, including the IRA, and apparently is believed by British intelligence sources to be the Belfast PIRA commander, graduating as one of the three-man group running PIRA after the arrest of Sean MacStiofain in 1973. He has never been convicted of membership in PIRA, however, and denies ever being in the IRA, though many believe it would have been extremely difficult for him to have risen to the position he now holds if that were not the case. It is rumored that he is responsible for many deaths in Northern Ireland and the United Kingdom throughout his alleged career as a terrorist, terrorist commander, and leader. Along with his close colleague, Martin McGuinness, he has been the key strategist in developing the political strategy of the republican movement: moving republicans from bullet to ballot box, having stated in 1979 that victory could not be achieved solely by military means—a concept the hunger strikes of the early 1980s helped to reinforce after the sympathy and electoral gains that ensued. Adams appears committed to the pursuit of a United Ireland through peaceful means, having recognized that an armed conflict will not produce the results republicans want. The main reason Adams and McGuiness allegedly maintain such close control over PIRA is that they need to avoid a split in the republican movement in order to have a strong negotiating position with the U.K. government. It is thought that Adams leaves the day-to-day, week-to-week running of PIRA to other figures such as Brian Keenan in order to concentrate on political matters, and only interjects on strategic matters.

In 1983 he was elected MP (Member of Parliament) as well as president of Sinn Fein, and was apparently more able to steer PIRA and Sinn Fein in the directions he wanted, and abandoned their policy of abstention from the Irish parliament. In 1984 he was shot and wounded when loyalist gunmen opened fire on his car in Belfast. His leadership was strongly challenged by Ruairi O'Bradaigh at the 1986 Sinn Fein Ard Fheis, which led to the formation of Republican Sinn Fein and the Continuity Irish Republican Army (CIRA). Adams began a series of contacts with John Hume, the SDLP leader, which later helped to form the basis of what became known as the peace process. At the same time the U.K. and Irish governments continued with intensive negotiations, which helped lead to the Downing Street Declaration in 1993, with the first IRA cease-fire in 1994. He was also challenged at the October 1997 General Army Convention by Mickey McKevitt, which led to the formation of the Real Irish Republican Army (RIRA) and the thirty-two-member County Sovereignty Movement (CSM). Since then, however, his leadership has been practically undisputed.

Cease-fires have often been used by terrorist groups as a stalling tactic in order to rearm and regroup. There are varying amounts of hope and doubt as to whether the current cease-fire is genuine, and the issue of decommissioning is one example that had run for years without a single weapon being placed "beyond use." Although there have been cease-fires and peace processes, PIRA has allegedly continued to operate, gather intelligence for targeting, commit punishment beatings, kill, maim, acquire funds and weapons, as well as network with other terrorist organizations and train them in tactics that cause maximum casualties, under the alleged leadership of Gerry Adams.

There is speculation that Adams has internal management problems regarding preventing further splits by disillusioned members joining dissident groups. If Adams can prevent further splits/defections while engaging the political institutions involved in the peace process, then some believe peace is possible. However, further defections are likely, as are coordination and links between dissident groups such as CIRA and RIRA, thus posing a real future threat.

## Countering the Leadership

Terrorist leadership consists of core and penultimate leaders. They formulate the ideology, develop concepts, delineate strategies, decide on the tactics, and direct the organization. Often terrorist campaigns continue for decades because the leadership recruits fresh members and generates support to replace the members killed or captured and the weapons and munitions wasted. Despite the high fatalities and casualties among the terrorists, terrorist groups have survived because the targeting has been at the membership and not the leadership.

Often the membership is expendable but not the leadership. The capture of Abimael Guzman, the founder/leader of Sendero Luminoso; Rohan Wijeweera, the founder/leader of the Janatha Vimukthi Peramuna; and Abdullah Ocalan, the founder/leader of the Kurdish Workers Party seriously weakens their groups. Similarly, after Shoko Asahara was captured, Aum Shinrikyo's new leader Fumihiro Joyu rejected the violent and apocalyptic teachings of its founder. After the arrest of Fusako Shigenobu, the leader of the Japanese Red Army, in November 2000, she announced her intention to abandon violence and pursue democratic politics. On April 4, 2002, shortly after the death of its leader Jonas Savimbi, the National Union for the Total Independence of Angola (UNITA) signed a cease-fire agreement with the government of Angola. Therefore, it is paramount to target the terrorist leadership—Osama bin Laden in the case of Al Qaeda, Prachanda and Bhattrai in the case of the Nepali Maoists, and Manuel Marulanda in the case of FARC. However, there are limitations to destroying or weakening a terrorist group by targeting the leadership. Although the Palestinian Islamic Jihad nearly suffered total collapse after MOSSAD operatives in Malta assassinated its leader, Shiqaqi, the conditions in Palestine led to the reemergence of the group under the leadership of Ramadan Shallah. Similarly, the new leader of the terrorist group can be much more effective, deadly, and unpredictable than the known assassinated leader. As an example, the assassination of Al Qaeda founder/leader Abdullah Azzam in Peshawar, Pakistan, by Egyptian terrorists created the conditions for Osama bin Laden to assume the mantle of Al Qaeda leadership. Especially if the group has widespread appeal and the support base is large, targeting the leadership is unlikely to be an effective strategy. Therefore, targeting the leadership will be effective when the group is at the formative phase. Nonetheless, targeting the leadership even at the mature phase of the campaign can break the momentum of the terrorist campaign and create opportunities for weakening the group's influence on the wider support base.

In general, a better tactic (in terms of being more manageable and more effective) is to target the "middle management" of the terrorist group. By taking out this level one separates the influential, charismatic leadership from the foot soldiers. Such a strategy will considerably weaken any of the larger groups, as most intelligence and expertise on operational and support structures and practices are held in the middle-management level.

The capture of a terrorist leader is preferred to the assassination of a terrorist leader. Upon capture, most leaders portray a poor image of themselves. With the elite forces of Turkey and Sri Lanka capturing Ocalan, the PKK leader, and Wijeweera, the JVP leader, they pleaded not to be tortured. Like the execution of a terrorist leader, the assassination of a terrorist leader inevitably elevates the dead leader to the rank of a martyr. Thereafter, the dead leader's ideals are likely to be the inspiration for a new generation of committed terrorists. However, there is a danger that a terrorist group will engage in hostage taking and kidnappings to seek the release of their imprisoned leaders. For instance, the Abu Sayaaf Group kidnapped a number of Americans in the Philippines and in Malaysia to seek the release of Ramzi Ahmed Yousef (the World Trade Center bomber of 1993) and Sheikh Omar Abdel Rahman (the leader of the New York landmarks bomb plot of 1995). Similarly, Ahmed Saeed Omar Sheikh of Harakat-ul Mujahedin kidnapped three Britons, one Norwegian, and one American in New Delhi, India, in 1994 to seek the release of Maulana Masood Azhar. When the Indian government did not respond positively, the group kidnapped five Western tourists and killed four of them in Kashmir in 1995. Finally, Harakat-ul Mujahedin secured the release of its leaders in Indian custody by hijacking an Indian airliner with 155 passengers and crew in 1999. One tactic to preempt and prevent this is to discredit or disgrace the leader, such as through publicly stating that the leader told the authorities *everything* or broke down and repented or realized that the aims (and activities) of the group are wrong and they should stop. This dampens the morale of the group as well as affecting support. The important thing is to ensure that the leader does not become a martyr, legend, or folk hero, as this strengthens the resolve of the group and encourages others to join. This is why a captured and discredited leader is better than a dead one, especially as the potential intelligence gleaned from such a person if he or she cooperates is of extreme value. Another tactic is to develop and strengthen the international court that has the authority to try and sentence such persons. An imperative aspect here is that the court must be seen to be fair and not a satellite for any superpower in order to minimize any backlash from the terrorist group/supporters.

As mentioned earlier, while the leaders provide the broad framework for action, the middle-level cadres or experts plan, prepare, and execute operations. Therefore, in the counterterrorist agenda, targeting the penultimate leaders or the middle-level cadres is equally important. After identifying potential recruits, the experienced middle-level cadres indoctrinate and train them to become full-fledged terrorist operatives. Acting as coordinating officers or agent-handlers, the middle-level cadres provide tactical direction. For instance, the losses of Al Qaeda military commander Muhammed Atef and head of external operations Abu Zubaidah have been major blows to the organization. Similarly, with the Shin Bet assassination of Yahiya Ayyash, "the Engineer," Hamas suffered the loss of its most experienced bomb maker. However, dependent on the availability of human and material resources, terrorist groups adapt to the changing circumstances and recover. For instance, Ayyash's death made Hamas aware of the risk of providing training in bomb-making only to a few, and provoked the group to retaliate. Hamas thus trained an unprecedented number of Palestinian terrorists in bomb-making and dispersed them throughout the West Bank and the Gaza Strip to counter or prevent such a problem from recurring.

# Profiles of Counterterrorism Leaders

An apparent problem in counterterrorism is that counterterrorist leaders are often restricted by chains of command, the law, bureaucracy, "red tape," accountability, budgets, and so on, whereas terrorist leaders are not.

## Department of Homeland Security— http://www.dhs.gov

### Tom Ridge—http://www.dhs.gov/dhspublic/
**Significance:** Secretary/leader
   **Background:** Born Aug. 26, 1945, in Pittsburgh's Steel Valley, Tom Ridge was raised in a working-class family in veterans' public housing in Erie. He earned a scholarship to Harvard, graduating with honors in 1967. After his first year at the Dickinson School of Law, he was drafted into the U.S. Army, where he served as an infantry staff sergeant in Vietnam, earning the Bronze Star for Valor. After returning to Pennsylvania, he earned his law degree and was in private practice before becoming assistant district attorney in Erie County. He was elected to Congress in 1982. He was the first enlisted Vietnam combat veteran elected to the U.S. House and was overwhelmingly reelected six times. He and his wife, Michele, the former executive director of the Erie County Library system, have two children, Lesley and Tommy.
   **Career:** Ridge was twice elected governor of Pennsylvania, serving from 1995 to 2001. He kept his promise to make Pennsylvania "a leader among states and a competitor among nations." His aggressive technology strategy helped fuel the state's ad-

vances in the priority areas of economic development, education, health, and the environment. He cut taxes every year he was in office. To ensure Pennsylvania was home to the jobs of the future, he also created industry-led Greenhouse initiatives in advanced computing technologies and the life sciences. He signed into law the Education Empowerment Act, to help more than a quarter-million children in Pennsylvania's lowest-performing schools. His education technology initiatives brought "anytime, anywhere" learning to Pennsylvanians from preschool to adult education. During his years in the governor's office the number of children receiving free or low-cost health care through Pennsylvania's nationally recognized Children's Health Insurance Program increased by 145 percent. His common-sense Land Recycling Program is a national model. He won passage of "Growing Greener" to make Pennsylvania's largest environmental investment ever, nearly $650 million.

**Current:** On January 24, 2003, Tom Ridge became the first secretary of the Department of Homeland Security. He now works with more than 180,000 employees from combined agencies to strengthen U.S. borders, provide for intelligence analysis and infrastructure protection, improve the use of science and technology to counter weapons of mass destruction, and create a comprehensive response and recovery division.

Tom Ridge was given his initial assignment by President George W. Bush in October 2001, just weeks after 9/11. The charge to the nation's new director of homeland defense was to develop and coordinate a comprehensive national strategy to strengthen the United States against terrorist threats or attacks. In the words of President Bush, Ridge has the strength, experience, personal commitment, and authority to accomplish this critical mission.

## State Department Counterterrorism Office— http://www.state.gov

**J. Cofer Black—http://www.state.gov/r/pa/ei/biog/15367.htm**
**Significance:** Coordinator, Office of the Coordinator for Counterterrorism

**Background:** Black was born in Stamford, Connecticut, and received his bachelor's and master's degrees in international relations from the University of Southern California.

**Career:** Black has had a distinguished 28-year career in the Directorate of Operations at the Central Intelligence Agency. Prior to joining the State Department, he was the director of the CIA Counterterrorist Center. In this capacity he served as the CIA director's special assistant for counterterrorism as well as the national intelligence officer for counterterrorism.

During his CIA career, Black served six foreign tours in field management positions. In 1995 he was named the Task Force Chief in the Near East and South Asia Division. From June 1998 through June 1999 he served as the deputy chief of the Latin America Division.

In addition to numerous exceptional performance awards and meritorious citations, Black received the Distinguished Intelligence Medal, the George H. Bush Medal for Excellence, and the Exceptional Collector Award for 1994.

**Current:** J. Cofer Black was sworn in on December 3, 2002, as the State Department Coordinator for Counterterrorism with the rank of ambassador at large. The State Department is the lead federal agency dealing with international terrorism, and Ambassador Black's office, S/CT, has primary responsibility for developing, coordinating, and implementing U.S. counterterrorism policy. On behalf of the secretary of state, Ambassador Black represents the department on the Counterterrorism Security Group. His office plays a leading role on the Department of State's counterterrorism task forces, organized to coordinate responses to international terrorist incidents. Among Black's responsibilities are coordinating U.S. government efforts to improve counterterrorism cooperation with foreign governments, including the policy and planning of the department's Anti-Terrorism Training Assistance Program.

# Group Profiles

An apparent problem in counterterrorism is that terrorist groups often have more funds than the agencies that work against them and sometimes even the states they operate in. Furthermore, many groups are so sophisticated, with structures and networks spanning across the world, that it becomes almost impossible for national agencies to counter them without help and coordinated efforts internationally. A comprehensive analysis of terrorist groups is necessary to challenge this threat.

# FARC—Fuerzas Armadas Revolucionarias de Colombia (Revolutionary Armed Forces of Colombia)

**Symbols:** Shield (white or black) with region placed on Colombian flag, upon which is placed the name FARC-EP (EP stands for "peoples army") and two crossed rifles

**History/Development:** Established in 1964 as the military wing of the Colombian Communist Party (original aims of land reform), the FARC is Colombia's oldest, largest, most capable, and best-equipped Marxist-Leninist insurgency.

The FARC-EP developed its "war of resistance in an uninterrupted manner" beginning on May 27, 1964, "when 48 patriots . . . took up arms in the municipality of Marquetalia (Tolima) against the aggression of the establishment, which the different governments have continued" (http://www.farcep.org).

**Aims:** "The construction of a new Colombia, without exploited or exploiters, in peace, with dignity and sovereignty and for the fundamental rights of the majority of Colombians" (http://www.farcep.org).

Other than self-determination, FARC has hidden its actual aims under an ideological struggle that is no longer credible. Following three years of peace talks (1998–2001) with former Colombian president Andres Pastrana, FARC obtained an area the size of Switzerland (42,139 square km) known as "Zona de Despeje" (demilitarized zone). FARC uses it as a sanctuary from which to launch operations, rest and refit its forces, move drugs and arms, and hold prisoners and hostages (Rabasa and Chalk 2001, 43). To make matters worse, the territory was ceded without enough controls, and now FARC uses it to arrange kidnappings, carry out summary executions, and sponsor coca plantations. After FARC started to charge war taxes to the drug producers, it was able to obtain enormous sums of money to buy weapons on the black market.

**Areas of Operation:** Colombia—extortion, kidnapping, logistics, drug trafficking, and "taxation." Venezuela, Panama, Ecuador, Peru, Brazil, and Paraguay—used for rest and recuperation, procurement, drug trafficking, extortion, and kidnapping. Mexico—for more than ten years FARC operated an office in Mexico City with the authorization of the Mexican government and the knowledge of the Colombian government. Marco León

Calarca, a member of FARC, directed the office. On April 12, 2002, the Mexican government closed the office. However, a line of investigation by Mexican authorities shows that FARC is still operating in Mexico, involved with hard-line left-wing students or "pseudo-students" at the National University of Mexico (UNAM), the FARP (Fuerzas Armadas Revolucionarias del Pueblo), and EPR (Ejercito Popular Revolucionario) guerrillas that operate in the states of Oaxaca and Guerrero (and who had presence in Mexico City). The real aims of these links remain unknown. There are two theories: to open drug corridors through the areas under EPR-FARP control, or to strengthen political support from left-wing radicals in Mexico to justify their activities (Becerra 2003).

In 2000, the Peruvian government launched investigations over allegations that a small group of Peruvian military officers sold a substantial quantity of small arms to FARC. Drug traffickers and producers had moved to remote regions of Colombia, and some of them had already crossed the porous Colombian borders and arrived in Ecuador as well as Peru. The northern part of Peru was the area where the Shining Path (Senderoso Luminoso) maintained its presence during its years of guerrilla activity. This area is well known for its poppy plantations, which had been used by the Shining Path to finance itself. It is possible that FARC is involved in heroin production and trafficking in that area.

Ecuador has become a strategic corridor for arms, ammunition, and explosives destined for FARC. Ecuador has weak control over its porous borders, turning them into passages for drug traffickers and terrorist groups. The regions of Nariño and Putumayo, Colombian departments bordering on Ecuador, are the main areas of drug production and are partially under FARC control. This "gray area" adjoining Ecuador is creating instability on both sides of the border. The incursion of FARC into Ecuadorian territory has already set off danger signals. FARC's sympathizers in northern Ecuador are launching a campaign supporting FARC, and the Revolutionary Armed Forces of Ecuador (FARE), a copycat group imitating FARC, has already emerged in the country. It is possible that the so-called FARE is formed by Ecuadorian criminals who use this name to spread fear across the region.

Paraguayan counternarcotics police in October 2000 arrested an individual believed to be representing FARC for possible involvement in a guns-for-cocaine ring between Paraguay and FARC. (Despite these successes, an ineffective judicial system and

pervasive corruption, which facilitate criminal activity supporting terrorist groups, have hampered counterterrorism efforts in
Paraguay.)

**External Support:** Cuba provides some medical care and political consultation. In the past, Hezbollah-run camps, arming and
training would-be groups, had the potential of becoming a major
destabilizing force on the continent. However, so far the only
group that Hezbollah has been known to have had a connection
with, albeit circumstantially, is FARC, and even this is uncertain.

Iran, a known supporter of Hezbollah, had planned to build
an enormous refrigeration complex in the heart of the FARC-controlled demilitarized zone in the jungles of Colombia. The initial
plan was for Iran to build a $3 million–$5 million beef processing
and refrigeration plant in the FARC stronghold of San Vicente del
Caguan. There were legitimate reasons for the Colombian government to approve the project. The Colombian government, in
need of direct foreign investment, used the project as a negotiating tool during difficult peace negotiations with FARC. However,
it turned out that the location of the plant was approximately 300
miles (480 km)—and on the other side of the Andes—from the
main Colombian ranching areas. The United States was worried
that the plant could, sooner or later, become a terrorist training facility, and the investment plan was soon exposed as an Iranian intelligence operation. The Iran Press Service revealed in December
2000 that the factory was a cover for the Iranian Ministry of Intelligence and Security and the Revolutionary Guards to give assistance to FARC. It is likely that Hezbollah cells would have been
involved in some way or other with this project. However, the
Colombian government canceled the project reportedly after
Iranian "project" officials refused to let their luggage be inspected
by Colombian Customs. There is speculation that U.S. pressure
on Colombia hastened the project's demise.

**Strength:** Approximately 8,000–12,000 armed combatants.
Further (unknown) number of supporters, mostly in rural areas.

**Organizational and Command Structure:** The FARC is governed by a secretariat, led by septuagenarian Manuel Marulanda,
a.k.a. "Tirofijo," and six others, including senior military commander Jorge Briceño, a.k.a. "Mono Jojoy" (see leader profiles).

The national command of the FARC-EP, elected in the National Guerrilla Conference, is the Central High Command, of
which the National Secretariat is part. This is composed of seven
members: commander in chief Manuel Marulanda Velez and

commanders Raúl Reyes, Alfonso Cano, Timoleón Jimenez, Iván Marquez, Jorge Briseño, and Efraín Guzmán.

The National Guerrilla Conference is the highest level of authority in FARC and defines the politics of the organization, while the "Statutes" define the organic and hierarchical structure of FARC. The group is organized along military lines and includes several urban fronts:

1. Squad: the basic unit, consisting of twelve combatants
2. Guerrilla: consists of two squads
3. Compañía (company): consists of two guerrillas
4. Column: consists of two or more companies
5. Front: consists of more than one column. The Central High Command (Estado Mayor Central) designates the highest command of each front
6. Block of fronts: consists of five or more fronts. It coordinates and unifies the activity of the fronts in a specific zone of the country. The Central High Command or its secretariat designates the High Command of each block, which coordinates the areas of the respective blocks.
7. The Central High Command is the superior organism of direction and command of the FARC-EP. Its agreements, orders, and decisions rule over the entire movements and all its members.

**Political Capability:** The political wing is the Patriotic Union (UP), a legal political party formed by FARC and the Colombian Communist Party (PCC), also called Aida ABELLA.

**Significant Events:** In 2000, FARC continued a slow-moving peace negotiation process with the Pastrana administration, which has gained FARC several concessions, including a demilitarized zone (Zona de Despeje) used as a venue for negotiations. FARC continues to reach out to government and nongovernment groups throughout the world and especially in Europe and Latin America through international representatives and attendance at regional conferences and meetings, such as the Sao Paulo Forum, in order to strengthen its status, support, and negotiating powers. Recently, a high-level Venezuelan military officer met clandestinely with FARC leader Marulanda in FARC-controlled territory in Colombia to negotiate a nonaggression agreement. It is possible that Venezuela is concerned about its border security with

Colombia. However, other concerns may include the fact that corrupt law enforcement and military officers have sold weapons to FARC. According to Colombian authorities, half of the weapons confiscated from FARC had Venezuelan army markings.

**Tactics:** Bombings, murder, kidnapping, extortion, and hijacking, as well as guerrilla and conventional military action. In March 1999, FARC executed three U.S. Indian rights activists on Venezuelan territory after it kidnapped them in Colombia. Foreign citizens often are targets of FARC kidnapping for ransom. The group has well-documented ties to narcotics traffickers, principally through the provision of armed protection. In early 2003, three U.S. agents were kidnapped by FARC and continue to be held hostage.

**Targets:** Colombian political, military, and economic targets. Foreign tourists and businessmen (especially U.S. citizens), usually for ransom. U.S. military personnel (declared as "legitimate targets" in October 2000 by FARC leaders in response to U.S. involvement). Colombian state/government personnel. Oil companies and workers, and coal companies (e.g., Drummond Inc.)

**Supply/Financing:** Taxation and other involvement in the drug trade, along with armed "protection" of the "narcotraficantes." Kidnap and Ransom ("K&R")—in a five-year period ending in March 2001, there were approximately 13,000 kidnappings, with an average individual ransom of $400,000. Internet sites with an international network of sales of calendars, music, and books as well as collection of donations. Growing belief of possible involvement in piracy of software, CDs, and DVDs.

**Annual Budget:** According to *The Economist* (April 19, 2001): "The best estimate of [FARC's] income from drugs, extortion and kidnapping is perhaps $250 millions to $300 millions a year." However, a better-placed source is that of Jeremy McDermott, who states that FARC makes "at least $300 million from the drug trade alone every year, added to which is their income from kidnapping and extortion, making them probably the richest insurgent group in the world" (http://news.bbc.co.uk/2/hi/americas/1746777.stm).

**Links/Associations:** There are increasing links with international drug trade and international organized crime (especially with Mexican drug cartels), and Colombia is increasingly seen as a haven for criminal activity. The Russian mafia supplies FARC with weapons, mainly AK-47s, and is believed to have participated in the shipment of 10,000 AK-47s to FARC in 1998 through former Peruvian intelligence director Vladimiro Montesinos. There is speculation of tenuous links in the past with Hezbollah and Iranian Intelligence, and known links between the ELN, EPL, and ARG (all Colombia); PIRA; ETA; Cuba; and the Japanese Red Army.

**State Response:** In 2000 the peace negotiation process led to several concessions, including the aforementioned demilitarized zone used as a venue for negotiations. Using additional resources available under "Plan Colombia," President Pastrana in 2000–2001 launched a major antidrug effort that features measures to curb expanding coca cultivation. He is also cooperating with the United States on other important bilateral counternarcotics initiatives, such as extradition. An elite antiterrorist unit, GAULA, was developed and is seen as an international model because it includes its own intelligence, lawyers, psychologists/counselors, hostage rescue team, and so on. Alvaro Uribe, Columbia's president since 2002, has created a network of informants who received excellent rewards. Uribe's government has received millions in military aid from the United States for counterinsurgency activities.

**Projected Activities:** FARC and ELN have stepped up their attacks on Colombia's economic infrastructure. This has soured the country's investment climate and complicated government efforts to promote economic recovery, following a major recession in 1999. Moreover, the insurgent violence has fueled the rapid growth of illegal paramilitary groups, which are increasingly vying with FARC and ELN for control over drug-growing zones and other strategic areas of rural Colombia. Like FARC, the paramilitaries rely heavily on narcotics revenue and have intensified their attacks against noncombatants in recent months. Paramilitary massacres and insurgent kidnappings are likely to increase as groups move to strengthen their financial positions and expand their areas of influence. Furthermore, government concessions to FARC and ELN over land and demilitarized zones serve to encourage other groups to follow similar paths. Recent examples are of right-wing paramilitary groups that continue to expanded their reach, most notably in southern Colombia's prime coca growing areas. In addition to massacring civilians in their attempts to erode FARC and ELN areas of influence, the groups also abducted seven national congressional representatives in December 2000, demanding negotiations with the government. After FARC insisted the "anti-drugs" aspects of Plan Colombia be dropped, the peace process was opposed by large sections of the population (including civilians, businesses, and paramilitary groups), and as a result a new president was elected for his hard-line attitude and rhetoric. FARC has since resumed attacks and activities, and the peace process has dissolved.

FARC thus poses an immediate and long-term threat on its own, but it also serves as a greater threat through its influence and effects on other potentially insurgent groups causing growing instability, spreading violence, and eroding the rule of law in Colombia, its neighbors, and in Central America.

## Liberation Tigers of Tamil Eelam (LTTE)

**Other Names/Aliases:** Tigers, Tamil Tigers, Tamil National Army, Liberating Tigers of Tamil Eelam, *Tami-er chi hoo* (Mandarin name, as known in China and Mandarin media sources, translated as "Tigers of Tamil")

**Symbols:** Central Tiger's head and paws emerging from a ring, with crossed rifles in the background.

**History/Development:** The Liberation Tigers of Tamil Eelam (LTTE) saw its origins in 1972 when Vellupillai Prabhakaran (see his profile earlier in this chapter) formed the "Tamil New Tigers" as a reaction against the perceived discrimination of Tamils in Sri Lanka. It drew its support from both economically deprived Tamil agricultural workers whose families lost their livelihood due to economic reforms in the late 1970s, as well as unemployed urban Tamil youth who faced economic and social discrimination stemming from the accession to power of a Singhalese-majority government in 1956. The persistent feeling of neglect of Tamil grievances by the Colombo authorities led to the formation of various Tamil militant groups. The LTTE, which assumed this name on May 5, 1976, from Prabhakaran's "Tamil New Tigers," emerged as the most prominent among them. The LTTE demanded the secession of the Tamil-dominated areas of north and east Sri Lanka and the formation of a sovereign political unit, the state of Tamil Eelam. Capitalizing on the politicization of the Tamil public by the Tamil United Liberation Front (TULF) and the existing support for independence, the LTTE launched an armed campaign in 1983. Since the widespread anti-Tamil riots in July 1983, the LTTE emerged as the most powerful Tamil group in Sri Lanka. Initially the group targeted Tamil political and administrative figures affiliated with the government. Subsequently it widened the target set to engage in large-scale open confrontation with Sri Lanka's military establishment. By eliminating co-ethnic competitors and successfully engaging the Sri Lankan armed forces, the LTTE prevented the government from gaining access to and control of the northeast provinces of the country. By 1987, the LTTE effectively ruled the northern peninsula—levying taxes, implementing its own policing, and providing civil services such as transport and education.

Following the Indo–Sri Lanka Accord in 1987, Indian peace-keeping forces were stationed in Sri Lanka from October 1987. After three months of uneasy peace, LTTE declared war on the Indian peacekeeping forces and was successful in checkmating a much larger, resourceful, and formally trained military. In 1990 LTTE agreed to peace talks with the government in Colombo, which resulted in the withdrawal of the Indian peacekeeping forces on March 24, 1990. Within three months, LTTE went back on the cease-fire, declared war against Colombo, killed about 400 surrendered policemen, and quickly regained control of the Jaffna peninsula and established a quasi-administration.

In 1987 the group formally adopted suicide tactics and staged a number of high-profile suicide attacks, assassinating India's ex–prime minister Rajiv Gandhi, Sri Lanka's navy commander Clancy Fernando, and Sri Lankan president Ranasinghe Premadasa. The LTTE also used suicide terrorism to destroy economic and religious targets, such as the Central Bank of Colombo in January 1996, the World Trade Center in October 1997, and Sri Lanka's holiest Buddhist shrine, the Temple of the Tooth, in January 1998.

The LTTE initially based its ideology on Marxist-Leninist teachings, which it followed up to the early 1980s. The basic objective was to establish a casteless Tamil society by armed struggle. The LTTE also sought to play up its attempts to preserve the cultural and ethnic identity of Tamils, with various organized cultural activities and celebrated festivals. With the failure of communism, the LTTE abandoned its Marxist image and in contemporary times is more of a strongly ethnonationalistic outfit.

This group is notorious for suicide bombings. It was involved in 168 suicide attacks during a period from 1980 to 2000. In the post-9/11 environment, the LTTE declared a cease-fire in December 2001 in order to avoid being blacklisted by more governments. Currently, peace talks are going on between the LTTE and the Sri Lankan government under Norway's mediation. The first round of talks ended in Thailand on September 18, 2002. Since the assassination of Rajiv Gandhi in May 1991, the group has been proscribed as a terrorist group by India since 1991 and the United States since 1997.

**Aims:** To create a separate Eelam (nation) for ethnic Tamils out of the northern and eastern parts of Sri Lanka. (However, the group claimed on September 18, 2002, that they would demand a separate Eelam only as a last resort.)

**Areas of Operation:** The LTTE controls most of the northern and eastern coastal areas of Sri Lanka but has conducted operations throughout the country. The LTTE headquarters is currently in Kilinochchi (northern Sri Lanka). For a brief period the LTTE shifted its operational headquarters from Sri Lanka to the Palk Straits in the Indian state of Tamil Nadu where Prabhakaran remained from 1984 to 1986. The group makes a point of not carrying out terrorist acts outside Sri Lanka (except for one case in India), as it does not want foreign governments to act against the Sri Lankan Tamil diaspora. The LTTE has established offices in fifty-four countries, with the largest and most important ones operating in the United Kingdom, Canada, and Australia.

**External Support:** One million Sri Lankan Tamils are spread throughout the world, especially in Western countries. Many of them give financial support. The LTTE is said to have offices and cells in at least fifty-four countries. About 80 percent of over forty Tamil newspapers in North Atlantic countries are either managed by the LTTE or its front companies. There were reports that different Indian administrations at the central, as well as the state level, have provided training and armaments to the Tamil rebels in the past. Its international wing, which operates from London and Paris, was instrumental in procuring a substantial quantity of sophisticated weaponry. Most of the finances for the purchase of arms and other political and military activities is raised through expatriate activists. The LTTE remains very active in Canada. There is considerable speculation that the fear of proscription post-9/11 has not prevented the group from continuing its activities in Canada. The Canadian government has not listed the group under amendments to its criminal code even though more obscure groups such as the Islamic Movement of Uzbekistan are listed. There is speculation that the group has strong ties to the Liberal Party of Canada and has been able to exert some influence. One of its fronts, the Tamil Chamber of Commerce, held a substantial convention in Toronto in the summer of 2002. Paul

Martin, a former finance minister and prime minister, attended a LTTE fund-raising dinner in Canada.

**Strength:** LTTE has developed into a formidable fighting force with air, land, and sea capabilities. The group's armed wings also possess heavy weaponry, including artillery, surface-to-air missiles, and rocket launchers. The group uses both conventional and unconventional tactics, with few qualms about engaging and hurting civilians. However, such actions are deliberate—to serve some purpose or objective—and are not due to breakdown in discipline. Jane's Terrorism Intelligence Center, a center maintained by the Jane's Group of Publications, has estimated the strength of the LTTE at 15,000 and the Sea Tigers (the LTTE naval unit, usually suicide bombers tasked with using explosive-laden speedboats) to be between 3,000 and 4,000. The LTTE cadres wear uniforms with unique patterns of jungle camouflage resembling tiger stripes, which also act to identify the individual's affiliation ("The LTTE's Ideology").

Cadre members are highly disciplined and trained with a strict LTTE code. Upon completion of the basic military training and acceptance into the LTTE ranks, all cadres are given a cyanide capsule, to be consumed upon capture or in the event of mission failure. Cadres are trained to obey orders from their leaders unquestioningly. Severe and brutal punishments are meted out for crimes such as negligence, cowardice, and disobedience. Torture and execution by painful deaths are not uncommon. It is regarded as disgraceful if cadres are captured by Sri Lankan forces or should missions fail, and suicide is the only alternative. The LTTE code requires cadres to abstain from premarital sex, which is punishable by death. Cadres are allowed to marry after a five-year period of service to the LTTE. Suicide bombers are venerated and treated with great honor. This cadre consists of highly motivated men and women who turn themselves into human bombs by strapping explosives onto their bodies. Upon the death of a suicide attacker in performing his mission, his photograph and name are displayed in the LTTE headquarters as examples for future cadre. The group is also known to recruit underage children to fight—boys and girls sometimes as young as twelve years old.

All LTTE fighters undergo a program of rigorous training. A typical training schedule includes the handling of weapons, battle and field craft, communications, intelligence gathering, as well as an exhaustive physical regimen and rigorous indoctrination. Recruits are given little free time to idle or rest during their training phase.

A typical suicide bomber would go through about two years of training, including rehearsal training with dummy targets (goats and dogs). Prior to the actual operation, LTTE surveillance elements gather detailed and minute information of the target well beforehand. Surveillance operations take place with the LTTE scouts/spies/reconnaissance disguised as non-attention-seeking civilians typical of the environment they operate in. This information is then transferred to the Black Tigers (suicide bombers), who will train the selected suicide bomber specifically in the unique mission. The selected suicide bomber studies the route and other relevant details about the target meticulously and spends much time prior to the actual mission itself rehearsing the entire route so as to ensure maximum success.

The LTTE also has extensive funding, research, and development capabilities, which it uses to develop mini-submarines, stealth attack boats, new types of mines, etc.

**Organizational and Command Structure:** The group is led by Vellupillai Prabhakaran (alias Tambi). Anton Balasingham, who lives in the United Kingdom, is the political ideologue and spokesman of the group. Tamil Selvam leads the political wing, and Pottu Amman heads the intelligence wing. The entire LTTE hardcore leaders are from Velvettihura or from the "fisher" caste, which has achieved some social standing because of the AK-47s carried by many of its militant members. However, several of the important Tiger groups are led by Tamils who are relatively uneducated and nonprofessional, from a middle-status caste. The LTTE organization includes a political wing, military wing, intelligence wing, women's wing, Sea Tigers (suicide bombers tasked with using explosive-laden speedboats), and Black Tigers (suicide bombers tasked to assassinate earmarked targets by the LTTE).

Its international operations can be broadly divided into three categories: political representation and propaganda; arms procurement; and fund-raising. Its international activity is mostly in two dozen Western countries and certain states in the Australasian region. Since 1999, it runs public offices in eleven countries, operating under four centralized fronts—the Tamil Co-coordinating Committee (TCC), the World Tamil Co-coordinating

Committee (WTCC), the United Tamil Organization (UTO), and the Tamil Co-coordinating Group (TCG) (Kloos 1999). The fifth front, the World Tamil Movement (WTM), active in Canada and Germany, has recently downscaled its operations after the arrest of some of its members for extortion. The LTTE indoctrinates the expatriate Tamil public by encouraging participation in public rallies, seminars, and political demonstrations in support of the Tamil cause. All proceeds from ticket sales, goods purchases, and donations during these events go to fill LTTE's coffers. To reinforce public interaction between the group and the Tamil population, the LTTE runs community organizations providing social services and benefits—namely, welfare, housing, immigration assistance, legal aid, information, education, communication, money transfers, etc.

*Political Wing:* The LTTE has its own press and newspaper and propaganda section. It is the first group to make use of the Internet to spread its messages and disseminate propaganda to garner support.

*Military Wing:* Land Army—The conventional army consists of an artillery regiment, a bodyguard unit (for protecting Vellupillai Prabhakaran), and an engineer regiment, apart from other guerilla formations and units. The commanders of these three special units report directly to Vellupillai Prabhakaran. The LTTE reputedly tried to build two airfields for the Air Tigers. Black Tigers are suicide bombers tasked to assassinate targets earmarked by the LTTE. Leopard Commandoes are believed to be the elite troops selected from other units and given special training and better equipment similar to that of special forces in conventional state armies. Sea Tigers is the naval wing of the group, with its suicide bomber section using explosive-laden speedboats, ramming into seagoing vessels, usually in coastal waters. The LTTE owns and operates a fleet of at least ten freighters, equipped with the most up-to-date surveillance technology. The role of these seagoing ships is to provide logistical support by transporting explosives, arms, ammunitions, and other war-related materials to Sri Lanka. The LTTE also has exclusive female units for each wing, for example in the Sea Tigers unit, the suicide brigade, etc. The female suicide volunteers have played a major role in LTTE targeted killings. For example, Rajiv Gandhi, the former Indian prime minister, was killed by "Dhanu," a female suicide bomber.

*Intelligence Wing:* The LTTE has built a secure, sophisticated, and efficient intelligence network. It encompasses military and political aspects and has units in all units of the LTTE organizational structure. The chief of the intelligence wing is Pottu Amman, who was one of the key planners for the assassination of Rajiv Gandhi, the former prime minister of India. Pattu Amman was trained in military warfare in India.

*Command Structure:* The LTTE Central Committee is the highest decision-making body; Prabhakaran is the chairman. The structure has both political and military wings. Area commanders are responsible for tactical decision making. The LTTE hierarchy uses army ranks and grades similar to the Sri Lankan Army—with the three categories of enlisted ranks, non-commissioned officers, and commissioned officers. The military subunits also typically follow such formation patterns, with squads as the smallest tactical unit and the regiment as the largest (http://www.tamiltigers. net/fallencomrades/fallen.htm).

*Research and Development (R&D) Wing:* LTTE maintained considerable interest in R&D, especially applying this to marine use. Its maritime R&D wing was operating out of Mangai Tikkam under Moorthy Master, alias Major Moorthy, for many years, constructing and modifying boats, maintaining and repairing boat engines, and drawing blueprints for new boats. About one hundred paid civilians worked in this unit. Moorthy, also responsible for the LTTE submarine project (discussed below), was interdicted by air and killed in Mulathivu. The Sea Tigers are highly innovative. In addition to manufacturing floating mines and underwater improvised explosive devices (IEDs), they produced several craft, including three mini-submarines. There are records about attempts to construct, and at least to procure, a midget submarine. The LTTE attempted to buy a midget submarine from the former USSR (most likely Ukraine) in the early 1990s and from North Korea in the late 1990s, and made enquiries about the sale of submarines from South Africa in the late 1990s. In mid-July 1990, within three months of the departure of the Indian peacekeeping forces from Sri Lanka, the LTTE launched a secret, bold, and ambitious project in Tiruvanmiyur, Tamil Nadu. The project to construct a midget submarine suffered when MV *Sunbird*, a LTTE ship transporting batteries and accessories for the vessel, was seized in Malaysia, and the LTTE crackdown by the Tamil Nadu police forced the LTTE to move the vessel to Pattipulam, Madras. Two years later on April 20, 1992, parts of the disassembled submarine were recovered by the Indian police from a house in Mahapalipuram, Madras. The submarine, with the outer body made of steel, measured 15 feet in length and 5 feet in width. The radar manufacturing unit, which was manufactured by Raytheon Marine Company, was type M-88391, and another one by Mariner Path Finder was type M-88391. To build the body alone Rs 400,000 (about $10,000) had been spent. The construction—the pressure hull, ballast tanks, rudder, engine cabin, and conning tower—was completed by December 1990. The brass pump set, compressors, propellers, and propeller shaft were fabricated in Tamil Nadu. In early 1991, the LTTE initiated a project to design, build, test, and manufacture an underwater vehicle for the purpose of conducting suicide attacks against Sri Lankan naval craft. David, a celebrated Sea Tiger who died with eight others in a sea accident, initiated the project. The vessel was designed in the base complex in the Mulathivu jungles and tested at sea, east of Polikandy. Since the vessel was unstable, the test was a failure. The LTTE redesigned a second vessel, and the task of building it was given to Moorthy Master, who was in charge of the Sea Tiger mechanical workshop in Polikandi. The vessel, known as *Neer Mulhi*, when completed was 14 feet in length, had a wingspan of 6 feet, and height of 4 feet. The power for the craft came from two externally fitted 55-horsepower outboard motors. Within the craft, there was considerable space for packing explosives. A watertight hatch, sealed and armed from outside, permitted the suicide driver into the vehicle. The suicide driver was given a device for maintaining sea-to-shore communication. A trailer fitted with tractor wheels was used to transport the vehicle. However, during a test-cum-training run, conducted in the sea near Polikandy junction during daylight hours, the vessel failed to perform.

**Political Capability:** The LTTE has refused to participate in mainstream Sri Lankan politics but tacitly supports some Tamil politicians, who can further the cause of the LTTE by striking some clandestine deals. Fear of assassinations of elected government candidates even led to the LTTE indirectly influencing political elections in Sri Lanka. Areas under LTTE's control are run like a government (LTTE has even set up police stations in its territory). The LTTE enjoys widespread support from a network of overt, legitimate front and cover organizations of overseas Tamils and their various communities. These international contacts are also used to procure funds, weapons, technologies, communications, and bomb-making equipment. These organizations also lobby for international support from foreign governments and the United Nations. Residents and businesses in areas under LTTE control and influence must demonstrate support to the group by contributing in financial or manpower terms. A certain "tax" of fixed amount is imposed on every family. Only families of cadre members (alive or dead) are exempted from this tax.

**Significant Events:** Founded in 1972 as a Sri Lankan political opposition group. Every year on November 27, LTTE marks Hero's Day, the day after Prabhakaran's birthday, to honor the sacrifice of LTTE "martyrs." LTTE emerged as an armed insurgency following the anti-Tamil riots of July 1983 in which some 160 people were killed, mainly Tamils. The riot was triggered by a LTTE ambush on an army patrol, which killed thirteen soldiers.

| | |
|---|---|
| May 21, 1991 | LTTE female suicide bomber, Dhanu, killed India's former prime minister Rajiv Gandhi. |
| August 8, 1992 | Army chief Lt. Gen. Denzil Kobbekaduwa was killed in a land mine blast in Kayts, northern Sri Lanka. |
| November 16, 1992 | In a suicide attack, the LTTE killed the commander of the Sri Lankan navy, Vice Admiral Clancy Fernando. |
| May 1, 1993 | President Ranasinghe Premadasa was assassinated by an LTTE suicide attacker at a rally. |
| October 24, 1994 | Opposition leader Gamini Dissanayake and fifty-six others were killed in Colombo. |
| January 31, 1996 | An estimated ninety-one persons were killed in an attack on the Central Bank of Sri Lanka in Colombo. |
| July 24, 1996 | Seventy persons were killed and approximately 600 others were injured as LTTE bombed a passenger train near the capital Colombo. |
| December 18, 1999 | LTTE made an unsuccessful attempt on the life of President Chandrika Kumaratunga, in which she lost eyesight in one eye. |

| July 24, 2001 | LTTE attacked Bandaranaike International Airport, destroying eleven aircraft and damaging another thirteen planes. |
| February 8, 2003 | Three LTTE cadres blew themselves up in a boat carrying arms and ammunition off Delft Island. |
| March 20, 2003 | Sea Tiger cadres of the LTTE sank a Chinese fishing trawler 33 kilometers northwest of Mullaithivu. Sixteen fishermen were reported missing and sixteen more were rescued. |

**Tactics:**

- Building up of strength during cease-fire periods
- Surveillance and target selection
- Suicide attacks, assassinations, bombings, kidnapping, extortion, hijacking, as well as guerrilla and conventional military action
- Propaganda and the deliberate spreading of fear

**Targets:** The LTTE has assassinated many Sri Lankan politicians, election candidates, and other political figures and even two national leaders. They also target Sri Lankan military and police personnel, as well as Sinhalese civilians. Sometimes, Tamil civilians are also caught between the conflict and cross fires between the LTTE and the government. The LTTE justifies this fact as being inevitable. The LTTE is known to be anti-Buddhist and they have also destroyed rival Tamil political and insurgent groups, becoming the sole insurgent group in Sri Lanka. Traitors or ex-cadre who have left the group are targeted as well.

**Supply/Financing:** LTTE enjoys diaspora financial support and procurement of arms and nonparamilitary products. Some estimates state that the LTTE receives up to $5–$10 million every month. For instance, the LTTE demands that Tamil families living in Germany contribute an estimated DEM1,000 (about $630) per family annually. Internet sites have an international network of sales of calendars, music, books, etc., as well as a collection of donations. Methods used for collecting funds are reported to vary from extortion, illegal trade, and front organizations to legitimate business and charities. There is a growing belief about the group's possible involvement in piracy of software, CDs and DVDs. Its international contacts are also used to procure funds, weapons, technologies, communications, and bomb-making equipment as well as international support from foreign governments and the United Nations.

The LTTE has harnessed many sources of funding through front, cover, and sympathetic organizations. In Canada, LTTE-affiliated associations—such as the WTM, the Federation of Associations of Canadian Tamils (FACT), and especially the Tamil Eelam Society of Canada (TES)—received grants amounting to over CAD$1 million (about $750,000) from the money earmarked to assist Tamil "newcomers" to adapt, resettle, and integrate into Canada. The Tamil Rehabilitation Organization (TRO) in France obtained monetary support from the Lions Club of Cergy. Similarly, the TCC received both governmental and nongovernmental humanitarian, refugee, and welfare grants in France. In Germany, the LTTE-affiliated WTM obtained financial assistance from the German government to provide informational, educational, legal, housing, immigration, financial, and cultural services to incoming Tamil refugees. In the United Kingdom, the LTTE-affiliated TCHA and its precursor, the Tamil Refugee Housing Association (TRHA), both received donations from local borough councils ("LTTE Abusing London Housing Assn., Allege Lankan Members," 2001). The LTTE-affiliated Medical Institute of Tamils (MIOT) received sponsorship from pharmaceutical companies, most notably the Boehringer Ingelheim.

**Annual Budget:** Not known but believed to be $60 million.

**Links/Associations:** Some LTTE elements are known to have trained in Palestinian camps but not known to have any direct links with external terrorist groups. The LTTE is also alleged to have helped the United Liberation Front of Assam (ULFA). The group has many front and cover organizations overseas, such as the World Tamil Association (WTA), the World Tamil Movement (WTM), the Federation of Associations of Canadian Tamils (FACT), the Ellalan Force, and the Sangillan Force.

**State Response:** Since February 2002, the LTTE had been engaged in peace talks with the Sri Lankan government. After many years of hiding, Prabakaran spoke to the world press in a press conference on April 10, 2002, with an uncompromising stand of continual insistence that a separate state of Tamil Eelam was the desire of the Tamil people of Sri Lanka. Since peace talks began, there had been only isolated incidents of violence in violation of the truce. Loans and grants worth $4.5 billion were promised but were made contingent on satisfactory progress in the peace process.

In March 2004, there was a major division in the LTTE organization after its special commander for Batticaloa-Amparai whose overall charge of the LTTE's military operations in the eastern province, Vinayagamoorthi Muralitharan (alias Colonel Karuna), was sacked by Prabhakaran for alleged treachery against the Tamil people and the Tamil leadership party and also for conspiring to leave the liberation organization. Karuna was replaced by Ramesh as special commander. Prabhakaran also ordered about 500 cadres from the eastern province to be disarmed and placed under house arrest. Karuna reportedly approached the Sri Lankan authorities and the Norwegian monitoring mission for a recognition of the separate role of his setup in the now stalled peace process, for physical protection and for ensuring safe passage for the nearly 2,000 eastern cadres. Though Karuna is not in a very strong position to effectively challenge Prabhakaran's leadership, the emerging rift and the possibility of a bloody encounter between the factions may contribute to a weakening of the strength of the group.

Negotiations, however, broke down in April 2003 after the LTTE pulled out. The LTTE accused the Sri Lankan military of a series of provocative measures, including the sinking of its vessels and demands from Washington to disarm. At the same time, it faced growing hostility from the Tamil masses as living conditions failed to improve following the February 2002 ceasefire. The peace process also ran into rough weather after the sacking of ministers by the Sri Lankan president and subsequent elections that returned a new government to power in Sri Lanka. For the time being there has been no progress in peace talks though the Norwegian interlocutors were hopeful of getting it back on track.

**Projected Activities:** Governments' "zero-tolerance" attitude toward terrorism since 9/11 has delayed the return of the group to open hostilities. However, during the stalled peace process the LTTE has continued to recruit, train, collect intelligence, and procure weapons. Some believe that it is only a question of *when* they will return to war rather than *if*.

**LTTE Web Sites:** http://eelam.com; http://www.eelamweb.com; http://www.Tamilnet.com

# References

"Colombo Lifts Ban on Tamil Tigers." 2002. *Straits Times,* September 6, 29.

Dias, Wije. 2003. "Moves to Restart Sri Lankan Peace Talks." (August 14). Available at http://www.wsws.org/articles/2003/aug2003/sril-a14.shtml (accessed May 14, 2004).

Fanney, Rob. 2002. "Liberation Tigers of Tamil Eelam (LTTE), Jane's World." *Insurgency and Terrorism* 15, no. 24 (May).

FAS Intelligence Resource Programme. "Liberation Tigers of Tamil Eelam." Available at http://www.fas.org/irp/world/para/ltte.htm (accessed May 14, 2004).

Gunaratna, Rohan. 2000. "The LTTE and Suicide Terrorism." *Frontline* 17, no. 3 (February 5–8). Available at http://www.frontlineonnet.com/fl1703/17031060.htm (accessed March 22, 2004).

———. 2002. "Peace Talks: The Transformation of Terror." *South Asia Intelligence Review* 1, no. 10 (September 23).

———. 2003. "Factors Facilitating and Inhibiting Escalation and De-Escalation of Political Violence by the Liberation Tigers of Tamil Eelam (LTTE)." Unpublished article.

Harrison, Frances. 2003. "Sri Lanka's Child Soldiers." BBC News (January 31). Available at http://news.bbc.co.uk/1/hi/world/south_asia/2713035.stm (accessed May 14, 2004).

http://eelam.com/

http://www.tamiltigers.net/fallencomrades/fallen.htm

Kloos, Peter. 1999. "Violent Youth Movement in Sri Lanka: The JVP and LTTE Compared." *Antropologische Bijdragen* 3. Available at http://cas-nws.scw.vu.nl/publicaties/kloos-jvp.html (accessed March 22, 2004).

Krishnan, S. 1999–2000. "The Internationalization of Ethnic Conflicts—Tamil Separatism and LTTE." IDSS MSc Dissertation.

"Liberation Tigers of Tamil Eelam (LTTE): Organization and Leadership, Military.com." Available at http://www.military.com/Resources/ResourceFileView?file=LTTE-Organization.htm (accessed May 14, 2004).

"LTTE Abusing London Housing Assn., Allege Lankan Members." 2001. *The Island,* November 8.

"LTTE Tamil Tiger Atrocities." Available at http://www.spur.asn.au/ltteatrp.htm (accessed May 14, 2004).

"LTTE Terrorism in Sri Lanka." Available at http://members.tripod.com/~sosl/terror.html (accessed May 14, 2004).

"The LTTE's Ideology." Available at http://www.military.com/Resources/ResourceFileView?file=LTTE-Ideology.htm (accessed March 22, 2004).

Raman, B. 2004. "Prabhakaran's Eastern Challenger." The Rediff.com (March 9). Available at http://www.rediff.com/news/2004/mar/09spec1.htm (accessed May 14, 2004).

"Sri Lankan Suicide Bomb Kills 13." 2000. Available at http://news.bbc.co.uk/1/hi/world/south_asia/591352.stm (accessed March 22, 2004).

Straw, Jack. 2001. "Tigers Raid Colombo Airport." *Sri Lanka Monitor* (July). Available at http://brcslproject.gn.apc.org/slmonitor/july2001/raid.html (accessed March 22, 2004).

"Tamil Tigers: A Fearsome Force." 2002. BBC News (May 2). Available at http://news.bbc.co.uk/1/hi/world/south_asia/526407.stm (accessed May 14, 2004).

"Wanted: VELUPILLAI, Prabhakaran." Lyon, France: Interpol General Secretariat. Available at http://www.interpol.int/public/Wanted/Notices/Data/1994/54/1994_9054.asp (accessed May 14, 2004).

# 5

# Framework for Counterterrorism Policy

The basis of U.S. counterterrorism policy is regarded as deriving from two presidential directives signed by President Clinton in 1995 and 1998. Reinforced by legislation, these directives treat terrorism as a crime and instigate procedures to apprehend and punish perpetrators worldwide (http://www.opsec. org/opsnews/Sept99/opscounterterroristsept99.htm). On the practical side, the U.S. Congress has appropriated funds to enhance federal agencies' capabilities to prevent, counter, and manage the consequences of international terrorism (http:// www.opsec.org/opsnews/Sept99/opscounterterroristsept99. htm). Furthermore, the National Security Council is mandated with coordinating the U.S. policy on combating terrorism. The director of the Central Intelligence Agency is charged with coordinating intelligence community issues and sharing information through the Counterterrorist Center (CTC) and the Interagency Intelligence Committee on Terrorism (IICT) (http://www. cia.gov).

In the global domain there are twelve major multilateral conventions that form an international counterterrorism framework that relate to states' counterterrorism efforts and responsibilities. It is imperative for the success of countering terrorism that as many states as possible sign and adhere to such conventions. States that do not sign or adhere to such conventions leave loopholes and room for terrorists to maneuver, survive, and continue their activities. Most of these conventions provide that parties must establish criminal jurisdiction over offenders. Nation-states are encouraged to develop the necessary legislation to empower their law enforcement and judicial authorities to take action by considering the location of the offense or the nationality of the perpetrator or victim (http://wwwserver.law.wits.ac.za/salc/report/pr105-chs1–5.pdf).

In addition to the twelve multilateral conventions, there are other instruments that are relevant in particular circumstances. They are bilateral extradition treaties, the 1961 Vienna Convention on Diplomatic Relations, and the 1963 Vienna Convention on Consular Relations. A significant number of important regional treaties and initiatives have taken place especially since September 11, 2001 (http://www.informationheadquarters.com/September_11_2001/Terrorism.shtml). Furthermore, there are several important UN Security Council and General Assembly Resolutions on international terrorism. They include three important Security Council resolutions dealing with Libya's conduct in connection with the 1988 sabotage of Pan Am 103, which includes UN Security Council Resolutions 731 (January 21, 1992), 748 (March 31, 1992), and 883 (November 11, 1993) (http://www.state.gov/www/global/terrorism/980817_terror_conv.html).

Most counterterrorism conventions are penal in nature. They have a common format. Typically, they:

- Define a particular type of violence as an offense under the convention, such as seizure of an aircraft in flight by threat or violence
- Require state parties to penalize that activity in their domestic law
- Identify certain bases upon which the parties responsible are required to establish jurisdiction over the defined offense, such as registration, territoriality, or nationality
- Create an obligation on the state in which a suspect is found to establish jurisdiction over the convention offense and to refer the offense for prosecution if the party does not extradite pursuant to other provisions of the convention. This is commonly known as the principle of "no safe haven for terrorists." (http://www.unodc.org/unodc/en/terrorism_conventions.html)

The UN Security Council in Resolution 1373 of September 28, 2001, stressed that member states have an essential antiterrorism obligation.

For the full text of international and regional conventions and protocols pertaining to terrorism, see http://www.state.gov/www/global/terrorism/980817_terror_conv.html, http://untreaty.un.org/English/Terrorism.asp, or http://www.ict.org.il/. We will now look at specific dates in history on which counterterrorism policy was made:

1963 *Tokyo Convention on Offenses and Certain Other Acts Committed on Board Aircraft*

   Concerns actions affecting in-flight safety; gives captain/pilot authority to restrain any person believed to have committed or about to commit an act that would endanger the safety of the flight. Requires contracting states to take custody of offenders and to return control of the aircraft to the lawful commander.

1970 *December 16. Hague Convention for the Suppression of Unlawful Seizure of Aircraft*

   This convention was in response to a string of hijacking attempts after the "success" of PFLP in highlighting its cause, and makes it an offense to threaten or attempt to seize control of an aircraft. Signatories are required to impose severe punishment on hijackers as well as to cooperate with other signatories including for extradition and prosecution.

1971 *February 2. Convention to Prevent and Punish the Acts of Terrorism Taking the Form of Crimes against Persons and Related Extortion That Are of Significance*

   This convention was formed by the Organization of American States (OAS) after the series of kidnappings in Latin America beginning in 1968, with signatories expected to cooperate in the prosecution or extradition of any persons attempting or committing such actions.

1971 *September 23. Montreal Convention for the Suppression of Unlawful Acts against the Safety of Civil Aviation*

This convention was a reinforcement of The Hague convention but focused more on aviation sabotage such as bombings aboard aircraft in flight, and extends it to direct or indirect (e.g., accomplice) attempts to place IEDs or bombs.

1973    *December 14. UN Convention on the Prevention and Punishment of Crimes against Internationally Protected Persons, Including Diplomatic Agents*

This convention was a response to the increasing trend for kidnappings of diplomats. It defines an internationally protected person as a "Head of State, a Minister for Foreign Affairs, a representative or official of a state or of an international organization who is entitled to special protection from attack under international law." This covers the person at work, home, in transport, and so on, and is also aimed at standardizing strict response internationally to any such attempts or acts in order to deter and prevent them. Signatories are required to cooperate in the investigation, prosecution, and extradition of any persons attempting or committing such actions.

1979    *December 17. International UN Convention against the Taking of Hostages*

The drafting of this convention began in 1976. It was spearheaded by Western states, most notably West Germany (http://wwwserver.law.wits.ac.za/salc/discussn/chs1_5.pdf). However, during the drafting it was weakened to the point of inefficacy. This convention states that "any person who seizes or detains and threatens to kill, to injure, or to continue to detain another person in order to compel a third party, namely, a State, an international intergovernmental organization, a natural or juridical person, or a group of persons, to do or abstain from doing any act as an explicit or implicit condition for the release of the hostage commits the offense of taking of hostages within the meaning of this Convention." The signatories are required to cooperate in the investigation, prosecution, and extradition of any persons attempting or committing such actions.

1980      *March 3. Convention on the Physical Protection of Nuclear Material*

Adopted in October 1979 and signed in 1980, this convention was designed to combat and criminalize any unlawful possession, taking, transfer, moving, or use of nuclear material with the intention of using the threat or use of such material to kill, injure, or damage. Signatories are required to cooperate in the investigation, prosecution, and extradition of any persons attempting or committing such actions/breaches.

1984      *Comprehensive Crime Control Act*

This act (18 U.S.C. 1203) authorized federal prosecution of hostage taking overseas that involves U.S. citizens/targets, providing a basis for extraterritorial jurisdiction on terrorism.

1986      *Omnibus Diplomatic Security and Antiterrorism Act*

This act (18 U.S.C. 2331) enhanced extraterritorial jurisdiction to any terrorist act against U.S. citizens or interests.

1988      *February 24. Protocol for the Suppression of Unlawful Acts of Violence at Airports Serving International Civil Aviation, Supplementary to the Convention for the Suppression of Unlawful Acts against the Safety of Civil Aviation*

This convention was an extension of the 1971 Montreal convention to include terrorist acts at airports serving international civil aviation.

1988      *March 10. Convention for the Suppression of Unlawful Acts against the Safety of Maritime Navigation*

This convention applies to terrorist activities on ships and makes it an offense for a person to seize or exercise control over a ship by force, threat, or intimidation, as well as to perform an act of violence against a person on board a ship if that act is likely to endanger the safe navigation of the ship. It also makes it illegal to place a destructive device or substance aboard a ship or any other acts against the safety of ships, and requires signatories to cooperate in extradition and prosecution.

1988     *March 10. Protocol for the Suppression of Unlawful Acts against the Safety of Fixed Platforms Located on the Continental Shelf*

This protocol applies to terrorist activities on oil rigs and, similar to other conventions, requires signatories to cooperate in prosecution and extradition following any such attempt or action. In the United Kingdom this resulted in the formation of Commachio, the royal marines special forces unit with the responsibility of protecting nuclear bases and oil rigs, and providing assaults and rescues if necessary.

1991     *March 1. Convention on the Marking of Plastic Explosives for the Purpose of Detection*

This convention was organized in response to the problems of unmarked plastic explosives and the difficulties in monitoring and tracing it. The convention initiated chemical marking to facilitate detection of plastic explosives, to combat aircraft sabotage, for example. The convention consisted of the convention itself and a technical annex that together aim to control and limit the used of unmarked and undetectable plastic explosives (negotiated in the aftermath of the Pan Am Flight 103 bombing). Each signatory must take necessary and effective measures to prohibit and prevent the manufacture, movement, possession, and transfer of unmarked plastic explosives, as well as monitoring and enforcing the holding and disposal of such materials held by the police or military.

1993     *September 13. Oslo Accords*

The Oslo Accords, also known as the "Declaration of Principles," are the basis of current Israeli-Palestinian peace negotiations. They were secretly negotiated by

Israeli and Palestinian delegations in 1993 in Oslo, Norway. The Norwegian foreign minister, Johan Jorgen Holst, played a pivotal role in the negotiations. They laid out the long-term goals to be achieved, including the complete withdrawal of Israeli troops from the Gaza Strip and the West Bank. Furthermore, they guaranteed the right of the Palestinians to self-rule in those territories. Palestinian leader Yasser Arafat and Israeli prime minister Yitzhak Rabin famously shook hands during the signing in Washington (http://www.cnn.com/interactive/specials/0007/mideast.documents/oslo.html). The PLO was no longer seen as a terrorist organization but as a peaceful political movement, demonstrating that terrorism can be successful in achieving its objectives. Many analysts saw the Israeli-Palestinian conflict as the catalyst for the rise of international terrorism. Therefore, they assumed that if peace could be reached between the two parties, it would reduce international terrorism.

1995    *September 28. Oslo Accords*

At this extension to the 1993 agreements, Israelis and Palestinians signed another deal known as the Interim Agreement or, popularly, as "Oslo 2." The 400-page pact allowed further autonomy for the Palestinians. It gave them self-rule in the cities of Bethlehem, Jenin, Nablus, Qalqilya, Ramallah, Tulkarm, parts of Hebron, and 450 villages. It also allowed Israeli-guarded Jewish settlements to remain in Palestinian-controlled land.

1996    *April 24. U.S. Antiterrorism and Effective Death Penalty Act* (AEDPA)

This act established the death penalty for certain terrorist crimes. As most other Western governments do not support the death penalty, the act also reduced cooperation (or the likelihood of cooperation) between foreign governments and the U.S. government. It is widely regarded that not enough attention was paid to the implications for U.S. foreign policy with this act.

1996     *June 27. G-7 Declaration on Terrorism*

Released at the G-7 Economic Summit in Lyon, France, following and condemning the June 25 fuel truck bomb attack in Dhahran, Saudi Arabia, that killed nineteen people and injured around four hundred others, this declaration attempted to unite and strengthen resolve, actions, and opinion against terrorism activity and support.

1997     *December 15. International Convention for the Suppression of Terrorist Bombings*

This convention attempted to internationalize the response against terrorism due to growing transnational phenomena and the problems in countering it by expanding the legal framework (against unlawful and intentional use of explosives and other lethal devices in or against public places with intent to kill, injure, or damage) for international cooperation in the investigation, prosecution, and extradition of persons who engage in terrorist bombings.

1999     *December 9. UN International Convention for the Suppression of the Financing of Terrorism*

An attempt to internationalize a response and combat the financial infrastructure of terrorists, this UN convention signified the acknowledgment of the international scale and sophistication of terrorist overseas support structures exploiting sovereignty and state loopholes. The United States signed the convention on January 10, 2000.

2001     *Patriot Act*

This act enhanced U.S. intelligence and law-enforcement powers in a number of areas, including investigating and monitoring of electronic transmissions, communications, and banking. For a summary and analysis of key sections, see http://www.cdt.org/security/011031summary.shtml.

# 6

# Directory of Counterterrorism Agencies and Organizations

"Since September 11, 2001, more than 3,000 Al-Qaeda leaders and foot soldiers have been taken into custody around the globe; nearly 200 suspected terrorist associates have been charged with crimes in the U.S.; and as many as a hundred terrorist attacks or plots have been broken up worldwide."

*FBI Web site (http://www.fbi.gov/terrorinfo/*
*counterrorism/waronterrorhome.htm)*

The achievements against terrorism have been due to the efforts of the following agencies and their international allies. This list is a select guide, as there are many more organizations in operation around the world.

## Government Agencies

### U.S. National Agencies

#### Bureau of Diplomatic Security (DS)
**Background:** The DS was formally established in 1916 under Secretary of State Robert Lansing. The office was headed by a chief special agent, who also carried the title of special assistant to the

secretary and reported directly to the secretary of state on special matters. Since the 9/11 terrorist attacks, the DS has played an active role in the global war on terrorism, utilizing over 486 special agents assigned to diplomatic missions in 157 countries.

**Mission:** To provide a secure environment for the conduct of American diplomacy.

**Activities/Responsibilities:** To design tailor-made security programs for every U.S. diplomatic mission in the world; investigate domestic passport and visa fraud; conduct personnel security investigations; protect VIPs such as the secretary of state at home and abroad, as well as high-ranking foreign dignitaries and officials visiting the United States; and train foreign civilian law enforcement officers in disciplines designed to reduce the threat and repercussions of terrorism throughout the world.

The DS also works with other federal agencies, the intelligence community, international law enforcement agencies, and the private sector to prevent terrorism against U.S. nationals both at home and abroad.

### References
http://www.defenselink.mil

http://www.state.gov/m/ds/

### Central Intelligence Agency (CIA)
**Headquarters:** Langley, Virginia

**Background:** Created in 1947 with the signing of the National Security Act by President Harry Truman, which charged the director of Central Intelligence (DCI) with coordinating the nation's intelligence activities and correlating, evaluating, and disseminating intelligence affecting national security. The agency is accountable to the president through the DCI and to the U.S. nation through the intelligence oversight committees of the U.S. Congress.

**Mission:** To support the president, the National Security Council, and all officials who make and execute the U.S. national security policy.

The activities of the CIA include providing accurate, comprehensive, and timely foreign intelligence on national security topics, conducting counterintelligence and special activities, and any other functions related to foreign intelligence and national security (as directed by the president).

**Activities:** In order to do this, research, development, and deployment of high-leverage technology for intelligence purposes are undertaken. The CIA acts as an independent source of analysis on topics of concern and works closely with other organizations in the intelligence community (see http://www.intelligence.gov) to ensure that the intelligence consumer receives the best intelligence product possible. The CIA also works closely with its U.K. equivalent, known as MI6/SIS—"Secret Intelligence Service," based at Vauxhall Cross, London, England, as well as MI5, or "the Security Service," based in Thames House, London.

As new challenges and threats arise in the international system, the CIA responds by creating and operating multidisciplinary centers to address high-priority issues (e.g., nonproliferation, counterterrorism, counterintelligence, international organized crime and narcotics trafficking, environment, and arms control intelligence), being proactive in forging stronger partnerships between the several intelligence collection disciplines, and producing all-source analysis on all issues affecting national security.

### References
http://www.cia.gov

### Counterterrorism Division (CTD) of the FBI
**Headquarters:** Washington, D.C.

**Mission:** To consolidate all FBI counterterrorism initiatives.

**Activities:** The National Infrastructure Protection Center (NIPC) and the National Domestic Preparedness Office (NDPO) are assigned to this division. The NIPC serves as the U.S. government's focal point for threat assessment, warning, investigation, and response for threats or attacks against the nation's critical infrastructures. The NDPO coordinates all federal efforts to assist state and local first responders with planning, training, and equipment needs necessary to respond to a conventional or nonconventional weapons of mass destruction incident.

The Tactical Support Branch of the FBI is made up of the Hostage Rescue Team (see entry) and Operations Training Unit. They ensure that the FBI has a full-time, national-level tactical team capable of being deployed to protect the American people at home and overseas. (See also Federal Bureau of Investigation.)

### References
http://www.fbi.gov/hq.htm

### Counterterrorism Security Group (CSG)

**Background:** During a crisis, representatives from the U.S. counterterrorism agencies meet to form the CSG. The CSG is chaired by the national coordinator for security, infrastructure protection, and counterterrorism. The other core members of the CSG are the heads of the counterterrorist elements of the CIA, FBI, Joint Chiefs of Staff, and departments of State, Justice, and Defense. Any other entity that could be affected by, or have a bearing on, either the situation or recommended course of action is brought in to consider specific matters that bear on its responsibilities. The current charter for the CSG is Presidential Decision Directive 62, signed in May 1998.

**Mission:** To produce a recommendation for the national security advisor on how to react to a terrorist threat.

**Activities:** Prior to the CSG meeting, members often have limited time to review news reports, intelligence reports, and briefings from other members/representatives involved in the crisis. Each representative meets with the following points in mind: The counterterrorism capabilities and resources of their agency, the equity their agency has in coordinating its efforts with other agencies, the concerns and criteria their agency considers in making decisions, and the primary goals of their agency in a crisis. From the information and advice available, as well as their own professional expertise and opinions, they are then asked to build their case and formulate their recommendations. During the meeting they work with other agency representatives to make their case to the CSG chairperson and reach consensus on a recommendation for the national security advisor to submit to the president. The national security advisor will then make the final decision on what recommendation goes forward from the CSG to the Principals Committee.

### References

Pillar, P. R. 2001. *Terrorism and U.S. Foreign Policy.* Washington, D.C.: Brookings Institution Press.

### Counterterrorist Center (CTC)

**Headquarters:** Washington, D.C.

**Background:** In the mid-1980s a series of high-profile terrorist attacks galvanized U.S. policymakers to take the offensive against international terrorism. A task force chaired by the vice president at the time, (former CIA member) George H. Bush, was formed in 1986 to address the problem of international terrorism. The task force concluded that U.S. government agencies collected information on terrorism but did not aggressively operate to disrupt terrorist activities. As a result of these findings, the DCI at that time, William Casey, created the DCI Counterterrorist Center (CTC) and directed it to *preempt, disrupt, and defeat terrorists.*

**Mission:** To assist the DCI in coordinating intelligence community counterterrorism in preempting, disrupting, and defeating terrorism.

**Activities:** The CTC is charged with implementing a comprehensive counterterrorist operations program to collect intelligence on, and minimize the capabilities of, international terrorist groups and state sponsors; exploiting all-source intelligence to produce in-depth analyses of the groups and states responsible for international terrorism; ensuring that counterterrorism activities are coordinated so as not to be detrimental to other counterterrorism activities; and disseminating to all of the departments and agencies any terrorist threat report that cannot be disproved.

Around a dozen agencies have personnel assigned at the CTC, including intelligence agencies such as the FBI and CIA as well as law enforcement agencies such as the Secret Service, and policy or regulatory agencies such as the Federal Aviation Administration (FAA).

The chief of the CTC also serves as special assistant to the director of Central Intelligence for counterterrorist matters. CTC's charter allows it to draw on all CIA resources and the talent of other U.S. government agencies.

### References
http://www.cia.gov

Pillar, P. R. 2001. *Terrorism and U.S. Foreign Policy* Washington, D.C.: Brookings Institution Press.

### Delta Force
**Headquarters:** Fort Bragg, North Carolina

**Background:** Formed in 1977 by Charlie Beckwith, a U.S. Special Forces officer who had served with the SAS (U.K.), the new unit was modeled after the SAS and called the 1st SFOD-Delta, or Delta Force (also known as CAG, for Combat Applications Group). Delta Force soldiers are mainly recruited from Special Forces Green Berets and Rangers. Estimates are of up to 2,500 personnel at Fort Bragg, with smaller numbers in other bases.

**Mission:** Military counterterrorism; maintaining and executing effective rapid response counterterrorism/hostage rescue capability and operations.

**Activities:** The Delta Force maintains an operational proficiency on land, sea, and air, with a variety of weapons, vehicles, and equipment pertaining to its mission. Activities also include the defense of territories, long-range and close-target reconnaissance (CTRs), intelligence gathering, crisis response/management, and covert/clandestine operations. The force also takes part in exchange programs with other counterterrorism units and some training of other countries' units. It is integrated with Seal Team 6 (now known as NSWDG), which conducts maritime operations but retains the ability to function as an independent unit. Delta Force personnel work closely with the 160th SOAR for air support, but they also have their own "civilian" fleet of helicopters (the aviation platoon) for air support and transport for covert operations. They also work with the CIA's Special Activities Staff. Delta Force and the FBI's Hostage Rescue Team (HRT) train together at the $80 million upgraded Range 19 in Fort Bragg. The Delta Force and HRT train together at Quantico, Virginia, where they have exclusive use of a new airstrip with enlarged C-141 capability. The 160th SOAR out of Fort Campbell, Kentucky, flies the Delta Force and HRT to their urban assault assignments. (See also FBI HRT, SOAR, and JSOC.)

### References

Davies, B. 2003. *Terrorism: Inside a World Phenomenon.* London: Virgin.

http://www.bragg.army.mil/

http://www.globalsecurity.org/military/agency/dod/jsoc.htm

http://www.specialoperations.com/Army/Delta_Force/default.html

http://www.specwarnet.net/americas/delta.htm

### Department of Defense (DoD)

**Headquarters:** The Pentagon, Washington, D.C.

**Background:** The War Department, established in 1789, was the precursor to what is now the Department of Defense. In 1947, the U.S. Congress established a civilian, cabinet-level secretary of defense to oversee the national military establishment. Subsequently, the three services, army, navy, and air force, were placed under the direct control of the secretary of defense. In 1949, as a result of congressional amendments, the national defense structure was consolidated further to create what is now known as the Department of Defense.

**Mission:** According to the Department of Defense Web site, "To provide the military forces needed to deter war and to protect the security of the United States."

### References
http://www.defenselink.mil

### Department of Homeland Security (DHS)

**Background:** After 9/11, President George W. Bush decided that twenty-two previously disparate domestic agencies needed to be coordinated into one department to better protect the nation against threats to the homeland. For a list (and links) of the agencies that fall under the DHS, see http://www.dhs.gov/dhspublic/display?theme=13.

**Mission:** To protect the United States against further terrorist attacks.

**Activities:** Component agencies analyze threats and intelligence, guard U.S. borders and airports, protect critical infrastructure, and coordinate the response of the United States for future emergencies. Besides coordinating U.S. defense efforts, the DHS also dedicates offices to missions such as those protecting the rights of U.S. citizens, as well as enhancing public services, such as natural disaster assistance and citizenship services.

### References
http://www.dhs.gov/dhspublic/

### Defense Intelligence Agency (DIA)

**Headquarters:** Pentagon, Washington, D.C.

**Background:** The DIA became operational on October 1, 1961, as the nation's primary producer of foreign military intelligence. It filled the need for a central intelligence manager for the Department of Defense to support the requirements of the secretary of defense, the Joint Chiefs of Staff, and the armed forces.

**Mission:** To provide combat support to the Department of Defense (DoD).

**Activities:** With estimates of over seven thousand military and civilian employees worldwide, the DIA is a major producer and manager of foreign military intelligence, which it provides to armed forces and policy makers in support of U.S. military planning and operations and weapon systems acquisition. Activities include improving threat assessment and counterterrorism preparation, enhancing intelligence integration and interoperability, and building a skilled response community.

The DIA also has major operational activities at the Defense Intelligence Analysis Center (DIAC) in Washington, D.C.; the Armed Forces Medical Intelligence Center (AFMIC) in Frederick, Maryland; and the Missile and Space Intelligence Center (MSIC) in Huntsville, Alabama.

**References**
http://www.dia.mil

### Director of Central Intelligence (DCI)

The DCI is the head of the CIA, but he or she also acts as the head of the United States intelligence community and thus is also the principal adviser to the president on intelligence matters pertaining to national security.

George J. Tenet is the current DCI (since July 10, 1997—see profile in Chapter 4) and is charged with coordinating intelligence community issues and sharing information through the Counterterrorist Center (CTC) and the Interagency Intelligence Committee on Terrorism (IICT).

**References**
http://www.cia.gov

### Federal Aviation Administration (FAA)

**Headquarters:** Washington, D.C.

**Background:** The Federal Aviation Act of 1958 created a new independent body, the Federal Aviation Agency, which had broader authority to combat aviation hazards and deal with various aspects of aviation safety. The act gave the agency the sole responsibility of developing and maintaining a common civil-military system of air navigation and air traffic control. In 1966, Congress authorized the creation of a cabinet department—Department of Transportation (DOT)—that would combine major federal transportation responsibilities. On April 1, 1967, the FAA became one of several model organizations within DOT.

**Mission:** "FAA provides a safe, secure, and efficient global aerospace system that contributes to national security and the promotion of U.S. aerospace safety. As the leading authority in the international aerospace community, FAA is responsive to the dynamic nature of customer needs, economic conditions, and environmental concerns."

**Activities:** The Federal Aviation Administration is responsible for the safety of civil aviation. The agency's major roles include:

- regulating civil aviation to promote safety;
- encouraging and developing civil aeronautics, including new aviation technology;
- developing and operating a system of air traffic control and navigation for both civil and military aircraft;
- researching and developing the National Airspace System and civil aeronautics;
- developing and carrying out programs to control aircraft noise and other environmental effects of civil aviation;
- and regulating U.S. commercial space transportation

**References**
http://www.faa.gov

### Federal Bureau of Investigation (FBI)
**Headquarters:** Washington, D.C.

**Background:** The FBI was established on July 26, 1908, with a small group of special agents as an investigative force of the Department of Justice. Today, the FBI is the principal investigative arm of the U.S. Department of Justice. The FBI has the authority and responsibility to investigate specific crimes assigned to it. Furthermore, the FBI is authorized to provide other law enforcement agencies with cooperative services. This includes fingerprint identification, laboratory examinations, and police training. The FBI is headed by a director who is appointed by the president and confirmed by the Senate for a term not exceeding ten years. The current director of the FBI is Robert S. Mueller III.

**Mission:** The FBI has the main counterterrorism responsibility within the United States. It is part of a vast national and international campaign dedicated to defeating terrorism, and it works closely with other agencies in law enforcement, intelligence, the military, and diplomacy. Part of its mission is to neutralize terrorist cells and operatives within the United States as well as helping dismantle international terrorist networks.

**Activities:** The FBI has dual functions. It collects domestic intelligence and enforces the law. As such, the FBI can pursue investigations, detect terrorist threats through surveillance, and engage in human source development and careful analysis. The FBI can also act against those threats through arrest and incarceration. Over the years, the FBI has developed an international network of dedicated special agents that liaise with federal, state, local, and international partners. Using this network, the FBI can react rapidly and mobilize to prevent attacks.

The Awareness of National Security Issues and Response (ANSIR) Program is the FBI's national security awareness program. ANSIR disseminates unclassified national security threat and warning information to U.S. corporations, law enforcement, and other government agencies. ANSIR e-mail provides this information at no charge to any interested person meeting the subscription prerequisites. In addition, to making potential targets of intelligence and terrorist activities less vulnerable through awareness, the FBI has unique response capability to act when these activities are identified. (See also Counterterrorism Division; Hostage Rescue Unit.)

### References
http://www.angelfire.com/weird/flash333/official.html

http://www.fbi.gov

### Federal Emergency Management Agency (FEMA)
**Headquarters:** Washington, D.C.

**Background:** Since its creation in 1979, FEMA has faced many unusual challenges including refugee crises, energy and nuclear power-plant incidents, disaster relief, and recovery operations. Al Qaeda's attacks on September 11, 2001, tested the agency in unprecedented ways, refocusing FEMA on issues of national preparedness and homeland security. FEMA coordinated its activities with the newly formed Office (now Department) of

Homeland Security, and FEMA's Office of National Preparedness was given responsibility for training and equipping the nation's first responders to deal with weapons of mass destruction. After 9/11, billions of dollars of new funding were directed to FEMA to help the United States face the threat of terrorism.

**Mission:** FEMA has a vision of "A Nation Prepared." Its mission is to lead the United States to prepare for, prevent, respond to, and recover from disasters, natural and man-made, as well as mitigating against them.

**Activities:** In March 2003, FEMA was reorganized to fall under the auspices of the newly created Department of Homeland Security (see entry). About 2,500 full-time employees of FEMA in the Emergency Preparedness and Response Directorate are supplemented by more than five thousand stand-by disaster reservists.

### References
http://www.fema.gov

### Foreign Terrorist Asset Tracking Center (FTATC)
**Headquarters:** Washington, D.C.

**Background:** The National Commission on Terrorism (composed of ten members from the House and Senate) urged the creation of the Foreign Terrorist Tracking Task Force and its attendant tracking center.

**Mission/Activities:** To blend the expertise of the Department of Treasury, CIA, FBI, and National Security Agency in tracking and disrupting the flow of money to terrorist groups. (See Foreign Terrorist Tracking Task Force.)

### References
http://www.webcom.com/hrin/magazine/footdragging.html

### Foreign Terrorist Tracking Task Force (FTTTF)
**Headquarters:** Washington, D.C.

**Background:** As there are a number of U.S. government agencies engaged in fighting terrorism, both at home and abroad, the U.S. government needed a central body to take the responsibility for tracking terrorists. The National Commission on Terrorism urged the creation of the Foreign Terrorist Tracking Task Force and its attendant tracking center. Both were instituted in 2001.

**Mission/Activities:** The Foreign Terrorist Tracking Task Force was empowered by law to coordinate programs to deny entry into the United States of aliens who are associated with, suspected of being engaged in, or supporting terrorist activity. The FTTTF was tasked to coordinate the efforts to locate, detain, prosecute, or deport any such aliens already present in the United States. The U.S. attorney general and the DCI are charged with ensuring, to the maximum extent permitted by law, the effective function of FTTTF. For instance, all U.S. agencies are mandated to provide FTTTF with access to all available information necessary to perform its mission. When appropriate, cooperating countries are invited to serve as liaisons to FTTTF to expedite investigation and data sharing. Other federal entities provide FTTTF with any relevant information they possess concerning aliens suspected of engaging in or supporting terrorist activity. They include the Migrant Smuggling and Trafficking in Persons Coordination Center and the Foreign Leads Development Activity.

**References**
http://www.whitehouse.gov/news/releases/2001/10/20011030-2.html#quicksearch

## Hostage Rescue Team (HRT) of the FBI
**Headquarters:** Quantico, Virginia
**Background:** The U.S. Justice Department made a key decision in 1982 to create an elite unit to offer a tactical option for any extraordinary hostage crisis occurring within the United States. The attorney general authorized the formation of a specialist counterterrorist unit within law enforcement known as the Hostage Rescue Team (HRT). Handpicked, highly motivated, and experienced FBI agents comprised the HRT. Assigned to the Washington Metropolitan Field Office, the HRT was originally allocated fifty agent positions; it has since grown to ninety-one personnel.
**Mission:** The HRT mission is to conduct a successful rescue of U.S. persons and others who may be held illegally by a hostile force, either terrorist or criminal in nature. Depending upon the magnitude of a crisis, the HRT is structured to deploy with part or all of its personnel and resources to any location within four hours of notification by the director of the FBI or his/her designated representative.

**Activities:** The HRT is part of the Tactical Support Branch of the FBI's Critical Incident Response Group (CIRG) and can be augmented by other CIRG entities with specialists trained in areas of negotiation, behavioral science, and communications. In support of FBI field divisions, HRT is deployed to perform a number of law enforcement tactical functions. It operates in all environments and under a variety of conditions. In the first two decades of its activity, the HRT has deployed on over two hundred occasions in support of combating terrorism, violent criminals, foreign counterintelligence, and other investigations. The unit has performed missions involving hostage rescue and barricaded subjects and has engaged in high-risk arrests and warrant services, raids, and dive searches. The HRT has also performed traditional law enforcement roles during hurricane relief operations, dignitary protection missions, tactical surveys, and provides support of special events such as the Olympic Games, presidential inaugurations, and political conventions.

When not operationally deployed, the HRT conducts full-time training at sites across the United States. HRT trains alongside the 1st Special Forces Detachment-Delta (SFOD-D/Delta Force) at the $80 million upgraded Range 19 in Fort Bragg, North Carolina. The HRT also maintains an office at the Joint Special Operations Command headquarters at Pope Air Force Base adjacent to Fort Bragg. HRT personnel train together with the Delta Force at Quantico, Virginia, where they have exclusive use of a new airstrip with enlarged C-141 capability. (See Delta Force; Joint Special Operations Command.)

The HRT trains for a wide variety of scenarios and climates including hostage rescue and barricaded subjects, high-risk arrest/searches, mobile assaults, manhunt and rural operations, maritime operations, helicopter operations, weapons of mass destruction (WMD), and cold weather operations.

**References**
http://www.fbi.gov/hq/isd/cirg/tact.htm

# Intelligence Community

The term *intelligence community* describes all of the agencies with an intelligence role and capability that collectively form a community of those involved in similar activities, with similar goals, that complement each other when used collectively.

### Bureau of Intelligence and Research (INR)

**Background:** The INR has the task of assessing and disseminating intelligence under the State Department.

**Mission:** Primarily to harness intelligence to serve U.S. diplomacy.

**Activities:** Using all-source intelligence, the INR provides analysis of events to State Department policy makers, ensures that intelligence activities support foreign policy and national security purposes, and serves as the focal point in the State Department for ensuring policy review of sensitive counterintelligence and law enforcement activities. The bureau also analyzes geographical and international boundary issues and developed the Geographic Learning Site (GLS) for K–12 students.

### References

http://www.state.gov/s/inr/

### Joint Special Operations Command (JSOC)

**Headquarters:** Pope Air Force Base, North Carolina, and Fort Bragg, North Carolina

**Background:** Established in 1980.

**Mission/Activities:** A joint headquarters designed to study special operations requirements and techniques, ensure interoperability and equipment standardization, plan and conduct joint special operations exercises and training, and develop joint special operations tactics. Although JSOC's stated purpose is to provide a unified command structure for conducting joint special operations and exercises, it is widely reported that JSOC is actually the command responsible for conducting U.S. counterterrorism operations. JSOC is reported to command the U.S. military's Special Missions Units (SMUs). These SMUs are tasked with conducting counterterrorism operations, strike operations, reconnaissance in denied areas, and special intelligence missions.

JSOC units regularly conduct training with similar units from around the world and provide training to nations that request U.S. support. JSOC has also provided support to domestic law enforcement agencies during high-profile or high-risk events such as the Olympics, the World Cup, political party conventions, and presidential inaugurations.

The full text of PDD-25 is reported to exempt the JSOC from the Posse Comitatus Act of 1878 18USC Sec.1385, PL86–70, Sec.

17[d], which makes it illegal for military and law enforcement to exercise jointly.

### References

http://www.globalsecurity.org/military/agency/dod/jsoc

### Interagency Intelligence Committee on Terrorism (IICT)

**Background:** Established under a 1990 DCI directive.

**Mission:** The IICT assists the DCI in coordinating national intelligence and promoting the effective use of intelligence community resources on terrorism issues.

**Activities:** A senior-level intelligence community officer manages both the Community Counterterrorism Board (CCB) and the IICT. IICT membership consists of U.S. intelligence, security, law enforcement, regulatory, and defense communities. The IICT's seven subcommittees examine a range of issues from intelligence requirements to threat warning. On a need-to-know basis, the CCB produces coordinated Terrorism Alerts and Advisories for wide government audiences. The Terrorism Warning Group, established in 1997, is hosted by the CCB. To senior military and civilian policy makers, the group provides timely warnings of impending terrorist attacks. The IICT includes more than forty federal agencies that have counterterrorist intelligence functions either as producers or consumers, ranging from the National Security Agency to the U.S. Capitol Police. It also has subcommittees on intelligence requirements, technical countermeasures, training, warning, handling of information, CBRN matters, and research and development.

### References

http://www.cia.gov

http://www.intelligence.gov

Pillar, P. R. 2001. *Terrorism and U.S. Foreign Policy.* Washington, D.C.: Brookings Institution Press.

### National Infrastructure Protection Center (NIPC)

**Mission:** To support law enforcement counterterrorism efforts in the domain of "Critical Infrastructure Protection."

**Activities:** The National Infrastructure Protection Center provides threat assessments, warnings, investigations, and response for threats or attacks against critical infrastructures. With the growing threat to critical infrastructure, NIPC has devised a Critical Infrastructure Protection Plan for the emergency law enforcement sector. The plan provides agencies with guidance and tools for risk assessment and strategic planning.

### References
http://www.counterterrorismtraining.gov/plan/

http://www.nipc.gov

### National Intelligence Council (NIC)
**Background:** The NIC is a critical component of the intelligence community. Whereas the bulk of the intelligence community focuses on the immediate term, the NIC's focus is on mid-term and long-term strategic thinking.

   **Mission/Activities:** The NIC provides a focal point for policy makers to task the intelligence community to answer their questions. As such, it reaches out to nongovernment experts in academia and the private sector to broaden the intelligence community's perspective, thereby contributing to the intelligence community's efforts to allocate its resources in response to policy makers' changing needs. The council produces National Intelligence Estimates (NIEs), which are the DCI's most authoritative written judgments concerning national security issues. Based on the common denominator of a number of agencies, they contain the coordinated judgments of the intelligence community. Regardless of whether analytic judgments conform to U.S. policy or not, they are intended to forecast the likely course of future events. The NIC's goal is to provide policy makers with the best, unvarnished, and unbiased information.

### References
http://www.cia.gov/nic/

### National Intelligence Officers (NIO)
**Mission/Activities:** Members of the National Intelligence Officers advise the director of Central Intelligence; interact regularly with senior intelligence consumers and support their current and longer term needs; produce top-quality estimative intelligence; engage with outside experts to tap their knowledge and insights; help assess the capabilities and needs of intelligence community analytic producers; promote collaboration among those producers

on strategic warning, advanced analytic tools, and methodologies; and articulate substantive priorities to guide intelligence collection, evaluation, and procurement.

## References
http://www.cia.gov/nic/

## National Security Agency (NSA)

**Headquarters:** Fort Meade, Maryland

**Background:** President Harry Truman and the National Security Council issued a revised version of the National Security Council Intelligence Directive (NSCID) on October 24, 1952, which resulted in the formation of NSA on November 4, 1952.

**Mission:** The NSA's mission of "information assurance" provides solutions, products, and services, and conducts defensive information operations for information infrastructures critical to U.S. national security interests. The NSA is charged with the collection and dissemination of intelligence information from foreign electronic signals for national foreign intelligence and counterintelligence purposes and to support military operations. The foreign signals intelligence (SIGINT) mission allows for an effective, unified organization and control of all the foreign signals collection and processing activities of the United States. The NSA is authorized to produce SIGINT in accordance with objectives, requirements, and priorities established by the DCI with the advice of the National Foreign Intelligence Board. The agency also is tasked with preventing foreign adversaries from gaining access to classified national security information.

**Activities:** Provides signals intelligence pertaining to national security and interests domestically and internationally. The NSA also conducts one of the U.S. government's leading research and development programs. Some of the agency's R&D projects have significantly advanced the state of the art in the scientific and business worlds. The NSA's early interest in cryptanalytic research led to the first large-scale computer and the first solid-state computer, predecessors to the modern computer. The NSA pioneered efforts in flexible storage capabilities, which led to the development of the tape cassette. It also made groundbreaking developments in semiconductor technology and remains a world leader in many technological fields. The NSA works closely with its U.K. equivalent, the Government Communications Headquarters (GCHQ), headquartered in Cheltenham, England.

## Reference
http://www.nsa.gov

## National Security Council (NSC)

**Background:** Created under President Truman, the National Security Council is the president's principal forum for considering national security and foreign policy matters with his/her senior national security advisers and cabinet officials. The NSC is chaired by the president and attended by the vice president, secretary of state, secretary of the treasury, secretary of defense, and the assistant to the president for national security affairs. The chairman of the Joint Chiefs of Staff is the statutory military adviser to the council, and the director of Central Intelligence is the intelligence adviser. The chief of staff to the president, counsel to the president, and the assistant to the president for economic policy are invited to attend any NSC meeting. The U.S. attorney general and the director of the Office of Management and Budget are invited to attend meetings pertaining to their responsibilities. The heads of other executive departments and agencies, as well as other senior officials, are invited to attend meetings of the NSC when appropriate.

**Mission/Activities:** To advise and assist the president on national security and foreign policies. The council also serves as the president's principal arm for coordinating these policies among various government agencies.

## References
http://www.whitehouse.gov/nsc/

## National Terrorist Asset Tracking Center (NTAC)

**Background:** In May 2000 the Clinton administration took steps toward establishing an interagency National Terrorist Asset Tracking Center (NTAC), to be supervised by the Secret Service (see entry).

**Mission/Activities:** To investigate and counter terrorist financing activities, as well as to strengthen the Office of Foreign Assets Control (see entry).

## Office of Foreign Assets Control (OFAC)

**Background:** OFAC is the Treasury Department's equivalent of the NTAC. OFAC itself was formally created in December 1950, following the entry of China into the Korean War, when President Truman declared a national emergency under the Trading with the Enemy Act (TWEA) and blocked all Chinese and North Korean assets subject to U.S. jurisdiction.

**Mission/Activities:** OFAC acts under presidential wartime and national emergency powers, as well as authority granted by specific legislation, to impose controls on transactions and freeze foreign assets under U.S. jurisdiction. Many of the sanctions are based on United Nations and other international mandates, are multilateral in scope, and involve close cooperation with allied governments. OFAC administers and enforces economic sanctions programs based on U.S. foreign policy and national security goals against targeted foreign countries, terrorists, international narcotics traffickers, and those engaged in activities related to the proliferation of weapons of mass destruction. The sanctions can be either comprehensive or selective, using the blocking of assets and trade restrictions to accomplish foreign policy and national security goals.

### References

http://www.ustreas.gov/offices/enforcement/ofac/faq/index.html

Pillar, P. R. 2001. *Terrorism and U.S. Foreign Policy.* Washington, D.C.: Brookings Institution Press.

### Naval Special Warfare Development Group (NSWDG)

**Headquarters:** Dam Neck, Virginia

**Background:** Founded in 1980, the NSWDG (also known as Dev Group or DEVGRU, and formerly known as SEAL Team SIX) comes under the direct command of NAVSPECWARGRU (Naval Special War Group). It is also a component of the Joint Special Operations Command, along with other counterterrorism units such as Delta Force and the 160th Special Operations Aviation Regiment (SOAR). (See Delta Force; Joint Special Operations Command; SOAR.)

**Mission:** To conduct and oversee U.S. maritime counterterrorist operations.

**Activities:** Maintains an operational proficiency on land, sea, and air, with a variety of weapons, vehicles, and equipment pertaining to its mission. Activities also include hostage rescue, defense of territories, long-range and close-target reconnaissance (CTRs), intelligence gathering, crisis response/management, and covert/clandestine operations. It has been reported that the

NSWDG is one of only a handful of U.S. units authorized to conduct *preemptive* actions against terrorists and terrorist facilities. It is integrated with the Delta Force but retains the ability to function as an independent unit. The group takes part in exchanges with other counterterrorism teams around the world.

### References

Davies, B. 2003. *Terrorism: Inside a World Phenomenon*. London: Virgin.

http://www.terrorism.com

### Secret Service

**Background:** The Secret Service Division was formed on July 5, 1865, in Washington, D.C., to suppress counterfeit currency. The 2001 Patriot Act (Public Law 107-56) increased the Secret Service's role in investigating fraud and related activity in connections with computers.

**Mission:** Mandated by the U.S. Congress to carry out two missions: protection and criminal investigations.

**Activities:** The Secret Service is responsible for the protection of the president and vice president and their families, heads of state, and other designated individuals; the investigation of threats against these protectees; protection of the White House and vice president's residence, foreign missions, and other buildings within Washington, D.C.; and security design, planning, and implementation at designated national special security events. The Secret Service is also responsible for the enforcement of laws relating to counterfeiting of obligations and securities of the United States, investigation of financial crimes including access device fraud, financial institution fraud, identity theft, computer fraud, and telecommunications fraud; and computer-based attacks on U.S. financial, banking, and telecommunications infrastructure. The Secret Service also runs the National Threat Assessment Center (NTAC), which provides law enforcement and related professionals with timely and effective assistance necessary to develop threat assessment programs and investigate and prevent targeted violence.

### References

http://www.secretservice.gov

http://www.ustreas.gov/usss/index.shtml

## SOAR—160th Special Operations Aviation Regiment

**Background:** SOAR is also known as the "Nightstalkers." Their motto is "Nightstalkers don't quit!" The regiment was formed from several different aviation battalions and was officially recognized as a unit on October 16, 1981. The Nightstalkers have been actively involved in counterterrorism operations since the early 1980s.

**Mission/Activities:** The 160th Special Operations Aviation Regiment (SOAR) uses specially modified rotary-winged aircraft and highly trained pilots to get special warfare teams to their mission through hostile territory or weather. It consists of three battalions, two "white" and one "black" (for classified missions). The 1st and 2nd Battalions are located at Fort Campbell, Kentucky, while the 3rd is located at Hunter Army Airfield in Georgia. SOAR operates a group of highly modified aircraft in its missions that are fitted with special avionics to allow them to fly at low level at night or in inclement weather. In addition it has increased weaponry and armor that enables them to survive under enemy fire.

### References

http://www.specwarnet.net/americas/soar.htm

## State Department Counterterrorism Finance and Designation Unit

**Mission:** To target terrorist financial infrastucture: cutting off financial support to terrorists—starving terrorists of their access to money and resources—and helping to bring them to justice.

**Activities:** The CFD Unit coordinates the delivery of technical assistance and training to governments around the world that seek to improve their ability to investigate, identify, and interdict the flow of money to terrorist groups. It works closely with other governments to cut off the sources and flows of support to terrorists and coordinates with the U.S. Department of Treasury and the Department of Justice to designate foreign terrorist organizations.

### References

http://www.state.gov/s/ct/terfin/

### Special Mission Units (SMUs)

**Background:** The U.S. government invested significantly to reduce the threat posed by terrorism and proliferation by developing specialist units even during the Cold War. In 1998, a senior official of the U.S. Department of Defense acknowledged the existence of covert action teams to combat terrorism and to counter potential terrorist use of weapons of mass destruction (WMD). These "Special Mission Units" are staffed, equipped, and trained to deal with a wide variety of transnational threats.

**Mission:** The closely guarded SMUs are tasked with conducting counterterrorism operations. This includes strike operations, reconnaissance in denied areas, and special intelligence missions.

**Activities:** Much of the hunting for senior Taliban and Al-Qaeda members in Afghanistan is believed to have been conducted by a unit called Task Force 11, composed mostly of Delta Force soldiers and SEALs. These units also participated in the Iraq campaign in the hunt for Saddam Hussein and other regime leaders. JSOC units have reportedly been involved in a number of covert military operations during the 1980s and 1990s, including providing assistance to Italian authorities during their search for kidnapped U.S. Army General James Dozier; participating in the U.S. invasion of Grenada (Operation URGENT FURY); planning a rescue attempt of U.S. hostages being held in Lebanon; rescuing hostages being held aboard the cruise liner *Achille Lauro*; participating in the U.S. intervention in Panama (Operation JUST CAUSE); directing U.S. Scud-hunting efforts in Iraq during Operation DESERT STORM (1990); conducting operations in support of UN mandates in Somalia; and searching for suspected war criminals in the former Republic of Yugoslavia. (See also Joint Special Operations Command.)

### References

http://www.globalsecurity.org/military/agency/dod/jsoc.htm

### Technical Support Working Group (TSWG)

**Background:** The U.S. government recognized that countering terrorism requires close day-to-day coordination among many executive branch agencies. Part of the growing challenge was to identify needs, seek common approaches, and coordinate development of new technologies. Toward meeting this challenge, the government created the interagency Technical Support Working Group.

**Mission:** To identify, prioritize, and coordinate interagency and international research and development (R&D) requirements for combating terrorism; conduct the national interagency research and development program for combating terrorism through rapid research, development, and prototyping; identify requirements, develop solutions, and execute projects; and customize technology to specific user needs.

**Activities:** The TSWG involves more than fifty federal offices that participate with program direction provided by an executive committee consisting of representatives from the departments of State, Defense, and Energy, and the FBI. The TSWG rapidly develops technologies and equipment to meet the high-priority needs of combating the terrorism community and addresses joint international operational requirements through cooperative R&D with major allies. The TSWG also sponsors R&D not addressed by individual agencies and fulfills an intelligence support role in the collection and dissemination of terrorism-related information taken to oppose terrorism throughout the entire threat spectrum (including terrorist use of chemical, biological, radiological, or nuclear materials or high-yield explosive devices).

**References**

http://www.tswg.gov

Pillar, P. R. 2001. *Terrorism and U.S. Foreign Policy.* Washington, D.C.: Brookings Institution Press.

# International Government Agencies

## France

### Groupement d'Intervention de la Gendarmerie Nationale (GIGN)

**Headquarters:** Outside Versailles, France

**Background:** Formed in 1973 to enable a French counterterrorism (CT) and hostage rescue (HR) capability. The unit recruits from the Gendarmerie (French police force).

**Mission:** To maintain and execute effective rapid response CT/HR capability and operations.

**Activities:** Maintains an operational proficiency on land, sea, and air, with a variety of weapons, vehicles, and equipment pertaining to its mission. Also takes part in exchange programs with other CT units, and some training of other countries' CT units.

### References
Davies, B. 2003. *Terrorism: Inside a World Phenomenon.* London: Virgin.

## Germany

### Grenzschutzgruppe 9 (GSG9)
**Headquarters:** St. Augustin barracks, Bonn, Germany

**Background:** Formed after the disastrous attempt at hostage rescue at the 1972 Munich Olympic Games, the unit recruits from the German federal border police. It has close ties with the United Kingdom's Special Air Service (see entry).

**Mission:** To maintain and execute effective rapid response CT/HR capability and operations.

**Activities:** Maintains an operational proficiency on land, sea, and air, with a variety of weapons, vehicles, and equipment pertaining to its mission. Also takes part in exchange programs with other CT units, and some training of other countries' CT units.

### References
Davies, B. 2003. *Terrorism: Inside a World Phenomenon.* London: Virgin.

### Kommando Spezialkraefte (KSK)
**Background:** Formed in 1996 in response to the need to have a military CT/HR unit capable of deploying and operating internationally. It predominantly recruits from the German Army airborne units.

**Mission:** Military CT/HR operations outside German borders.

**Activities:** Maintains an operational proficiency on land, sea, and air, with a variety of weapons, vehicles, and equipment pertaining to its mission. Activities also include hostage rescue, the defense of territories, long-range and close-target reconnaissance (CTRs), intelligence gathering, crisis response/management, and covert/clandestine operations. Also takes part in exchange programs with other CT units, and some training of other countries' CT units.

### References
Davies, B. 2003. *Terrorism: Inside a World Phenomenon*. London: Virgin.

# Israel

### Mista'Aravim (Hebrew for "To become an Arab")
**Headquarters:** undisclosed location in Israel

**Background:** Origins are unknown; one of the original units, Duvdevan (West Bank), is still in operation.

**Mission:** Proactive covert intelligence gathering operations.

**Activities:** Maintains an operational proficiency with a variety of weapons, vehicles, and equipment pertaining to its mission. Agents/members are trained in close quarter combat (CQB), disguise, and surveillance techniques in order to operate covertly and to conduct the activities of hostage rescue, intelligence gathering, counterterrorism missions, and assassination of leading Intifada members.

### Reference
Davies, B. 2003. *Terrorism: Inside a World Phenomenon*. London: Virgin.

### Mossad (Hebrew for "Institute")
**Headquarters:** Tel Aviv, Israel

**Background:** The Institute for Intelligence and Special Tasks (ha-Mossad le-Modiin ule-Tafkidim Meyuhadim), formerly known as the Central Institute for Coordination and the Central Institute for Intelligence and Security, was formed by Prime Minister David Ben Gurion on April 1, 1951.

**Mission:** To enhance and aid the defense of Israel through human intelligence collection, covert action, and counterterrorism.

**Activities:** Mossad's focus is on Arab nations and organizations throughout the world. It also is responsible for the clandestine movement of Jewish refugees out of Syria, Iran, and Ethiopia. Mossad agents are active in the former communist countries, in the West, and at the United Nations. Mossad has eight departments, which include collections (HUMINT, or human intelligence), liaison, "black" or special operations, psy-ops, research/analysis, and technological development.

### References
http://fas.org/irp/world/israel/mossad/

### Sayaret Mat'Kal ("General Staff Recon" or "The Unit")
**Background:** Formed in 1957 and based on the United Kingdom's SAS.

**Mission:** To undertake domestic military counterterrorism within Israel.

**Activities:** CT/HR operations, as well as surveillance/reconnaissance. Maintains an operational proficiency with a variety of weapons, vehicles, and equipment pertaining to its mission. Activities also include the defense of territories, long-range and close-target reconnaissance (CTRs), intelligence gathering, crisis-response/management, and covert/clandestine operations. Unit 269 is an elite unit within Sayaret Mat'Kal that members can apply for; it executes counterterrorism operations outside Israeli territory. Both units have taken part in hostage rescue missions.

### References
Davies, B. 2003. *Terrorism: Inside a World Phenomenon.* London: Virgin.

http://www.isayeret.com

### Yechida Meyuchedet Le'Milchama Baterror (YA'MA'M; "Special Unit for War against Terrorism")
**Background:** Formed in 1974 in response to high-profile mission failures of Sayaret Mat'Kal in dealing with terrorist hostage incidents. Another domestic CT unit is "LOTAR Eilat," which operates solely in the Eilat city area.

**Mission:** Domestic military counterterrorism (within Israel).

**Activities:** Maintains an operational proficiency with a variety of weapons, vehicles, and equipment pertaining to its mission. Activities also include the defense of territories, long-range and close-target reconnaissance, intelligence gathering, crisis-response/management, and covert/clandestine operations. Supports counterterrorism operations using snipers, surveillance, covert, and clandestine long-range reconnaissance missions.

### References
Davies, B. 2003. *Terrorism: Inside a World Phenomenon*. London: Virgin.

http://www.isayeret.com

## Russia

### Alpha Units
**Background:** Created in 1974 by the KGB in response to the sweeping international wave of terrorist acts, and under the control of the KGB until it sided with Boris Yeltsin in the coup against Mikhail Gorbachev in 1991 against orders, after which it was moved to the jurisdiction of the Ministry of Internal Affairs (MVD); now falls under the Federal Security Service. Alpha's counterterrorism efforts and capabilities (along with Vega and the USO) are coordinated by the Anti-Terrorist Center in Russia's federal Securtiy Service (FSB) system.

    **Mission:** To conduct military counterterrorism and hostage rescue operations.

    **Activities:** Maintains an operational proficiency on land, sea, and air, with a variety of weapons, vehicles, and equipment pertaining to its mission. Activities also include VIP protection, hostage rescue, the defense of territories, long-range and close-target reconnaissance, intelligence gathering, crisis response/management, and covert/clandestine special forces operations.

### References
Davies, B. 2003. *Terrorism: Inside a World Phenomenon*. London: Virgin.

## United Kingdom

### Special Air Service (SAS)
**Headquarters:** Credenhill, Hereford, England

    **Background:** Formed during World War II, the SAS is first and foremost a special forces unit, and is used as a model for all other similar units. Its counterterrorism wing (CT-Wing) is thought to be the best in the world. The SAS did not form a counterterrorism/hostage rescue capability in response to any event, but predicted the need for one and so trained and equipped a team in anticipation. The first SAS counterterrorism team led the way in developing CT tactics, formation, organization, strategy, and training. The SAS remains, and is regarded by its peers to be, at the forefront of counterterrorism operations.

**Mission:** To provide 24-hour rapid and effective response (in activities listed below) to any situation anywhere in the world.

**Activities:** Conducts military counterterrorism operations. Maintains an operational proficiency on land, sea, and air, with a variety of weapons, vehicles, and equipment pertaining to its mission. Activities also include VIP protection, hostage rescue, the defense of territories, long-range and close-target reconnaissance, intelligence gathering, crisis response/management, and covert/clandestine special forces operations. The SAS is trained to operate in any environment. Also takes part in exchange programs with other counterterrorism units and trains other countries' CT units.

### Special Boat Service (SBS) (UK)

**Headquarters:** Poole, Dorset, UK

**Background:** Like the SAS, the SBS was formed during World War II and is first and foremost a Special Forces Unit, but also the leading maritime CT unit.

**Mission:** To provide 24-hour rapid and effective response (in activities listed below) to any situation anywhere in the world.

**Activities:** Conducts military maritime counterterrorism operations. Maintains an operational proficiency on land, sea, and air, with a variety of weapons, vehicles, and equipment pertaining to their mission. Activities also include VIP protection, hostage rescue, the defense of territories, long-range reconnaissance and close-target recce's (CTRs), intelligence gathering, crisis response/management, and covert/clandestine Special Forces operations. The SBS is capable of operating in any environment. Also takes part in exchange programs with other CT units and trains other countries' CT units.

### References

Davies, B. 2003. *Terrorism: Inside a World Phenomenon.* London: Virgin.

# Nongovernmental Organizations (NGOs)

### International Centre for Political Violence and Terrorism Research (ICPVTR)

**Headquarters:** Institute of Defence and Strategic Studies, Nanyang Technological University, Singapore

**Background:** The Political Violence and Terrorism Programme of the Institute of Defence and Strategic Studies in Singapore was upgraded to a center of excellence in 2004. The specialist center, staffed by personnel from the United States, Europe, the Middle East, Africa, and Asia, is the largest and the most resourceful terrorism center located outside the West.

**Mission:** The ICPVTR aims to reduce the threat of terrorism by conducting research into terrorist, guerrilla, extremist, and other organizations of security interest. In addition to advising government and business leaders, the ICPVTR trains future leaders in countering terrorism.

**Activities:** The primary activities include the management of state-of-the-art integrated databases on domestic and international terrorist incident, group, and personality profiles and attack profiles; training the specialized branches of governments to strengthen and enhance their counter- and antiterrorism capabilities and capacities; and imparting informal and formal public education to increase public awareness of the terrorist threat as well as to build an ethic and norm against the use of violence as a form of political expression. In addition to offering a module in counterterrorism at the master's level, the center supervises doctoral students specializing in counterterrorism.

### Centre for the Study of Terrorism and Political Violence (CSTPV)

**Headquarters:** University of St. Andrews, Scotland, UK

**Background:** The CSTPV was established in 1994 by academics (Dr. Bruce Hoffman and Professor Paul Wilkinson) who have been studying terrorism since the late 1960s.

**Mission:** Aims to investigate the roots of political violence, to develop a body of theory spanning its various disparate elements, and to study the impact of violence, and responses to it, at societal, governmental, and international levels.

**Activities:** Monitors and predicts trends of terrorism and political violence worldwide as well as profiling groups' strengths, tactics, funding, links, and so on. Conducts research projects such as assessing and planning measures for response to major incidents/attacks and organizes regular seminars with representatives from academia, private and public sectors, policy makers and politicians, and security practitioners in order to increase understanding and bridge the gaps between.

### References
http://www.st-andrews.ac.uk/academic/intrel/research/cstpv/

### International Policy Institute for Counter-Terrorism (ICT)
**Headquarters:** Herzliya, Israel

**Background:** Formed in 1996 at the academic Interdisciplinary Center (IDC) in Israel, the ICT is a research institute and think tank that focuses solely on the subject of counterterrorism, both domestically and internationally.

**Mission:** To develop innovative public policy solutions to international terrorism. The institute applies an integrated, solutions-oriented approach built on a foundation of real-world and practical experience.

**Activities:** Although the ICT provides situational recommendations to the private sector, this is a peripheral activity. The institute aims to affect policy at the highest levels, in joint cooperation with the world community. It conducts applied research concerning the roots of terrorism, its motivations, and causes—with the aim of defining more effective ways of combating terrorism as a phenomenon. It formulates and publishes research papers, situation reports, and informational publications for worldwide distribution, as well as organizing seminars with representatives from academia, policy makers, and security practitioners in order to increase understanding of terrorism.

### References
http://www.ict.org.il/

### National Memorial Institute for the Prevention of Terrorism (MIPT)
**Headquarters:** Oklahoma City, Oklahoma

**Background:** Incorporated on September 23, 1999, as a nonprofit corporation in Oklahoma and recognized as a charitable organization by the Internal Revenue Service, the MIPT grew out of the desire of the survivors and families of the Murrah Federal Building bombing of April 19, 1995, to have a living memorial.

**Mission:** Dedicated to research pertaining to the prevention of terrorism or mitigating its effects.

**Activities:** Sponsors research to discover equipment, training, and procedures that might assist "first responders" (police officers, firefighters, emergency medical technicians, and all of the others who are first on the scene in the aftermath of terrorist activity) in preventing terrorism and responding to it. Engages in research and academic activities that fit its mission. Currently funded by a special congressional appropriation that directs it to conduct "research into the social and political causes and effects of terrorism and the development of technologies to counter biological, nuclear, and chemical weapons of mass destruction as well as cyberterrorism."

### References
http://www.mipt.org/

### RAND Corporation
**Headquarters:** Washington, D.C.

**Background:** RAND (a contraction of the term *research and development*) was the first organization to be called a "think tank." It was created in 1946 by its original client, the U.S. Air Force.

**Mission:** To help improve policy and decision making through research and analysis.

**Activities:** Developing new knowledge to inform decision-makers without suggesting any specific course of action, as well as spelling out the range of available options and by analyzing their relative advantages and disadvantages. For nearly three decades, RAND's work has included investigating the origins, development, and implications of terrorism; developing a body of theory; and examining policy options for democratic governments and the private sector.

### References
http://www.rand.org

# Intergovernmental Organizations

Most of the effective counterterrorist work is carried out through and by the national agencies working jointly with other national agencies and/or bilaterally. Thus, "international counterterrorist agencies" are less effective due to the associated problems mentioned earlier of proliferation of sensitive information and the like. Furthermore, international agencies often do not have any real powers or opt-out clauses to enforce international obligations. In addition, they are dependent on all members agreeing to cooperate. For these reasons we have concentrated more on U.S. national counterterrorism agencies and made short reference to international organizations.

### Inter-American Committee against Terrorism (CICTE)

**Background:** The Second Specialized Conference on Terrorism, held in Mar del Plata, Argentina, on November 23–24, 1998, concluded with the adoption of the Commitment of Mar del Plata. That commitment called for establishing within the Organization of American States an "Inter-American Committee against Terrorism" composed of "competent national authorities" of the member states. Within the inter-American system, the Inter-American Committee against Terrorism (CICTE) serves to coordinate efforts to protect the citizens of the member nations from terrorism. Preeminent leaders, subject matter experts, and decision makers exchange information and work together to strengthen hemispheric solidarity and security.

**Mission:** As set forth in the Commitment of Mar del Plata to enhance the exchange of information via the competent national authorities, including the establishment of an inter-American database on terrorism issues; formulate a proposal to assist member states in drafting appropriate counterterrorism legislation in all states; compile the bilateral, subregional, regional, and multilateral treaties and agreements signed by member states and promote universal adherence to international counterterrorism conventions; enhance border cooperation and travel documentation security measures; and develop activities for training and crisis management.

**Activities:** At the twenty-third Meeting of Consultation of Ministers of Foreign Affairs on September 21, 2001, in Washington, D.C., the CICTE adopted a resolution strengthening cooperation to prevent, combat, and eliminate terrorism. Resolution RC.23/RES.1/01 called upon CICTE (1) to strengthen cooperation between the member states, at the regional and international levels, to pursue, capture, prosecute, and punish and, as appropriate, to expedite the extradition of the perpetrators, organizers, and sponsors of these terrorist acts, strengthen mutual legal assistance, and exchange information in a timely manner; (2) to instruct the Permanent Council to convoke, as soon as possible, a meeting of the Inter-American Committee against Terrorism so that it may identify urgent actions aimed at strengthening inter-American cooperation to prevent, combat, and eliminate terrorism in the hemisphere; (3) to entrust the Permanent Council with preparing a draft Inter-American Convention against Terrorism with a view to presenting it to the next session of the OAS General Assembly; (4) to urge the states to study the international legal repercussions of the conduct of government authorities who provide financial support to, protect, or harbor terrorist individuals or groups.

During 2002, the secretariat designed and deployed the CICTE On-Line Antiterrorism Database in support of the 2002–2003 work plan. Additionally, CICTE has participated in the drafting of model regulations for the prevention of terrorist financing with OAS-CICAD's group of experts. CICTE has also participated in meetings of the Caribbean Financial Action Task Force (CFATF) and the United Nations Security Council Counterterrorism Committee (CTC).

A key milestone in 2002 was the drafting and signing of the OAS Convention against Terrorism. This landmark document was signed by thirty of the organization's member states at the OAS General Assembly in Bridgeton, Barbados, on June 3 of that year.

### References

http://scm.oas.org/doc_public/ENGLISH/HIST_03/CP10953E04.doc

http://www.cicte.oas.org/history.htm

### Interpol (International Criminal Police Investigation)

**Headquarters:** Lyons, France

**Background:** Interpol's involvement in the fight against international terrorism materialized during the fifty-fourth General Assembly in Washington in 1985 when Resolution AGN/54/RES/1 (Washington, D.C., 1985) was passed, calling for the creation of a specialized group within the then Police Division and set out the group's mission (see below). The same resolution also called for the preparation of an instruction manual "outlining the practical possibilities that currently exist for cooperation in dealing with terrorist cases."

**Mission:** To coordinate and enhance cooperation in combating international terrorism.

**Activities:** The Public Safety and Terrorism subdirectorate (PST) deals with matters relating to terrorism, firearms and explosives, attacks and threats against civil aviation, maritime piracy, and weapons of mass destruction. It attempts to encourage the widest possible cooperation and exchange of information and makes maximum use of communication networks and central records capabilities to maximize subsequent analyses or responses to queries from member countries from all information it receives. Interpol also liaises with a number of international organizations and organizes various symposia and working groups for people involved in the fight against terrorism. Interpol has the authority to address all criminal activity, including terrorism.

### References

http://www.interpol.int/Public/Terrorism/default.asp

http://www.interpol.int/Public/Terrorism/financing.asp

http://www.interpol.int/Public/Terrorism/resolutions.asp

### North Atlantic Treaty Organization (NATO)

**Headquarters:** Brussels, Belgium

**Background:** In the years following the end of World War Two, many Western European countries and their North American allies had legitimate concerns with the U.S.S.R.'s growing military presence and threats of international intervention from the Communist Russian government. NATO was officially created as an alliance of twelve Western countries in April 1949 with the signing of the North Atlantic Treaty (also known as the Washington Treaty). The alliance evolved during the Cold War years to include more countries. Presently, twenty-six countries form the mulinational NATO alliance. On September 12, 2001, NATO members invoked Article 5 of the Washington Treaty, declaring the September 11 attack against the United States to be an attack against all nineteen allies. Each NATO member committed itself to assisting the United States by taking actions deemed necessary to do so. In response to requests by the United States, the allies agreed on October 4, 2001, to take eight measures to expand the options available in the campaign against terrorism. These initial measures included enhanced intelligence sharing, blanket overflight rights and access to ports and airfields, assistance to states threatened as a result of their support for coalition efforts, the deployment of NATO naval forces to the eastern Mediterranean, and airborne early warning aircraft to patrol U.S. airspace.

At NATO's Prague Summit in November 2002, heads of state and government of NATO member countries adopted a package of measures that will strengthen NATO's preparedness and ability to take on the full spectrum of security challenges, including terrorism and the spread of weapons of mass destruction.

**Mission:** To play an important role as a platform for political support and multinational military action. NATO continues to engage its Euro-Atlantic Partnership Council (EAPC) partners in its response to terrorism and is working to enhance its dialogue with seven southern Mediterranean nations. NATO's new military concept for defense against terrorism underlines the alliance's readiness. It includes development of measures to act against terrorist attacks, or the threat of such attacks, directed from abroad against their populations, territory, infrastructure, and forces; to provide assistance to national authorities in dealing with the consequences of terrorist attacks; to support operations by the European Union or other international organizations or coalitions involving allies; and to deploy forces as and where required to carry out such missions. These activities will be supported by measures to further improve intelligence sharing among allies. The activities include: "Active Endeavour," the continuing maritime operation of patrolling the eastern Mediterranean, monitoring merchant shipping, and boarding suspicious vessels. The NATO-Russia Council identifies terrorism as one of several areas for NATO-Russia consultation and practical cooperation. NATO member forces in the Balkans have acted against terrorist groups with links to the Al Qaeda network by focusing on the illegal movement of people, arms, and drugs and by working with the authorities throughout the region on border security issues. Bringing together elite forces from both sides of the Atlantic has resulted in the formation of the NATO Response Force (NRF)—a technologically advanced and highly flexible force that is ready to move quickly to wherever needed, as decided by the NATO Council. It will have initial operating capability at the latest by October 2004, and full operating capability no later than October 2006. NATO has five anti-WMD initiatives under way: a deployable nuclear, chemical, and biological (NBC) analytical laboratory; an NBC event response team; a virtual center of excellence for NBC weapons defense; a NATO biological and chemical defense stockpile; and a disease surveillance system. Efforts are also under way within the alliance to better protect against and otherwise prepare for a possible disruption of NATO and national critical infrastructure assets, including information and communications systems.

## References

http://www.nato.int

http://www.nato.int/terrorism/factsheet.htm

http://www.nato.int/terrorism/five.htm

http://www.nato.int/terrorism/index.htm#c

http://www.un.org/Docs/sc/committees/1373/nato_contribution.doc

## United Nations Terrorism Prevention Branch (UN-TPB)

**Headquarters:** Vienna, Austria

**Background:** Commenced operations in April 1999.

**Mission:** "To promote international cooperation in terrorism prevention, conduct research activities on terrorism in all its forms and manifestations, and engage in technical cooperation activities in efforts to prevent terrorism."

**Activities:** Maintenance and updating of databases of international terrorist incidents, threat assessments, research projects, and preparation of technical cooperation manuals.

## References

http://www.unodc.org/unodc/en/terrorism.html

http://www.un.org/Docs/sc/committees/1373/

http://www.un.org/terrorism/index.html

# 7

# Print and Nonprint Resources

## Print

Adams, J. 1989. *Secret Armies.* London: Pan.

A dated but useful book that details the history, evolution, and uses of international covert units.

———. 1999. *The Next World War.* London: Arrow.

Outlines the threats and possible scenarios of asymmetric warfare.

Bergen, P. L. 2002. *Holy War Inc.* London: Phoenix.

A comprehensive account of Osama bin Laden and Al Qaeda, from unprecedented access.

Buzan, B. 1991. *People, States, and Fear: An Agenda for International Security Studies in the Post–Cold War Era.* London: Harvester Wheatsheaf.

Provides a useful debate on redefining security to meet the new security challenges of a post–Cold War environment.

Chalk, P. 1998. **"The Response to Terrorism as a Threat to Liberal Democracy."** *Australian Journal of Politics and History* 4, 3 (September): 373.

Provides guidelines for response.

Claridge, D. 2000. **"Exploding the Myths of Superterrorism."** *The Future of Terrorism.* London: Frank Cass.

Useful analysis of the reality of the WMD threat.

Collins, E. 1998. *Killing Rage.* London: Granta.

A personal account of a former terrorist and informer.

Combs, C. C. 1997. *Terrorism in the Twenty-first Century.* Upper Saddle River, NJ: Prentice Hall.

Examines the nature of terrorist perpetrators from varying perspectives and responses.

Combs, C. C., and Slann, M. 2002. *Encyclopedia of Terrorism.* New York: Facts on File.

Presents terrorism as a means of surrogate warfare and argues that a growing number of governments are themselves using terrorist tactics, employing terrorist groups, or exploiting terrorist incidents.

Crenshaw, M., ed. 1995. *Terrorism in Context.* University Park: Pennsylvania State University Press.

Experts from different disciplines—politics, economics, and so on—examine terrorism.

Davies, B. 2003. *Terrorism: Inside a World Phenomenon.* London: Virgin.

Interesting analysis from the perspective of a former SAS member.

Gunaratna, R. 2002. *Inside Al Qaeda.* London: Hurst.

Definitive book on Al Qaeda's organization, networks, ideology, training, funding, and how to counter it, based on interviews with Al Qaeda members and intelligence organization members.

Gurr, N., and Cole. B. 2000. *The New Face of Terrorism.* London: I. B. Tauris.

Examines the threat from WMD terrorism, arguing that a balance should be found between overexaggeration/hysteria and preparedness/contingency planning. Contains useful database of WMD-related terrorist events.

Harmon, C. C. 2000. *Terrorism Today.* London: Frank Cass.

Wide-ranging coverage of groups and trends as well as threat assessment.

Hoffman, B. 1999. *Inside Terrorism.* London: Indigo.

A leading expert on terrorism outlines the nature, trends, evolution, and future of terrorism.

Hudson, R. A., and Federal Research Division of the Library of Congress. 1999. *Who Becomes a Terrorist and Why: The 1999 Government Report on Profiling Terrorists.* Guilford, CT: Lyons.

Data and findings from attempts to research and formulate "terrorist profiles."

Jamieson, A. 1989. *The Heart Attacked.* London: Marion Boyars.

Interesting insight into terrorism in Italy during the 1970s, using interviews with former terrorist group members.

Jenkins, B. M. 1985. **"The U.S. Response to Terrorism: A Policy Dilemma."** *Armed Forces Journal* (April): 39, 41, 44–45.

Presents terrorism as a means of surrogate warfare and argues that a growing number of governments are themselves using terrorist tactics, employing terrorist groups, or exploiting terrorist incidents.

Kegley, C. W., Jr., ed. 2003. *The New Global Terrorism.* Upper Saddle River, NJ: Prentice Hall.

Useful collection from a number of expert contributors on the characteristics, causes, and possible ways to combat terrorism.

McGartland, M. 1998. *Fifty Dead Men Walking.* London: Blake.

Personal account of a former terrorist and informer.

————. 2000. *Dead Man Running.* London: Mainstream.

Updated personal account of a former terrorist/informer.

O'Callaghan, S. 1999. *The Informer.* London: Corgi.

Personal account of a former terrorist turned informer.

Pedahzur, Ami, and Ranstorp, Magnus. 2001. **"A Tertiary Model for Countering Terrorism in Liberal Democracies: The Case of Israel."** *Terrorism and Political Violence* 13, no. 2 (summer): 1–26.

Provides a theoretical framework to make emergency measures more accountable and democratic.

Pillar, P. R. 2001. *Terrorism and U.S. Foreign Policy.* Washington, DC: Brookings Institution Press.

The U.S. perspective on terrorism and counterterrorism measured in relation to U.S. foreign policy.

Rapoport, D. 1996. **"Editorial: The Media and Terrorism; Implications of the Unabomber Case."** *Terrorism and Political Violence* 8, 1 (Spring): viii.

Case study examining U.S. experiences of complexities of relationship between terrorism and the media.

Reich, W., ed. 1996. *Origins of Terrorism.* Cambridge: Cambridge University Press.

Valuable collection of papers covering psychologies of terrorism, ideologies, theologies, states of mind of terrorists, and implications for research and practice.

Schmid, A., and Crelinsten, R. 1993. *Western Responses to Terrorism.* London: Frank Cass.

Valuable collection of contributions from academics and practitioners examining various national experiences of and responses to terrorism.

Sprinzak, E. 1998. **"The Great Superterrorism Scare."** *Foreign Policy* 112 (Fall): 110–124.

Details the balance between being prepared and making ourselves more of a target through panic and hysteria.

Taylor, M., and Horgan, J. 2000. *The Future of Terrorism*. London: Frank Cass.

Excellent collection of papers from academics and practitioners covering the most pressing issues concerning terrorism, future predictions, and response.

Viotti, P., and Kauppi, M. 1993. *International Relations Theory*. New York: Macmillan.

A useful dictionary explaining paradigms and theories.

Wilkinson, P. 2001a. *Aviation Terrorism and Security*. London: Frank Cass.

Invaluable collection of contributions from academics and practitioners examining threats, vulnerabilities, and recommendations for revising security.

———. 2001b. *Terrorism Versus Democracy*. London: Frank Cass.

Examines trends, emergence, and tactics of terrorism before assessing options and problems of liberal democratic response in countering terrorism.

# Nonprint

BBC News: http://news.bbc.co.uk/

Canada's Counterterrorism Program: http://www.csis-scrs.gc.ca/eng/operat/ct_e.html

Center for Democracy and Terrorism: http://www.cdt.org/policy/terrorism/

Commentary published by the Canadian Security Intelligence Service: http://www.csis-scrs.gc.ca/eng/operat/ct_e.html

Counterterrorism home page: http://www.counterterrorism.com/

Counterterrorism bills and proposals: http://www.epic.org/privacy/terrorism/

Electronic Frontier Foundation: http://www.eff.org/pub/Privacy/Terrorism_militias/

Emergency Response Guide to Terrorism: http://www.emergency.com/cntrterr.htm

Federal Emergency Management Agency: http://www.fema.gov

Financial Action Task Force on Money Laundering: http://www.fatf-gafi.org/

Foreign and Commonwealth Office (HMG-UK): http://www.fco.gov.uk

Home Office (HMG-UK): http://www.homeoffice.gov.uk/

International Association of Counterterrorism and Security Professionals: http://www.securitynet.net

International Center for Counterterrorism Studies: http://www.potomacinstitute.org/academic/icts.cfm

International Policy Institute for Counterterrorism: http://www.ict.org.il/

Jane's Intelligence Review, Terrorism and Security Monitor, etc. (follow links): http://www.janes.com

National Criminal Intelligence Service, UK: http://www.ncis.com

North American Treaty Organization: http://www.nato.int

Office of the Coordinator for Counterterrorism, U.S. State Department: http://www.state.gov/www/global/terrorism/index.html

Oklahoma City National Memorial Institute for the Prevention of Terrorism: http://www.mipt.org/

Olivares, S. "Terrorist Leader Profile: A Working Research Project." http://www.iacsp.com/mp.html 2001.

Organization for Security and Co-operation in Europe: http://www.osce.org

Patterns of global terrorism: http://www.hri.org/docs/USSD-Terror/http://www.state.gov/s/ct/rls/pgtrpt/2000/index.cfm?docid=2460&clid=2408

Security Service (UK): http://www.mi5.gov.uk

Terrorism group profiles (mainly taken from the U.S. State Department): http://library.nps.navy.mil/home/tgp/tgpmain.htm

The Terrorism Research Center: http://www.terrorism.com/index.shtml

Terrorist and insurgent organizations: http://www.au.af.mil/au/aul/bibs/tergps/tg98tc.htm

United Nations: http://www.un.org

U.S. Department of Defense: http://www.defenselink.mil/other_info/terrorism.html

William R. Nelson Institute for Public Affairs: http://www.jmu.edu/orgs/wrni/

Miscellaneous: http://www.antiterrorism.org

http://www.cdi.org/terrorism/

http://www.counterterrorismtraining.gov/

http://www.cromwell.50megs.com/security/netusers.html#professionals

http://www.emergency.com/cntrterr.htm

http://www.fas.org/irp/

http://www.iacsp.com/mp.html

http://www.ict.org.il/

http://www.loc.gov/rr/frd/Sociology-Psychology%20of%20Terrorism.htm

http://www.monitor.bbc.co.uk

http://www.terrorism.com

http://www.terrorismfiles.org/individuals/ramzi_yousef.html/

# Appendix

## List of Abbreviations

**ANM**  Arab Nationalist Movement

**ASG**  Abu Sayaf Group (Philippines)

**CBRN**  chemical, biological, radiological, nuclear (weapons)

**CIA**  Central Intelligence Agency

**CT**  Counterterrorism

**FARC**  Fuerzas Armadas Revolucionarias de Colombia (Revolutionary Armed Forces of Colombia)

**FBI**  Federal Bureau of Investigation

**FRU**  Force Research Unit

**GIA**  Groupe Islamique Armée, or the Armed Islamic Group (Algeria)

**GIGN**  Groupement d'Intervention de la Gendarmerie Nationale (French CT Unit)

**GSG9**  Grenzschutzgruppe 9 (German CT Unit)

**HR**  Hostage Rescue

**JRA**  Japanese Red Army

**JSOC**  Joint Special Operations Command

**LTTE**  Liberation Tigers of Tamil Eelam (Tamil Tigers)

**MILF**  Moro-Islamic Liberation Front (Philippines)

**MRF**  Mobile Reaction Force

**NIOCTF**  Northern Ireland Organised Crime Task Force

**NGO**  nongovernmental agency

**NSA**  National Security Agency

**PFLP**   Popular Front for the Liberation of Palestine

**PIRA**   Provisional Irish Republican Army

**PLO**   Palestine Liberation Organization

**RUC**   Royal Ulster Constabulary

**SAS**   Special Air Service (U.K.)

**SBS**   Special Boat Service

**SMUs**   special missions units

**TSWG**   Technical Support Working Group

**WMD**   weapons of mass destruction

# Index

# About the Authors

**Graeme C. S. Steven** has both practical and theoretical experience with counterterrorism in the private and public sector. He is a research associate at the Centre for the Study of Terrorism and Political Violence at the University of St. Andrews, Fife, Scotland, specializing in counterterrorism, tri-border areas, the role of intelligence in counterterrorism, threat assessment, suicide-bombers, terrorist financing, and profiling terrorist groups. He is currently writing his Ph.D. on the motivations behind joining, supporting, and leaving terrorist groups and the implications for security policy and practice.

**Dr. Rohan Gunaratna** has twenty years of policy, operational, and academic experience in counterterrorism. He is head, International Centre for Political Violence and Terrorism Research at the Institute of Defence and Strategic Studies in Singapore; senior fellow, Combating Terrorism Center at the United States Military Academy at West Point; and honorary fellow, International Policy Institute for Counter-Terrorism in Israel. At the invitation of the UN Monitoring Group, he led the specialist team that designed and built the UN database on the mobility, finance, and weapons of Al Qaeda, Taliban, and their entities. He is author of eight books including *Inside Al Qaeda: Global Network of Terror* (2002), an international bestseller. He chairs the NATO-Partnership for Peace Working Group on Counter Terrorism.